VOLUME 2

CHAPTERS 5:12–8:39

Romans

THE GOSPEL OF GOD

TITUS CHU

Romans: The Gospel of God
by Titus Chu

December 2017
Print on Demand

© 2017 by Titus Chu
Volume II of III Volumes
ISBN: 1-932020-58-6
ISBN for set: 1-932020-60-8

Distributed by
The Church in Cleveland Literature Service
3150 Warren Road
Cleveland, Ohio 44111

Available for purchase online.
Printed by CreateSpace,
an Amazon.com company.

Please send correspondence by email to
theeditors@ministrymessages.org

Published by
Good Land Publishers
Ann Arbor, Michigan

Unless otherwise noted,
Scripture quotations are taken from the
New American Standard Bible®,
© 1960, 1995
by The Lockman Foundation.

Contents

Section Four:
Sanctification

69. An Overview of Sanctification   9

70. Four Aspects of God's Gift   17
    Romans 5:15–16

71. The Entrance of Sin   29
    Romans 5:12

72. Death Reigned   35
    Romans 5:13–14

73. Transgression, Offense, and Disobedience   41
    Romans 5:14–21

74. The Gift of Life by Grace   47
    Romans 5:15

75. The Gift in Operation   53
    Romans 5:15–16

76. The Free Gift from Many Offenses   61
    Romans 5:16

77. Abundant Grace and Righteousness   65
    Romans 5:17

78. Reigning in Life   69
    Romans 5:17

79. Justification of Life   73
    Romans 5:18

80. The Life of Justification *Romans 5:18*	81
81. Unto Eternal Life through Jesus Christ *Romans 5:19-21*	87
82. Dead to Sin *Romans 6:1-2*	93
83. Baptized into Christ Jesus *Romans 6:2-4*	97
84. Newness of Life *Romans 6:4*	107
85. United with Him *Romans 6:5*	113
86. Our Crucified Old Man *Romans 6:6-7*	121
87. Two Kinds of Knowing *Romans 6:6-10*	127
88. Considering Ourselves to be Dead *Romans 6:11*	135
89. Not Letting Sin Reign *Romans 6:12*	141
90. Presenting Ourselves to God *Romans 6:13-16*	145
91. The Form of Teaching *Romans 6:17*	151
92. Unto Sanctification *Romans 6:18-23*	157

93. Married to Christ *Romans 7:1–4*	163
94. God's View of Our Body *Romans 7:5*	167
95. Released from the Law *Romans 7:6*	173
96. Sin's Opportunity *Romans 7:7–11*	177
97. The Commandment and Life *Romans 7:10–11*	183
98. Three Laws *Romans 7:12–23*	187
99. Sold into Bondage to Sin *Romans 7:14, 7:24–25*	193
100. The Law of the Spirit of Life *Romans 8:1–2*	199
101. No Condemnation in Christ Jesus *Romans 8:1–2*	207
102. Condemning Sin in the Flesh *Romans 8:3*	211
103. Fulfilling the Requirement of the Law (1) *Romans 8:4*	215
104. Fulfilling the Requirement of the Law (2) *Romans 8:4*	221
105. Walking according to the Spirit *Romans 8:4*	227

106. The Mind of the Flesh or the Spirit 231
    Romans 8:5-6

107. The Flesh Being Hostile toward God 237
    Romans 8:7-8

108. The Spirit of God: Union 243
    Romans 8:9

109. The Spirit of Christ: Mingling 247
    Romans 8:9-10

110. The Spirit of Him Who Raised 253
    Jesus from the Dead: Incorporation
    Romans 8:11

111. The High Peak of Sanctification: Our Living 257
    Romans 8:12-13

Section Five:
Glorification

112. An Overview of Glorification 265

113. Led by the Spirit of God 269
    Romans 8:14

114. The Spirit of Sonship 279
    Romans 8:15

115. The Testimony of the Spirit with Our Spirit 283
    Romans 8:16-17

116. Heirs, God's Heirs, and 287
    Fellow Heirs with Christ
    Romans 8:16-17

117. Glorified with Christ 291
    Romans 8:17

118. The Revealing of the Sons of God 297
Romans 8:18-22

119. The First Fruits 307
Romans 8:23

120. The Redemption of Our Body 311
Romans 8:23-25

121. The Help of the Spirit 315
Romans 8:26

122. Groanings Too Deep for Words 319
Romans 8:26-27

123. All Things Work Together for Good 327
Romans 8:28

124. Those Whom He Predestined 333
Romans 8:29-30

125. Conformed to the Image of His Son 339
Romans 8:29-30

126. The One Who Is For Us 343
Romans 8:31-32

127. The One Who Justifies 349
Romans 8:33

128. Intercession for Us 353
Romans 8:34

129. The Love of Christ 357
Romans 8:35

130. Overwhelmingly Conquering 361
Romans 8:36-37

131. The Love of God in Christ Jesus 365
Romans 8:38-39

Works Cited 371

SECTION FOUR

SANCTIFICATION

69

An Overview of Sanctification

I am speaking in human terms because of the weakness of your flesh. For just as you presented your members as slaves to impurity and to lawlessness, resulting in further lawlessness, so now present your members as slaves to righteousness, resulting in sanctification.

—*Romans 6:19*

WORD STUDY

The Greek word used at the end of this verse for "sanctification," *hagiasmos*, means "purification, holiness, sanctification" (Strong, #38). It is used in the New Testament to denote both the process and resultant state of sanctification, which is a life in fellowship with God and displaying His characteristics (Vincent, 3:72).

W. E. Vine explained the process of sanctification in this way: "This sanctification is God's will for the believer...and it must be pursued by the believer, earnestly and undeviatingly. For the holy character is not vicarious, that is, it cannot be transferred or imputed, [rather] it is an individual possession, built up, little by little, as the result of obedience to the Word of God and of following the example of Christ" (Vine, 545).

REVELATION AND APPLICATION

The section of Paul's letter to the Romans from 5:12 to 8:13 deals with sanctification. At the end of the section on justification is a summary description of sanctification: "For if while we were enemies we were reconciled to God through the death of His Son, much more, having been reconciled, we shall be saved by His life" (5:10). This leads right into the topic of sanctification and shows that sanctification is a process of being saved in the life of Christ.

A Christian's life involves both reconciliation with God and salvation in His life. Reconciliation points to a harmony between us and God, while being saved in His life is for our sanctification. Reconciliation has both judicial and organic aspects. It is not as simple as two lawyers shaking hands; it is also like the harmony of life within a family. Romans 5:10 makes it clear that it is on the foundation of reconciliation that we experience salvation in life, that is, sanctification.

The Life of Resurrection

Sanctification is the process of being saved in life. The Greek word for "life" in Romans 5:10, zōē, is the life of the Son of God, which means it is the resurrection life of Christ. We were reconciled to God through the death of Christ, and through His resurrection, we received the divine and eternal life that organically unites us with God. This resurrection life is eternal, imperishable, and for us to experience and enjoy day after day. This life is fresh, bright, and strong. It is full of vitality and overcomes all the limitations of death. These aspects exist because this life is Christ Himself, the resurrected One who dwells in us. In the gospel of John, Jesus said that He is the resurrection and the life (11:25). Now, because He is resurrected from the dead, we can continually be sanctified in His resurrection life.

As we follow the Lord, we can experience moments of strength and overcoming, yet we also have moments of weakness and discouragement. However, whether we are strong, overcoming, weak, or discouraged, we should not forget that Christ is resurrected. The resurrection of Christ is for our justification (Rom. 4:25) and allows Him to work and operate within us as the resurrection life.

Following the Lord is altogether related to the principle of resurrection. Our experience of God's divine life is only in resurrection. The resurrected Christ is our assurance and boast. Those who follow the Lord can say, "In my weaknesses and limitations, I have experienced the resurrection power of Christ." We dare not boast, saying things like, "I led five young men to salvation, read five chapters of the Bible again, and helped five sisters in the church love the Lord more." Whoever boasts like this does not understand life or resurrection. A person who knows the resurrection life will say, "I can lead people to salvation, I can help the saints, and I can read the Bible, pray, and pursue the Lord. However, what truly amazes me is that a weak and sinful person like me is united to the Lord and can love and follow Him." This is the feeling of a person who both lives in resurrection and is inwardly full of the resurrection life of Christ.

The Beginning, Process, and Result

To experience sanctification, we must take Christ's life as the beginning, process, and result of our sanctification. Paul wrote, "Much more, having been reconciled, we shall be saved by His life" (Rom. 5:10). This shows that once we are reconciled to God, His divine life (zōē) is the source and beginning of our experience of sanctification. Later, Paul wrote, "The free gift of God is eternal life in Christ Jesus our Lord" (6:23). If we put these verses together, it shows that the divine and eternal life is a gift from God for the process of our sanctification.

Paul also wrote, "Much more those who receive abundance of grace and of the gift of righteousness will reign in life through the One, Jesus Christ" (5:17). This shows that sanctification results in our reigning in the divine life.

Many Christians assume that sanctification means the outward change of a person. However, the Bible presents a picture far beyond this. Consider a man who does not gamble anymore, although he used to gamble obsessively. We might assume that this man has experienced a measure of sanctification. However, this may not be so. Some people stop gambling because it is "the Christian thing to do." Others stop because God's divine life has worked in them and caused them to lose interest in gambling. Both outwardly look the same to us; however, the two processes are very different. The Bible describes true sanctification as a matter of Christ's divine life. His life is the beginning, the process, and the result of true sanctification.

A Christian's Three Lives

There are three Greek words commonly translated "life" in the New Testament:

1. *Zōē*—the highest and most noble life; used in relation to God
2. *Bios*—used to denote the natural life of man
3. *Psuchē*—the soul life, related to our hearts, minds, and souls (Vine, 368)

People are complicated. We outwardly have a physical life, which is related to our physical body. Because of Adam's fall, our physical body has become sinful flesh. In the flesh dwells sin (Rom. 7:17), which has its source in Satan himself. This is the result of Adam's transgression (5:12). We also have our inward and natural soul life, which everyone has from their natural birth. Moving deeper, we also received the divine life in our spirits when we were regenerated by believing into Christ (John 3:6). Therefore, a Christian has three lives: physical life, soul life, and divine life.

We all have a different physical life. We grow up differently, and our physical life manifests itself in different ways in different stages. The physical life of a grandfather is expressed very differently than the physical life of his young grandson. Yet regardless of how different we are from one another, we all have sin dwelling in our flesh. However, even the way sin operates is different from person to person.

Additionally, our soul lives are different. Some have strong souls, some have big souls, and some have weak and small souls. If we only look at the realms of physical life and soul life, we all differ from one another. Yet the divine life every believer receives at regeneration is identical. It is the same life. Although this life manifests itself differently in different people, the life itself is the same.

The Process of Sanctification: The Growth of Life

Since sanctification is our being saved in life, our lifelong experience of the process of sanctification is the process of the growth of the divine life in us. In this growth process, we may find ourselves joyful, discouraged, strong, or weak. As the divine life operates and abides in us, we may feel joyful and victorious. As the divine life restrains us, we may feel sober and subdued. Whatever our experience is, however, this life is always operating and working the resurrection life of Christ into us according to His righteousness and holiness.

Sometimes we may feel like we could not possibly be weaker. Other times we may feel like we could not be stronger. However, these feelings are not very important. What is important is the divine life dwelling within us. It is by the growth of this resurrection life that we experience true sanctification.

The continual dispensing of the divine resurrection life into us is critical to our experience of sanctification. As we receive this dispensing of life, it becomes the source of the growth of God's life in us. The process of our growth and sanctification involves both our enjoyment of this life and our obedience as it is dispensed into us. Finally, the result of this process is the divine life bearing even more abundant life.

The Process of Sanctification: Union, Mingling, and Incorporation

Another way to talk about sanctification is to consider our union, mingling, and incorporation with God. Being united is a matter of life, being mingled is a matter of nature, and being incorporated is a matter of person. Firstly, we are united with God in life, then we are mingled with God in nature, and eventually we are incorporated with God in person. The union of life occurs when the divine life regenerates us. As we are constituted with the divine life, we become mingled with God in nature. Eventually, we experience incorporation with the person of the Lord. When our person is incorporated with the Lord, His thoughts become our thoughts, His delight becomes our delight, and we pursue what He pursues with a determination that is the Lord's. Our experience of sanctification is the progressing of our union, mingling, and incorporation with God.

Two Vital Experiences

Paul states that through Christ we obtained an introduction by faith into the realm of grace (Rom. 5:2). In this realm, we boast in the hope of the glory of God. On one hand, this is part of Paul's final word on justification. On the other hand, this is the beginning of our experience of sanctification. Justification gives us a boast, and this boast allows us to live a life of sanctification in the resurrection of Christ.

Two things are vital to the process of sanctification: salvation in the divine life, and boasting in the hope of God's glory. Many Christians can testify that even after loving and following the Lord for many years, they still feel like they have fallen short of the Lord in many ways. Yet they continue to follow Him. What is the secret to this ability to follow the Lord? The secret is to not depart from His life or from our boasting in the hope of God's glory. It is so simple, yet we often miss life and discount our boast. We must learn how important it is to continually receive the divine life for our salvation and how important it is to continually boast in the hope of the glory of God. When we learn this secret, our lives will be filled with experiences of sanctification.

Four Aspects of God's Gift

But the free gift is not like the transgression. For if by the transgression of the one the many died, much more did the grace of God and the gift by the grace of the one Man, Jesus Christ, abound to the many. ¹⁶The gift is not like that which came through the one who sinned; for on the one hand the judgment arose from one transgression resulting in condemnation, but on the other hand the free gift arose from many transgressions resulting in justification.

—Romans 5:15–16

Therefore it says, "When He ascended on high, He led captive a host of captives, and gave gifts to men."...And He gave some as apostles, and some as prophets, and some as evangelists, and some as pastors and teachers.

—Ephesians 4:8, 11

WORD STUDY

In Romans 5:15–16, three different Greek words are used in the four instances of "gift": *dōrea*, *dōrēma*, and *charisma*. The Greek word used for "gifts" in Ephesians 4:8 is *doma*. While all four words can simply be translated "gift," there are slight differences in how they are used in the New Testament.

Dōrea is typically a more formal gift than the word it is derived from—*doron*. *Dōrea* denotes formal endowment, and in the New Testament is always used of the gift of God or Christ to man. The grace of God is always implied with *dōrea*, and Paul used this word in Romans 3:24 to describe justification by grace as a gift from God (Kittel, 2:167).

Dōrēma is similar to *dōrea*, with the exception of the added suffix, *ma*. This suffix is a common noun ending in Greek that denotes an object, often the result of action (Robinson, 139).

The word *charisma* literally means a "gift of grace" (Vine, 264). It is often used in the New Testament in reference to the spiritual endowment of believers by the Holy Spirit. Thus, it is used in Romans 12 and 1 Corinthians 12 for the miraculous faculties possessed by believers, from the Holy Spirit, for the benefit of the church (Brown, 2:42).

The word *doma* is used in the New Testament only four times. This word lends a greater stress to the concrete character of the gift, rather than to its beneficent nature (Vine, 264). It is generally accepted that in Ephesians 4, the gifts are the gifted members of the church (Eph. 4:11) given by God for the benefit of the believers.

REVELATION AND APPLICATION

Paul discusses spiritual gifts in detail in several chapters of the Bible, including later in the book of Romans. Notice, however, that in Romans 5:15–16 the word "gift" is used four times. Paul very much related our experience of sanctification to the word "gift." Though our justification is a gift freely given by God (Rom. 3:24), we can also say our experience of sanctification is related to God's gift—the gift of life.

Four Aspects of God's Gift

There are several Greek words translated "gift," each representing a different aspect of God's gift. The ways these words are used in verses 15 and 16 are as follows:

But the free gift (*charisma*) is not like the transgression. For if by the transgression of the one the many died, much more did the grace of God and the gift (*dōrea*) by the grace of the one Man, Jesus Christ, abound to the many. The gift (*dōrēma*) is not like that which came through the one who sinned; for on the one hand the judgment arose from one transgression resulting in condemnation, but on the other hand the free gift (*charisma*) arose from many transgressions resulting in justification.

The words *charisma*, *dōrea*, and *dōrēma* are all used in this section. Firstly, the gift (*charisma*) is not like the transgression. Secondly, the gift (*dōrea*) is by the grace of the one Man, Jesus Christ. Thirdly, the gift (*dōrēma*) is not like that which came through the one who sinned. Finally, the gift (*charisma*) which came from many transgressions resulted in justification. In addition to these three words here, the Bible also uses the word *doma* for "gift" in Ephesians 4:8.

What are the differences among these four words? It seems that each word denotes a different aspect of the gift we receive from God. *Dōrea* indicates the gift we receive from God when we are born again. Over time, this gift of God grows within us and can be called *dōrēma*, since the added suffix *ma* indicates the result of an action. *Charisma* is the gift in its outward operation (see 1 Cor. 12:28–30 and Rom. 12:6–8). God's gift is first defined by life (*dōrea*), then simultaneously by its growth (*dōrēma*) and operation (*charisma*). *Dōrea* grows within us unto *dōrēma*, which is outwardly expressed as *charisma*. As *charisma* operates, it constitutes us as a gift (*doma*) to bless the church (Eph. 4:11).

Dōrea: The Gift of Life

Dōrea is the gift of God defined simply by His divine life. Just as a pair of earrings could be considered a gift of gold, this heavenly gift is a gift of life, the giving of which is based on God's judicial redemption. This gift of life allows us to serve God, and it grows as we serve Him.

We all have certain talents or abilities we possess from birth. Yet these abilities are not defined immediately by outward operation. Newborn babies do not work through mathematical equations or play complicated songs on the piano, even though they may become gifted mathematicians or pianists later in life. Rather, people's gifts and talents are at first defined and expressed simply by the life within them. It takes the growth of life to develop outward manifestations of the life within. Through redemption, we are given the gift of God, yet this gift is not immediately defined by its operation. Rather it is defined simply by the life of God. All people possess certain natural talent, but God's gift of life, *dōrea*, can only be obtained through salvation.

The eventual manifestation of God's life generally matches a person's natural talent. For example, many people who have the gift of prophecy (1 Cor. 14:1–3) are naturally eloquent speakers. In a parable found in Matthew, God gives one servant five talents, another two talents, and another one talent, "each according to his own ability" (25:15). The "ability" here is man's natural talent, while the one, two, and five talents represent the gift of God given according to each servant's ability.

Regardless of how talented we are, if we do not have the gift of God's life, our talent will be natural and useless to God. Some people are born with the natural ability of leadership, but if they are not regenerated and saved, they may become leaders in governments or corporations, but cannot be leaders in God's hands. In this way, people's talents cannot be considered true gifts until the divine life is within them.

No matter how talented people may be, they must be saved and regenerated to receive the divine life.

The Realization of the Gift of Life

Once we have been born again and have received God's gift of life, the question becomes how to experience and realize it. The realization of the gift of life lies in the person of the Lord, the One who gave the gift to us. In the gospel of John, Jesus said, "If you knew the gift of God, and who it is who says to you, 'Give Me a drink,' you would have asked Him, and He would have given you living water" (4:10). In the original Greek text, the "gift of God" Jesus refers to is *dōrea*. He was talking with a woman about His gift of life! Notice that Jesus said, "If you knew the gift," and, "[If you knew] who it is who says to you." Without knowing this "who"—the living Lord— the gift of life will be ineffective and remain hidden in us.

All who have been regenerated have received the gift of eternal life. This is a fact for every born-again Christian (John 3:16). However, this gift will not be revealed and realized without a relationship with the living Lord. When we are in oneness with the living Lord, the gift of life will become manifested. The Lord freely gives us the gift of life (*dōrea*), yet the enjoyment, manifestation, and realization of the gift are all related to our relationship with Him.

Its Different Measures

We should treasure the gift of life that has been given to us by God. If we treasure this life in a proper way, it will result in many different manifestations of the divine life. Paul uses the word *dōrea* in his letter to the Ephesians to say that each one of us was given grace according to the measure of God's gift (Eph. 4:7). This shows that the measure of the gift of life differs from person to person, just as the number of talents given to each servant was different (Matt. 25:15).

The word "measure" implies a limited portion or degree (Strong, #3358). We all receive the same divine life, yet the measure of the gift we receive according to our ability may not be the same. Even if we shared the same measure initially, our diligence in pursuing the Lord, seeking to grow, and carrying out our operation would result in different increases of measure. The more we pursue, experience, and enjoy Christ, the larger our measure of the gift will be. This is why Paul uses *dōrēma* to indicate the growth of the gift of life.

Dōrēma: The Gift as Defined by Its Growth

The second aspect of God's gift is *dōrēma*, which is the result of the inward growth of the gift of life. This aspect of the gift of God not only involves our experience of judicial redemption but also organic salvation. The suffix *ma* especially emphasizes this aspect as the result of God's organic salvation.

Romans 5:15-16 reveals the process of the growth of God's divine life in us. The section both begins and ends with the gift as it is defined by its operation (*charisma*). Between the two uses of charisma, Paul uses *dōrea* and *dōrēma*. The process of growth is from one *charisma* to another *charisma*, but this growth is intimately connected to the gift of life and this gift as defined by its inward growth. On the one hand, when we are saved, we receive the gift of life (*dōrea*); on the other hand, this gift will continually grow in us through our experiences of organic salvation, becoming richer and more abundant in the divine life. This is *dōrēma*.

Charisma: The Gift as Defined by Its Operation

Charisma is the gift of life defined by its outward operation.

As with *dōrēma*, *charisma* involves our experience of organic salvation, indicated by the suffix *ma*. The gift of God in someone full of the operation and working of the divine life has become charisma. The inward flowing and growth of life results in a proper ministry. The problem among many Christians today is a shortage of *charisma*, the gift of life in outward operation.

Paul told Timothy, "Do not neglect the spiritual gift (*charisma*) within you" (1 Tim. 4:14). This was Paul's encouragement to Timothy, but it is also a word the Lord would use to encourage us today. The gift of life (*dōrea*) given by the Lord must grow in us (*dōrēma*), and this inward growth should be manifested from us as the outward operation of life (*charisma*).

The process of the growth of life unto an outward manifestation is not easy. For example, our growth can be impeded by the pride that comes from an obvious measure of life and great natural talent. If people feel satisfied every time we open our mouths to speak, it would be easy to immerse ourselves in the elementary stages of the gift and forget about growing and moving forward in our Christian lives.

Some may inwardly grow well in the divine life (*dōrēma*), yet their operation is lacking. Their outward operation (*charisma*) does not match their inward knowledge and spiritual riches. For others, their operation is pushed beyond their inward growth. They may do many things in the church life, but without the riches of life's growth within them, they will not be able to adequately build up the believers. To have the healthy growth of the gift of life (*dōrēma*) with its proper operation (*charisma*) is not easy at all.

The Effectiveness of Charisma

The gift of life in operation (*charisma*) is dynamic and effective. Paul told the Romans, "For I long to see you so that

I may impart some spiritual gift (*charisma*) to you, that you may be established" (1:11). The operating aspect of God's gift can establish people. The apostle Peter wrote, "As each one has received a special gift (*charisma*), employ it in serving one another as good stewards of the manifold grace of God" (1 Pet. 4:10). The gift of God in operation makes people stewards of grace to serve the saints. These verses show that God's gift as defined by outward operation (*charisma*) is related to the operation of life, both in us and in those we serve. When God's gift operates in us and out from us, it is dynamic and effective.

Romans 12:6 is another good illustration of this aspect of God's gift: "Since we have gifts (*charisma*) that differ according to the grace given to us, each of us is to exercise them accordingly: if prophecy, according to the proportion of his faith." The gifts in this verse and those that follow are related to the operation of prophesying, leading, and all kinds of ministering. Paul also told the Corinthians, "Now there are varieties of gifts (*charisma*), but the same Spirit" (1 Cor. 12:4). Notice that there are varieties of gifts in operation. Though the divine life in all Christians is the same, the outward operation of our gifts may be very different and effective in different ways.

The Role of the Spirit of God

Notice that 1 Corinthians 12:4 emphasizes that although there are varieties of gifts, there is "the same Spirit." Those who experience the operating aspect of their gift must be rich in the Spirit of God. The Spirit is the One who gives life (John 6:63; 1 Cor. 15:45), and it is only through Him that this gift of life becomes manifested in operation.

It is impossible for a person who lacks or does not know the Spirit to have a richly operating gift. Even if we praised a naturally charismatic man, we may only be praising his eloquence and natural attraction. A *charisma* that would build up the church belongs to those who have the Spirit of God, know Him, and live by Him. The richer our fellowship with the Spirit is, the more our *charisma* will be manifested and profitable.

Our Earnest Desire

Paul encouraged Timothy, saying, "Do not neglect the spiritual gift (*charisma*) within you" (1 Tim. 4:14). Rather, Paul wanted Timothy to stir it up (2 Tim. 1:6). Within Timothy was the divine life, and Paul hoped that this gift could be stirred up again to operate and work. Timothy himself would be the deciding factor. It is important to understand that the operation of the gift of life is related to our desire. Paul said in 1 Corinthians, "Earnestly desire the greater gifts (*charisma*)" (12:31). This is the proper desire of those who are in one accord with God and who live in His life. Those who are trapped in religious rituals or natural zeal are unable to understand such desire.

This verse in 1 Corinthians uses the phrase "earnestly desire." On the one hand, it is very natural for the gift of life (*dōrea*) to grow and mature within us (*dōrēma*); on the other hand, this growth is related to our earnest desire. We should have the desire for our gift to grow from *dōrea* to *dōrēma*, and for this growth to be expressed as *charisma*. Christians should not only be filled with the riches of God's life but should operate and become blessings to the church.

The Role of Our Spirit

The operating aspect of God's gift is not only related to the Spirit of God but is also related to the burning, strength, and riches in our spirit. Let us again consider the interaction between Paul and Timothy. Paul told Timothy, "For this reason I remind you to kindle afresh the gift (*charisma*) of God which is in you through the laying on of my hands. For God has not given us a spirit of timidity, but of power and love and discipline" (2 Tim. 1:6–7). After reading these verses, many people may wish the apostle Paul could have laid hands on them. It is true that Paul's laying on of hands manifested a gift in Timothy, but we must realize that the reality of this manifestation was a matter of Timothy's spirit. Paul seems to have said to Timothy, "You have a gift in you through the laying on of my hands; now you should stir it up in your living! Do not let it be quenched and cold. You should stir it up again, for God has not given us a spirit of timidity or fear, but of power and of love and of discipline."

Paul based his whole encouragement to Timothy on the spirit. The emphasis of these verses in 2 Timothy is not the gift but rather the spirit. A person who has received God's life (*dōrea*) and allowed it to grow (*dōrēma*) must have a strong, burning spirit to manifest the operation of the gift (*charisma*). In turn, this operation must be related to God's heart's desire, the church.

Please note the essential place our spirit has in the reality and manifestation of an operating gift. A *charisma* can be rich, but its riches flow out of our spirit. A *charisma* can be full of truth, but the revelation of the truth occurs in our spirit. A *charisma* can be very virtuous and active in service, but this virtue and service are generated from our spirit.

Good Stewards of God's Grace

The apostle Peter wrote, "As each one has received a special gift (*charisma*), employ it in serving one another as good stewards of the manifold grace of God" (1 Pet. 4:10). Our operating gift must be used for the sake of those around us. We should desire *charisma*, and the Holy Spirit can give *charisma*, yet *charisma* should never be for itself.

Those with an operating gift must not live for their gift only, nor should they live in their gift. Those who grow from *dōrea* unto *dōrēma* and manifest *charisma* must see the will of God and become good stewards. This is what God wants— stewards of His manifold grace. When we have *charisma*, we must minister grace to one another as good stewards.

Doma: A Constituted Gift

So far we have considered three aspects of the word "gift"—*dōrea*, *dōrēma*, and *charisma*. Eventually, through the operating *charisma*, we ourselves will be constituted to be a gift (*doma*) that blesses the church. Having been constituted with the life of God, we will have a true ministry for the building up of the church.

Doma is a constituted gift, the result of *dōrēma* and *charisma* together. As the life of God grows within different people and develops different outward operations, it is constituted in them as different ministries. The ultimate result of the growth and operation of God's gift of life is the constitution of different ministries for the building of the church.

Everyone's ministry is different. When Ephesians 4:8 says that God gave gifts to men, it uses the plural form of *doma*. Verse 11 lists these gifts, saying, "And He gave some as apostles, and some as prophets, and some as evangelists, and some as pastors and teachers." Apostles, prophets, evangelists, pastors, and teachers are all constituted gifts (*doma*). The divine life in them has grown inwardly (*dōrēma*), operated outwardly (*charisma*), and now becomes their very constitution.

Those with a constituted gift are that gift. They not only have life but also have the riches of the growth and operation of this life. An apostle not only does the work of an apostle, but also has the constitution of an apostle. A prophet not only does the work of a prophet, but also has the constitution of a prophet. Evangelists, pastors, and teachers not only do the work of their ministry, but also have the constitution of their ministry. This is the result of the growth of life and the growth of the operation of that life.

God's Desire

Every regenerated believer has the gift of life (*dōrea*), every believer more or less grows (*dōrēma*), and every believer experiences some operation of their gift (*charisma*). Still we should ask, "Where are those today who truly have a ministry and have become constituted gifts?" This is what we lack today. God is not content to stop with the *dōrea*, *dōrēma*, or *charisma*. His desire is to eventually gain constituted gifts who have a ministry and can bless the church.

Doma is the highest aspect of God's gift and is indispensable for the building up of the body of Christ. We should pray, "Lord, may Your gift of life grow in me and develop an operation. May I become a person so constituted with Your life that no matter where I go I can minister to people in the operation of my gift. I hope that through the operation of my gift I can bring many to Your presence, one by one. Lord, I ask that I would grow to be a gift that could bless Your church through the ministry You have measured to me."

The Entrance of Sin

Therefore, just as through one man sin entered into the world, and death through sin, and so death spread to all men, because all sinned.

—*Romans 5:12*

WORD STUDY

Romans 5:12 introduces the beginning of a comparison that is not completed until verse 21. In this section of verses, the entrance of reconciliation and life by Christ is compared to the entrance of sin and death by Adam's fall (Alford, 2:359). The story of Adam's fall in the garden of Eden is found in Genesis 3.

Both man's sinful nature and sinful acts are displayed in Romans 5:12. The first time sin is mentioned is as the singular Greek noun *hamartia*, which W. E. Vine calls "a principle or source of action, or an inward element producing acts." When Paul writes at the end of the verse that "all sinned," he uses the Greek verb *harmartanō*, which literally means "to miss the mark...to sin against God" (Vine, 576). It is through the sinful nature that death entered the world. Death comes to all men because sin is universal, causing men to sin (Rogers, 326).

In his commentary on Romans, Martin Luther wrote a lengthy passage on the differences between "original sin" (or, the sinful nature) and "actual sin" (or, sinful actions). He wrote, "Actual sins...come from out of us....But original [sin] enters into us; we do not commit it, but we suffer it. We are sinners because we are the sons of a sinner. A sinner can beget only a sinner, who is like him" (Luther, 95).

REVELATION AND APPLICATION

Romans 5 begins by describing many of the glorious effects of justification by faith, culminating in our being "saved by His life" (5:10)—our sanctification. From Romans 5:12, Paul begins to discuss our experience of this sanctification.

Five Aspects of Subjective Experience in Adam

The "one man" mentioned in this verse is Adam. Sin entered the world through Adam. Another Man is mentioned in verse 15, who is the Lord Jesus Christ: "much more did the grace of God and the gift by the grace of the one Man, Jesus Christ, abound to the many." This passage uses these two men to demonstrate the difference between sin and grace and also to show that our experience of sanctification includes subjective experiences in both Adam and Christ.

There are only two men in God's eyes: Adam and Christ. Adam is the first man, while Christ is the second man, the last Adam (1 Cor. 15:45–47). All people are in one of these two. If we are not in Christ, then we are in Adam. If we are not in Adam, then we are in Christ. We have different subjective experiences depending on which man we are in.

Our subjective experiences in Adam match his experiences with regard to sin. Our subjective experience of sin in Adam has five aspects related to sin's source, our being, our realm, sin's effectiveness, and our living.

As to sin's source, it was through one man that it entered the world (Rom. 5:12). Regarding our being, we are now all under the authority of death (v. 14). Our realm changed when sin brought us into the realm of judgment (v. 18), and sin's effectiveness is seen in that it has constituted us all as sinners (v. 21). In terms of our living, we all live in sin and are isolated from God (v. 21). These few verses in Romans 5 present a broad view of our subjective experiences of sin in Adam.

According to Source: The Sinful Nature in All Men

Sin entered the world through one man. Romans 5:12 speaks of singular sin, pointing toward the sinful nature of man. Paul's emphasis here was not on our specific sins, but on the sinful nature we share in Adam. We are sinners because we have a sinful nature, and we cannot help but commit sins. The sinful nature within us results in sinful outward acts. We are not only people who commit sins, but our very essence is sin. This principle is reflected in the following stanzas from a hymn by Isaac Watts:

Backward with humble shame we look,
On our original;
How is our nature dashed and broke
In our first father's fall!...

How strong in our degenerate blood,
The old corruption reigns,
And, mingling with the crooked flood,
Wanders through all our veins!

Wild and unwholesome as the root

Will all the branches be;
How can we hope for living fruit
From such a deadly tree? (Rippon, #82)

We were born into Adam. Because Adam sinned and fell, our sinfulness and failures should not surprise us. We need no effort to express Adam's nature. When we are in Adam, we are only sinners who can do nothing but commit sins.

In Chinese history, it is possible that no one knew the sin nature more clearly than Confucius. One of his sayings was, "He who sins against heaven has no one to whom he can pray." He realized that because of sin, it was futile to pray, no matter how much or how hard he tried. We may sometimes feel the same way. We may say, "How can I pray? I am nothing but a sinner. Because of my sin, I have no reason to pray, for even if I did, heaven would not hear me. I am not a good person who sins; I am a sinner."

This understanding is very deep. We often associate sin with behavior. Many Christians pray with this thought, "Lord, I did something wrong, but now my behavior is proper again. Please forgive me for what I did earlier." Very few people understand that we ourselves are sin. If we were only people who commit sins, then God would only need to deal with those sins. However, because we are sinners, God must terminate who we are.

God desires not only to solve the problem of the many outward sins committed by people, but also the problem of sinners themselves. Through the cross, God not only deals with our sinful, outward deeds but also with our sinful, inward being, so that He can fill us with His divine life.

The Most Serious Consequence of Sin

The most serious consequence of sin is that it takes us away from God. This will also be discussed more in the next chapter.

Most Christians would consider an argument between a husband and wife as sin. However, sin already affects their relationship with God, whether an argument breaks out or not. We are separated from God by our sin nature. In our concept, sin involves doing something to offend God. To God, however, sin's greatest consequence is our separation from Him, whether a sinful action is committed or not. We often consider our most serious problem to be the violation of God's Law, but God considers our most serious problem to be our separation from Him. When the Bible mentions sin, it does not focus on the number of outward things we have done to offend God but rather on whether or not we have God and are one with Him.

The Principle of Sin

Satan was the highest archangel, even above the archangel Michael (Jude 9). He was under God, yet he was put over all of God's creation. However, one day he proudly said, "I will ascend above the heights of the clouds; I will make myself like the Most High" (Isa. 14:14). In this way, Satan became the very embodiment of sin.

When we think of Satan's first sinful act, we often think of a violent rebellion against God. However, our thoughts about this may be wrong. Satan's sin was that he declared independence from God and desired to be like God. In fact, Satan did not even have the thought to overthrow God's throne. It was as though he declared, "I will be just as God is. I will have independent sovereignty like Him. Though I do not have God's power, I have the ability to speak like Him. What God says counts, and what I say also counts!" This is the principle behind Satan's fall. In our experience, we might also unconsciously play the role of Satan by declaring that we are like God in our self. Whenever we consider ourselves like God, we commit a grave sin.

The reason human beings commit sins is because of the sin nature, which always desires to be like God. In the garden of Eden, Eve was tempted by the serpent to be like God, knowing good and evil (Gen. 3:5). When Adam ate the fruit of the tree of the knowledge of good and evil, he took in sin. Now, whenever people say in their hearts, "I want to be like God," they follow the principle of the tree of the knowledge of good and evil. Originally, only God's voice counted. Today, after God says something, we may stop to think about it and judge it. We think and feel that our own opinions about things matter. Such thinking is of the tree of the knowledge of good and evil.

The sinful nature entered into the world through one man to make everyone commit sins. We must realize the truth in Romans 5:12: through one man, Adam, we are sinners with sinful natures that cause us to commit sins and experience death. This is both an objective fact and our subjective experience in Adam.

72

Death Reigned

For until the Law sin was in the world, but sin is not imputed when there is no law. ^{14}*Nevertheless death reigned from Adam until Moses, even over those who had not sinned in the likeness of the offense of Adam, who is a type of Him who was to come.*
—*Romans 5:13-14*

WORD STUDY

Verse 14 contains the striking phrase, "death reigned." The Greek word used here for "death," *thanatos*, is used in the Bible to speak both of the physical separation of a man's soul from his body and of the spiritual separation of man from God (Vine, 149). In verse 12, sin operated in men to cause them to commit sins, bringing in death. In verse 14, death is personified by the word "reigned," translated from the Greek word *basileuō*, meaning "to rule as king, here in the sense of controlling or determining the destiny of [others]" (Rogers, 326). H. Alford writes, "The aim is to prove, that the seed of sin planted in the race by the one man Adam, has sprung up and borne fruit in all, so as to bring them under death;—death temporal, and spiritual" (Alford, 2:362).

Verses 13 and 14 show that though sin was not formally held against those who lived before God's Law was revealed, death reigned over them also (the consequence of sin). Death is the result of our sinful nature.

REVELATION AND APPLICATION

Our subjective experiences in Adam match his experiences with regard to sin. As we pointed out in the previous chapter, our subjective experience of sin in Adam has five aspects related to sin's source, our being, our realm, sin's effectiveness, and our living. In this chapter, we will consider the subjective experience of sin in Adam according to our being.

According to Being:
Under the Power of Death

The defining characteristic of those in Adam is that they have a sinful nature. This sinful nature not only results in sinful deeds but also in death. Paul shows us in Romans 5:14 that death reigns over all men, even over those who have not sinned in the likeness of Adam's offense. This further proves that death is the result of our sinful nature, which is the result of what we have in the first man Adam. All who are in Adam find themselves under the power, oppression, and suffering of death. Subjectively, this reign of death causes feelings of depression, oppression, and pain. Death is over all men, and there is nothing that can be done but be subject to it.

Death: Separation from God

Verse 14 says that "death reigned from Adam to Moses." Death is not an easy matter. People not only live in sin but also under death. People in Adam's day may have been astonished when death visited them for the first time. They may have said of the dead man, "Why won't he wake up when I call him? Why doesn't he move when I cry out to him?" Physical death separates people from one another. Spiritual death separates people from God.

In our experience, separation from God means losing feelings about God. God charged Adam not to eat the fruit of the tree of the knowledge of good and evil, for in the day he ate of it he would surely die (Gen. 2:17). When Adam ate the fruit, however, he did not immediately die, and instead lived for 930 years (Gen. 5:5)! This shows that the death Adam suffered in the day he ate the forbidden fruit was his separation from God, symbolized by his being cast from the garden of Eden (Gen. 3:23-24). Eventually this spiritual death also separated Adam from the physical world when he was 930 years old. Separation from God is death.

All who are in Adam have a sinful nature, commit sins, and have death reigning over them. If someone refuses the gospel and says, "I do not need God," we should understand what they really mean. What this response really means is, "I am a person in Adam who has a sinful nature and commits sins. I have been isolated from God, and death is reigning over me." There is not one person who doesn't need the gospel. When a person is in Adam, the gospel is immediately needed.

A person without God is not only a sinful human being committing sins but also a person under the reign of death. For death to reign over us is a terrible thing! Whenever we do not care to live before God, death will reign over us. For example, if a Christian brother feels far away from God yet ignores this feeling, he is allowing death to reign over him. For a day or two, such feelings may be strong, but gradually they will weaken and disappear, and death will completely take him. He will have no feelings about God, godly things, church meetings, following the Lord, living a church life, or consecration and service. Spiritual death separates us from everything that is involved in a life with God.

On the contrary, if believers who have not attended church meetings for a long time are sitting in a meeting today, we should be comforted and greatly encouraged. They have broken through the limitation and power of death and have now come back to enjoy the divine life again!

The Echoes of Sin and the World

Romans 5:12 tells us that through one man, sin entered the world. The "world" here could be a general term for mankind—the people of the world. Thus, sin entered mankind through one man. However, Satan also constructed a system we call "the world," which, while it caters to human needs and living, also mirrors and encourages the fallen human nature.

Verse 12 tells us that sin entered the world, and verse 21 tells us that sin reigned in death. The sinful nature dwells in our flesh, while Satan, the ruler of the world (John 12:31), controls the world system around us. The world around us is simply an echo of the sin within us, while the sin within us echoes the fallen world around us. The sin within us causes us to think of, love, and practice the fallen things of the world. Conversely, the world around us attracts us to sin. This echoing between our inward sinful nature and the worldly outward environment is a lifelong experience for all people. This echoing produces death, which reigns over man.

The entire world system that Satan has constructed is designed to cause fallen people to fall even farther. Much about the world is very attractive. Consider a place like Oxford University, an English university well known for its history and education. It has produced many talented and famous people and accumulated many academic achievements. Oxford may seem like a source of shining light. In every aspect, it is an attractive university. However, we must still realize that it is nothing but the satanic world.

The satanic world is everywhere. In Western countries, people go to bars and party. In China, people go to restaurants to eat, drink, and live a life apart from God. Both are aspects of the world and the reigning of death. A life without Christ is a life under the power of death, and this spiritual death will eventually bring in physical death. On our own, not one of us can escape the reality or power of death.

The Wonderful Christ

Romans 5:14 says that Adam was a type of Him who was to come. What good news! Though mankind fell, God has revealed His wisdom through the last Adam, Jesus Christ our Lord. It is in Christ that we can escape the power of sin and death. Praise the Lord! Even long before Adam's fall, God had prepared another Man to become our salvation. He is better, more attractive, and surpassingly great—Jesus Christ our Lord!

73

Transgression, Offense, and Disobedience

Nevertheless death reigned from Adam to Moses, even over those who had not sinned according to the likeness of the transgression of Adam, who is a type of Him who was to come. [15]But the free gift is not like the offense. For if by the one man's offense many died, much more the grace of God and the gift by the grace of the one Man, Jesus Christ, abounded to many. [16]And the gift is not like that which came through the one who sinned. For the judgment which came from one offense resulted in condemnation, but the free gift which came from many offenses resulted in justification. [17]For if by the one man's offense death reigned through the one, much more those who receive abundance of grace and of the gift of righteousness will reign in life through the One, Jesus Christ.

[18]Therefore, as through one man's offense judgment came to all men, resulting in condemnation, even so through one Man's righteous act the free gift came to all men, resulting in justification of life. [19]For as by one man's disobedience many were made sinners, so also by one Man's obedience many will be made righteous.

[20]Moreover the law entered that the offense might abound. But where sin abounded, grace abounded much more, [21]so that as sin reigned in death, even so grace might reign through righteousness to eternal life through Jesus Christ our Lord.
—*Romans 5:14–21 (NKJV®)*

WORD STUDY

Three words related to sin stand out in this passage: transgression (v. 14), offense (vv. 15–18), and disobedience (v. 19).

The Greek word used in verse 14 for "transgression," *parabasis*, means "a violation, breaking, transgression" (Strong, #3847), and the suffix *sis* indicates the action of transgressing (Robinson, 140). The thought is that when Adam ate of the tree of the knowledge of good and evil, he overstepped the boundaries set for him (Vine, 640). This overstepping was his transgression. Though no one has committed the same transgression as Adam, the verse says that death still reigned over all men. Martin Luther explains, "Adam became a cause of death to his descendants, though they did not eat of the forbidden tree....The figure of Adam's transgression is in us, for we die just as though we had sinned as he did" (Luther, 97).

The Greek word translated "offense" in verse 15 is *paraptōma*, which literally means "a side-slip...fall, sin, trespass" (Strong, #3900). This word ends with the Greek suffix *ma*, a common noun ending that emphasizes the result of action (Robinson, 139). These verses explain three results of the one man's offense:

1. All men died (v. 15)
2. Death reigned (v. 17)
3. Judgment came to all men, resulting in condemnation (v. 18)

The Greek word in verse 19 for "disobedience," *parakoē*, means "inattention, by implication disobedience" (Strong, #3876), and primarily indicates a failing to hear. Quoting J. Bengal, Vincent writes, "The word very [fittingly] points out the first step in Adam's fall—carelessness; as the beginning of a city's capture when the guards are not there" (Vincent, 3:64). Strikingly, it was by such a disobedience, or carelessness, that all men were made sinners (v. 19).

REVELATION AND APPLICATION

Our subjective experiences in Adam match his experiences with regard to sin. As we pointed out in the previous two chapters, our subjective experience of sin in Adam has five aspects related to sin's source, our being, our realm, sin's effectiveness, and our living. In this chapter, we will consider the subjective experience of sin in Adam according to our being, our realm, sin's effectiveness, and our living.

According to Being: Under the Power of Death

Romans 5:14 says that death reigned over those who lived after Adam, even over those who did not commit the same transgression as Adam. This is the case because all people are born in the Adamic race. Although only Adam ate of the forbidden fruit in the garden of Eden, all men have inherited Adam's sin nature and are under the power of death.

The fact is we can never commit the same sin as Adam. Adam ate the fruit of the tree of the knowledge of good and evil, yet we have never even seen this tree! However, the Greek word for "transgression" indicates the action and process of transgressing, rather than the transgression itself. It does not matter that our transgressing is not in the likeness of Adam's. The action of transgressing still continues today in us, because we walk according to the same principle of disobedience. We are continuing Adam's transgression and find ourselves under the power of death (vv. 12, 14).

According to Realm: Condemnation

Verses 15–18 speak of the results of Adam's sinful action, and so contain the Greek word *paraptōma* (offense) rather than *parabasis* (transgression). *Paraptōma* stresses the result of Adam's sin rather than his act of sinning. Adam not only acted sinfully, but his action also had results affecting all humanity.

Transgression (*parabasis*) contains the meaning of stepping beyond set boundaries. Some examples are taking someone's money, reading other people's books without permission, or using other people's office supplies without asking. In all of these cases, the action would be considered stepping over set boundaries. In the same way, the sin committed by Adam was a step beyond the boundaries within which God had commanded him to stay. Furthermore, his transgression affected his relationship with God, and so it became an offense. According to verse 18, the result of this offense was judgment coming to all men, resulting in condemnation.

Paul mentioned both Adam's transgression and offense because while people often consider Adam's transgression, God also considers his offense. We tend to focus on the overstepping of boundaries, but God's concern is the effect it has on our relationship with Him. Adam's offense affected the very realm in which we exist. Through his offense, we were shut up in the realm of condemnation, a realm apart from God.

According to Effectiveness: Constituting Us as Sinners

Romans 5:19 begins by asserting that by Adam's disobedience all mankind was made, or constituted, sinners. Sin and disobedience are closely linked. Through our disobedience, sin is able to act effectively in us. As sinners, our constitution of sin not only involves our position before God—the realm of condemnation—but also our disposition of being disobedient.

In the process of sanctification, there are four items that frustrate our experience: sin, transgression, offense, and disobedience. The first, sin, brings in the other three. Disobedience affects our constitution and disposition. It means to walk one's own road instead of God's road. If someone says, "I will walk this way and do what I want," they are manifesting disobedience.

According to Living: Separated from God

Adam ate the fruit of the tree of the knowledge of good and evil in an act of disobedience. Such an act had five aspects: sin entered him, he transgressed, he offended, he disobeyed, and eventually sin reigned in death over him, causing him to live separated from God.

We can use these five aspects to summarize our experience in Adam, as described by Romans 5:12–21. The source of sin was one man, and as descendants of that man, we are born with a sinful nature. This sinful nature results in transgressions, leading to death reigning over our being. Through Adam's offense, we are in the realm of condemnation, and through Adam's disobedience, sin effectively constitutes us as sinners. Finally, we live sinful lives that allow sin to reign in death, separating us from God.

Some may feel that these were only Adam's experiences and have nothing to do with us. However, our own lives testify that in Adam our experiences are the same as his. Those in Adam have a very clear sequence of falling. First, the sinful nature dwells in them. The sinful nature issues in transgressions that become offenses, resulting in disobedience, and eventually issuing in death that separates them from God. The beginning of this sequence is the sinful nature, the end is death, and in between are transgressions, offenses, and disobedience.

In Christ!

To be in Adam is wretched, but as Christians, we can praise the Lord because we are now in Christ! In Him, we are justified by God and experience sanctification in His divine life. We used to be in Adam, but through the redemption of Jesus Christ, we can now experience the working of His life within. We can allow Him to dwell in us, live in us, walk with us, and be with us, which causes us to grow and experience reigning in His divine life. Satan cannot rule over us anymore, for Christ is our Lord!

74

The Gift of Life by Grace

But the free gift is not like the offense. For if by the one man's offense many died, much more the grace of God and the gift by the grace of the one Man, Jesus Christ, abounded to many.
—*Romans 5:15 (NKJV®)*

WORD STUDY

This verse begins Paul's comparison between Adam and Christ, and discusses the effects brought about by each. Just as sin is of Adam, grace is of Christ. Before committing any sins of their own, all people were condemned by the one offense of Adam. However, much more the grace of God and the free gift of Christ abound to us without our merit (Luther, 97). The term "much more" could indicate the great results of Christ's effect or the fact that what is gained through Him is surer than what is gained through Adam (Vincent, 3:63).

Two items abound in this verse: the grace of God and the gift by the grace of Jesus Christ. The phrase "the gift" is joined to "the grace of the one Man, Jesus Christ" by the Greek word *en*. *En* is a common Greek preposition, most often translated "in" and used to indicate the spatial position of an object. However, it can also be translated "with" to indicate an association (often a close personal friendship), "because of" to indicate causation, or "by, with" to indicate instrumentation (Wallace, 742). Whichever way it is translated, it is clear that the gift and the grace of Jesus Christ are intertwined. H. Alford states that the grace here is not grace working in people, but the grace that is in, and flows from, God. This grace of our Lord Jesus Christ is then the medium by which the free gift abounds to all people (Alford, 2:362).

REVELATION AND APPLICATION

The Subjective Experience in Christ

Just like our subjective experience of sin in Adam, our subjective experience of sanctification in Christ has five aspects, related to sanctification's source, our being, our realm, the effectiveness of sanctification, and our living. The source of our sanctification is grace and the gift of life, *dōrea*. In our being, the gift of life has grown, *dōrēma*, and become a gift in operation, *charisma* (Rom. 5:15–16); Additionally, the realm of sanctification is the realm of grace (5:18). Sanctification is effective in constituting us with righteousness (5:19), and our living allows grace to reign in us through righteousness to eternal life (5:21).

In this chapter, we will consider the source of our experience of sanctification and our realm. In the next chapter, we will consider our experience of sanctification as it relates to our being. Finally, in chapter 81, we will consider our experience of sanctification's effectiveness and our living. As we consider these five items, we may be amazed at how many riches these verses contain concerning our subjective experiences in Christ.

According to Source: Grace

In Romans 5:14, we are told that Adam was a type of Him

who was to come, that is, Jesus Christ (v. 15). All people are born into Adam, but through the resurrection of Jesus, God regenerates us and transfers us from Adam into Christ. Now we are in Christ! In Christ, grace is the source of our experience of sanctification.

According to Realm: Grace

Grace is not only the source of our experience of sanctification but also a realm we can enter and stand in (Rom. 5:2). It is the divine and mystical realm. At the moment we were saved, God moved us from the realm of condemnation and death to the realm of grace. His desire is to richly dispense all of Himself, everything He has, and everything He has done into us. By this dispensing, we can live in the reality of our oneness with Him. In order to bring about such a reality and living, however, He had to bring us into a new realm—the realm of grace. Only in this realm can God's gift grow and be realized in us.

In Romans 5:15, Paul gives an advanced description of grace: it is of God, it is of Jesus Christ, and it abounds to many.

Grace is a realm, but we can also say our triune God Himself is grace. God the Father is the source of grace, Christ is the outflow of that grace to us, and the Holy Spirit brings that grace into us. Just as Satan is expressed as sin, God is expressed as grace. Because He is grace, when we are in the realm of grace, the triune God is our all-sufficient supply.

The Gift of Life by Grace

Grace is the triune God Himself. The gift by grace is also nothing but God Himself entering us to become our experience, enjoyment, and reality. How wonderful! When grace enters us, it becomes the gift of God's divine life (*dōrea*).

Christians sometimes struggle to define salvation. In fact, salvation is simply the gaining of the grace of God and the gift of life. Every Christian has both the grace of God and the gift of life, which is by this grace (Rom. 5:15). Because we have this gift, we can know, experience, and enjoy both grace and life.

Grace and the gift of life are closely related, although they are not the same. The outflow of the divine life from God is grace, and when this grace comes to us, the divine life flows into us as the gift of life. The Father is the source of life, the Lord Jesus is the outflow of life, which is grace, and the Holy Spirit brings the gift of life into us as the realization of this grace.

Throughout our Christian life, as we experience the flowing of God's life to us as grace, we are revived, which brings in the power of the Holy Spirit. The divine life brought in by our enjoyment of grace is both powerful and operative. Grace surrounds us (5:2), and the gift of life enters into us (John 4:10, 14). Grace upholds us, supplies us, and protects us. The gift of life restores our spiritual vitality by reviving our spiritual life and desire and enabling our spiritual growth. The gift of life freely given by God is full of revival and power in us!

The power of this life has the ability to change people. A man's friends may notice a change in him after he is saved. This change is not solely outward, like that of a circus monkey dressed as a human, yet still retaining the life of a monkey. When we are regenerated, the life we receive changes us inwardly and organically. It is the gift of life by grace that has this power to change us. The spontaneous manifestation of the inward gift of life is contrary to the life we lived according to our sinful nature. It is no wonder people notice the change in the life of a regenerated believer. Such a change is not the result of a determination for self improvement, but the result of the inward gift of life manifesting itself outwardly.

The Gift of Life Being the Triune God

By grace we were regenerated and received the gift of life. The divine life regenerated us, became our gift, and produced power in us. This life was and continues to be dynamic, not static. It is the very life of our triune God, and it brings us His attributes and operation. It not only comes into us and grows in us, but it is also manifested, lived out, and magnified from us.

All of the aspects of God, including His person, His attributes, His operation, and His expression, are in the gift of life. Because our triune God is life, this gift is full of life. Because He is powerful, this gift is full of the power of His life. Praise Him! We have received His grace and His life!

The Growth of Life

As we stand in grace and experience this life inwardly, the divine life grows in us. As this gift of life (*dōrea*) grows, it develops riches and becomes defined by its growth (*dōrēma*).

We should desire that this gift of life would grow in us. However, spiritual growth is always relative and never absolute. In other words, we are never absolutely mature; there is always more growth to experience. If someone asks how mature we are, we should answer, "It is based on who I am standing beside!" Compared to a new believer, we are hopefully more mature. Compared to an old and spiritual believer, we are probably less mature. Maturity is relative, and our growth is life-long.

Our experience of sanctification is altogether wrapped up in the growth of the divine life in us. Our enjoyment of grace, our knowledge of life, and our experience of this life's power are all tied to the growth of God's life in us. The grace of God as our realm and the gift of life by grace within us work together for the growth of the divine life. This is the growth of the triune God in us and produces the reality of sanctification.

The Gift in Operation

But the free gift is not like the offense. For if by the one man's offense many died, much more the grace of God and the gift by the grace of the one Man, Jesus Christ, abounded to many. ¹⁶And the gift is not like that which came through the one who sinned. For the judgment which came from one offense resulted in condemnation, but the free gift which came from many offenses resulted in justification.
—Romans 5:15-16 (NKJV®)

WORD STUDY

In this section, the Greek word *charisma* is twice translated "gift." The first time is in the beginning of verse 15: "But the *charisma* is not like the offense." The second time is at the end of verse 16: "The *charisma* which came from many offenses resulted in justification."

The word *charisma* simply means a "gift of grace, or a gift involving grace" (Vine, 264). This definition is derived from the root word *charis*, which means "grace, favor, and pleasure" (Strong, #5485). The suffix *ma* is a common ending for Greek nouns, and often denotes the result of an action (Robinson, 139). Thus, *charisma* could be considered a gift that is the result of God's grace given to men.

Within the context of the New Testament, *charisma* is used mostly in reference to the spiritual endowments of believers through the Holy Spirit (Brown, 2:42). These spiritual endowments are called gifts from God and include abilities like prophesying, teaching, and healing (see Romans 12 and 1 Corinthians 12). These gifts are given by the Holy Spirit in the context of the church (1 Cor. 12:4, 7).

REVELATION AND APPLICATION

The Key to Sanctification

The offense of one man, Adam, had a specific result, and the gift of life (*dōrea*) also has a specific result. The result of Adam's offense was death and condemnation, but the gift of life only results in more life as it grows in us. When grace visits us, it becomes the gift of life (Rom. 5:15). This gift grows in us richly (*dōrēma*) and issues in an outward operation (*charisma*).

Because *dōrea* is the most basic aspect of the gift of God, we may expect that this section of verses would begin with it. Amazingly, however, it begins with the aspect of this gift's operation—"the *charisma* is not like the offense" (v. 15). This section also ends with the aspect of operation—"the *charisma* that… resulted in justification" (v. 16). It would seem from this emphasis that Paul felt very strongly about the operation of the gift of life. Because of Paul's emphasis, we may say that *charisma* is the key to our experience of sanctification. The key is not simply life, nor is it the riches gained by the growth of life. Rather, the key is the operation of the riches gained by the growth of life.

A true spiritual gift will always involve the constitution of God's grace in a person. This is a good indicator of whether a believer's operation is spiritually inspired or not. Rather than focusing on things like eloquent speaking, high understanding, or even the fruit of labor, we should consider whether the source of a believer's operation is simply natural talent and ability or if it is a true *charisma*. A true *charisma* will always involve the constitution of God's grace in the believer who possesses it.

Do not think lightly of this. Today there are many Christians who serve God by their natural ability and not by His divine life. Our service should not come from our natural ability but from our growth, riches, and maturing in grace.

According to Being: The Gift in Operation

As we saw in the previous chapter, our subjective experience of sanctification in Christ has five aspects, related to sanctification's source, our being, our realm, the effectiveness of sanctification, and our living. The source of our sanctification is grace and the gift of life, *dōrea*. In our being, the gift of life has grown, *dōrēma*, and become a gift in operation, *charisma* (5:15–16); Additionally, the realm of sanctification is the realm of grace (5:18). Sanctification is effective in constituting us with righteousness (Rom. 5:19), and our living allows grace to reign in us through righteousness to eternal life (5:21).

In this chapter, we will consider the subjective experience of sanctification in Christ according to our being.

The Result of the Rich Growth in Grace

The progression in Romans 5:15–16 shows us that the process of sanctification is from grace (*charis*) to the gift of life (*dōrea*), to the growth of the gift of life (*dōrēma*), to the gift in operation (*charisma*).

Both *dōrēma* (the growth of the gift of life) and *charisma* (the gift in operation) have the Greek ending *ma*. Generally, this Greek suffix indicates the result of a process. Thus, *dōrēma* is the result of the rich growth of the gift of life. Likewise, the gift in operation, *charisma*, is the result of the rich growth of grace.

Grace and life can never be separated from each other. Romans 5:2 says, "Through whom also we have obtained our introduction by faith into this grace in which we stand." Today we are standing in abundant grace, which is a divine and mystical realm. Two things happened when we believed: we received the gift of life by grace, and we entered into the realm of grace. Over time, this gift of life grows within us (*dōrēma*). When this gift is in harmony with the realm of grace in which we stand, the operation of this gift is produced (*charisma*). *Charisma* is not simply another word for the free *dōrea*, nor is it merely the operation of our natural talent or ability. Instead, it is the operation produced by the harmony between the rich inward growth of the divine life and the rich realm of grace in which we stand.

The Importance of an Encouraging Environment

We may consider the gift in operation a simple thing. In fact, we may think that a person's charming or magnetic personality is such a gift. According to the revelation in Romans, however, a *charisma* is better thought of as the gift of life operating in grace. This indicates that the gift in operation is produced by the growth of the divine life within us in a harmonious relationship with God in the realm of grace. If the inward riches we have gained by the growth of life match grace, the result will be a proper gift in operation (*charisma*).

For the divine life to grow and for the gift to develop an operation, there must be a proper outward environment. This is also true in the natural realm. For example, a man may be naturally able to play very moving music. However, no matter how talented he is, his outward environment must be proper for this talent to develop and constitute him as a composer and musician.

Another example involves the period of history known as the Dark Ages, roughly from A.D. 500–1500. During this time, society was dormant in every aspect. No matter how talented people were, their abilities were not developed. This was because there was no proper environment for growth and development. It was not until the Renaissance that European society changed and became full of vitality. Now, people were encouraged to develop their abilities, to grow, and to think. In this environment, many talented writers, artists, and thinkers were manifested, whose works still shine today.

These examples are related to the natural realm. Regardless of how much natural talent a person has, it will not operate effectively without a proper environment. Spiritual things are no different, and the gift of God follows this pattern.

The Match between Our Growth and Operation

In a healthy Christian, *dōrēma* and *charisma* should match each other. In other words, the inward growth of the divine life should match the outward operation produced in grace. If the *dōrēma* does not match the *charisma*, an unhealthy situation will be produced in the church life.

In the New Testament, the church that emphasized spiritual gifts the most was the church in Corinth, which, according to Paul, was not lacking in any *charisma*, or outward gift (1 Cor. 1:7). However, the believers there were full of the fallen human nature, and they earned Paul's rebuke in several instances as fleshly people (1 Cor. 3:1–3). Church history shows us that Corinth was not unique. There have been many earnest Christian groups that have emphasized outward gifts, yet their members lived extremely corrupt lifestyles.

We may wonder how the most damaging things to the church could flourish alongside outward spiritual gifts. This happens when believers value the gift of life (*dōrea*), treasure the grace of God (*charis*), and emphasize the gift in operation (*charisma*), but do not pay much attention to the inward growth of life (*dōrēma*). Though the Bible very positively mentions outward gifts, if the gift in operation and the growth of life do not match, God's work in the church will be frustrated.

Believers generally have a far different understanding of the proper place of spiritual gifts than the Bible describes. For example, some Christians heavily emphasize speaking in tongues. This is a spiritual gift in the Bible, and neither the practice of speaking in tongues nor the teaching concerning it is wrong. What is wrong is to promote it and to force the saints to practice it. The danger of overly focusing on speaking in tongues, or on any spiritual gift, is that eventually there is not much life (*dōrea*), growth (*dōrēma*), or true operation (*charisma*). A proper, healthy, and effective operation in the church must come from the divine life and match the riches produced by the growth of life.

Not Like the Offense

Paul used the word *charisma* when he described what was the opposite of Adam's offense: "But the free gift (*charisma*) is not like the offense" (Rom. 5:15). He did not say forgiveness or salvation are not like the offense. Rather, he said that the gift is not like the offense. This is a profound statement and hard to understand.

Why is the gift in operation not like the offense? It is because they are completely opposite of each other. *Charisma* indicates that God has worked in us and that He has brought us from the realm of sin to the realm of grace. In the realm of sin are the sinful nature, transgressions, offenses, disobedience, and death. In the realm of grace are grace, the gift of life, the riches of life, and the rich operation and working of life. A genuine and spiritual *charisma* must be related to God and His desire, accomplish His eternal will, carry out His divine administration, and bring in His kingdom and satisfaction.

This thought regarding the gift in operation (*charisma*) is not simple. Our lifelong experience of sanctification is inseparable from the gift in operation. As this gift grows, it builds upon itself, becoming higher, richer, and more heavenly. Just as an old man has a higher understanding of life than a young boy, only as we mature and experience the process of sanctification is it possible to have a deeper and higher understanding of the stages of the growth of the divine life.

This is our lifelong experience of *charisma*. This gift is totally related to grace. In the gift in operation are the grace of God and the grace of one Man, Jesus Christ, which abounds unto all people. God is the source of grace, Christ is the outflow of grace, and the Spirit is the flow of grace into us. *Charisma* involves the gift of life, the rich growth of life, and the harmony between this life and grace. Praise the Lord that the *charisma* is not like the offense!

76

The Free Gift from Many Offenses

And the gift is not like that which came through the one who sinned. For the judgment which came from one offense resulted in condemnation, but the free gift which came from many offenses resulted in justification.
—Romans 5:16 (NKJV®)

WORD STUDY

This verse continues the contrast begun in verse 15 between the offense and the free gift. In verse 15, the entry of the gift of grace through Jesus Christ was compared to the entry of sin through Adam. The main distinction there was in the degree; the phrase "much more" shows that the gift of grace far surpassed the offense and its results (Morgan, 72).

Verse 16 contrasts two results, differentiating them immediately with the phrase, "the gift is not like that which came through the one who sinned." According to the verse, judgment came from the one offense and resulted in condemnation. The Greek word for condemnation, *katakrima*, indicates not only the sentence at the time it is pronounced but also suggests the carrying out of the punishment that follows (Vine, 119). In contrast, the gift came out of not one but many offenses and resulted in justification (*dikaiōma*).

Another way to describe the comparison in this verse is this: one offense brought in judgment, which resulted in condemnation; many offenses brought in the free gift, which resulted in justification.

REVELATION AND APPLICATION

The Result of the Gift in Operation

As we saw in previous chapters, Paul uses two different Greek words in Romans 5:16 for the word "gift." The first is *dōrēma*, which "is not like that which came through the one who sinned." The second is *charisma*, which "came from many offenses [and] resulted in justification." *Charisma* is the gift in operation, the manifestation of the growth of life within us in harmony with grace. This verse tells us that *charisma*, the gift in operation, issues in justification.

The Greek word translated "justification" in this verse is different than the one used in Romans 4:25, which reads, "He who was delivered over because of our transgressions, and was raised because of our justification." There, the Greek word used is *dikaiōsis*; in 5:16 the word used is *dikaiōma*. In Greek, the suffix *sis* is often used to denote action or process, while the suffix *ma* is often used to denote the result of an action or process. We could say that the resurrection of Christ is related to the process of justification (4:25), and that *charisma* is related to the result of this process (5:16). This result of justification can be described in a simple phrase that we will consider further: the reality of everlasting justification.

The Reality of Everlasting Justification

We who are in Christ are objectively justified before God, and this justification will last through eternity. If our everlasting justification is real to us, our subjectivity is less likely to affect us in negative ways. Christians often say things like, "Yesterday my spiritual situation was good. The Lord's presence was with me, my fellowship with Him was so sweet, and I overcame my sin. But today I am not doing so well! I lost the Lord's presence, I feel very far from Him, and I have incurred many offenses." All of these thoughts are related to subjective feelings that do not take the objective facts into view.

Our recognition of the reality of everlasting justification frees us from this kind of subjectivity. We can joyfully say in any situation, "Lord, thank You. I treasure the gift given to me by Your grace." Where can we find such firm assurance? It is by the outward manifestation of the gift of God that the assurance of our justification is found. When God's gift of life operates and functions from us, we are brought to realize how real our justification is. Whether our subjective responses to situations leave us feeling high, strong, sweet, and overcoming, or whether we feel low, weak, bitter, and failing, our everlasting justification is a reality to which we can cling.

The Process of Justification

The blessing of God can be brought in by justified believers, despite all our weaknesses and shortcomings. Some may wonder how such a thing could be. According to Romans 4:25, Christ was raised for our justification (*dikaiōsis*). When we fail or are weak, the resurrection life within us is able to bring in the subjective application of our justification. This is the process of justification.

Without the resurrection life and the process of justification (*dikaiōsis*), we would never be able to overcome a failure. Loving the world once would mean we could never love the Lord again. Experiencing weakness once would mean we could never be strong again. However, we can be thankful that justification is always operating in resurrection. Even if we fail, become weak, or love the world, through the process of justification in resurrection, we can come back to overcome, find strength, and love the Lord.

Paul says in 5:16 that the free gift came from many offenses and results in justification. Offenses are negative and do not please God. However, from our offenses the resurrection life operates to bring into us the process of justification (*dikaiōsis*). Through this process, the gift of God can operate from us (*charisma*), and we can be brought into the result of justification, the assurance of the reality of everlasting justification (*dikaiōma*). Thus, many offenses lead to *dikaiōma*, just as the verse says. Praise the Lord for His resurrection life and for His operating gift within us!

Abundant Grace and Righteousness

For if by the one man's offense death reigned through the one, much more those who receive abundance of grace and of the gift of righteousness will reign in life through the One, Jesus Christ.
—*Romans 5:17 (NKJV®)*

WORD STUDY

This verse completes Paul's comparisons between Adam and Christ, and the effects brought about by each. Paul mentions two things that are received in abundance through the One, Jesus Christ: grace and the gift of righteousness. The Greek word used here for "abundance," *perisseia*, means "surplus, i.e. superabundance" (Strong, #4050). It is used to indicate an exceeding measure or something above ordinary, and metaphorically can be translated, "overflowing," as liquid in a cup would overflow its rim (Vine, 5).

In the Greek text, the word for "righteousness" is a genitive noun describing "gift." In general, the genitive case is used to qualify a noun. This relationship could indicate, among other possibilities, that the gift is characterized by righteousness, that it could contain righteousness, or that it could even be for the purpose of righteousness (Wallace, 727–728).

REVELATION AND APPLICATION

Romans 5:17 mentions the abundance of two things: grace and the gift of righteousness. The Greek word used here for "gift" is *dōrea*, which here indicates the gift of God's divine life. It is not only called the gift of righteousness in this verse but is also called the gift by grace in Romans 5:15. We can say that the gift of life (*dōrea*) has two obvious characteristics: it has an abundance of grace, and it has the quality of righteousness.

Our Realm and Nature

In Romans 5:2, grace is a divine and mystical realm we can stand in. According to Romans 5:17, righteousness is the quality, or nature, of the gift of life. We receive an abundance of this gift, and so receive an abundance of righteousness. Abundant grace is the realm of God's gift of life (*dōrea*) and abundant righteousness is its nature. We have not only received abundant grace but also abundant righteousness.

When we think of gifts, we usually think of a person's ability to do things like speak, manage a church, serve, or preach the gospel. However, the gift mentioned here, *dōrea*, is not focused on outward manifestation or ability but on a realm and nature. On the one hand, we live in the realm of abundant grace. On the other hand, abundant righteousness will become a regulating factor within us. Abundant grace is our all-inclusive supply, energizing us to enjoy, experience, and follow the Lord lifelong. Abundant righteousness inwardly regulates and constrains us so that our living becomes righteous.

Constituted Righteous

The process of sanctification involves both grace and righteousness. Therefore, we should never lay them aside. We need abundant grace as well as abundant righteousness. Grace is the triune God becoming our enjoyment, and righteousness is the result of our enjoyment of the triune God as grace. The gift of life needs the abundance of grace to support its righteous nature, so that we are constituted righteous in grace. As we receive and enjoy grace, we are constituted righteous and live out righteousness.

Righteousness is a divine attribute. When we were saved, we received the gift of God and were changed in life, because this gift of life, with its quality of righteousness, came to dwell in us. Even more, through our growth in grace, righteousness will be manifested through our living. Such a living is the result of becoming constituted righteous by the gift of life.

Overflowing Grace and Righteousness

The gift of life (*dōrea*) is related to grace and righteousness. Because *dōrea* is life, it can overflow. Jesus is life (John 14:6), and He declared that He is living water to spring up within us (John 4:10-14). When the divine life overflows from us, it overflows with both grace and righteousness.

How wonderful this is! The gift of life, which we enjoy, overflows with grace and righteousness. Grace is the realm of the gift of life, and righteousness is its nature. Grace is enjoyment, and righteousness is a divine attribute. Grace fills us with enjoyment, and righteousness regulates our living. Our experience of the reality of sanctification is according to both abundant and overflowing grace and abundant and overflowing righteousness.

78

Reigning in Life

For if by the one man's offense death reigned through the one, much more those who receive abundance of grace and of the gift of righteousness will reign in life through the One, Jesus Christ.
—Romans 5:17 (NKJV®)

WORD STUDY

This verse completes Paul's comparisons between Adam and Christ, and the effects brought about by each. Specifically, it contrasts the reign of death with a reigning in life. The Greek word used here for "reign," *basileuō*, means "to rule as king." This word is also used in verse 14 for the reigning of death, and in this context it has the sense of controlling or determining the destiny of those it is over (Rogers, 326). The reign of death means death controls our destiny.

Although death reigned through the offense of Adam, through Jesus Christ those who receive the abundance of grace and the gift of righteousness will reign in life (for more on this aspect, see chapter 77). G. C. Morgan calls this reigning in life the reign of grace. He writes, "The phrase 'much more' reveals the fact that in grace overwhelming provision is made for victory over sin" (Morgan, 73).

The Greek word for "life" in this verse is *zōē*, which is God's divine and eternal life (Vine, 367). We would expect Paul to write that this life reigns, in antithesis to "death reigned." However, Paul wrote that we will reign in life. H. Alford explains that this is to bring out even more the idea of free personality: "Reigning is the highest development of freedom, and the highest satisfaction of all desires" (Alford, 2:364).

REVELATION AND APPLICATION

The Reigning Divine Life

According to this verse, the process of sanctification includes our reigning in life. The Greek word for "life" in this verse is *zōē*, the divine and eternal life. It is very crucial to know the *zōē* life. This is the life we are saved by (Rom. 5:10), grow in, and reign in through Jesus Christ. Before we can reign in life, however, this life must reign in us. We are in the reality of sanctification whenever we allow the divine and eternal life to reign in us.

Paul uses the phrase "abundance of grace and of the gift of righteousness" (v. 17). The "gift" here is *dōrea*, the gift of life. It is by this gift that we can reign in life. The divine life not only regenerates us and initiates our experience of sanctification, but also reigns in us. It does not take a certain amount of growth or spirituality for this reigning of the divine life to begin. This life came into us and began to reign the moment we believed.

The reigning life within us may manifest itself in different ways. For example, a man who liked to gamble before receiving the Lord continued to gamble after his regeneration. Outwardly, he seemed to still enjoy gambling, but he later testified that he was inwardly suffering and tormented. Gambling used to be a great enjoyment to him, but now it made him very uncomfortable. This was his experience of the reigning of the *zōē* life. By cooperating with this reigning life, this brother could eventually stop gambling—a manifestation of his reigning in life.

As believers, we have the gift of life within us, which not only saves us by life but allows us to reign in life. The rest of our human life will be filled with experiences of this reigning life. As the divine life within us grows, these experiences multiply and grow richer in us. As the inward reigning of the divine life is outwardly manifested through our reigning in life, we are living in the reality of sanctification.

Because we are regenerated, we should not allow death to reign in us. Rather, we should allow the reining of the divine life. We should not live in death but in life. We should not be one with the world but with the grace of Christ. We should not abide in the sinful flesh but in the realm of grace. The sin in us lives in the realm of the world, but the gift of life (*dōrea*) lives in grace. We used to live as sinners in the world, allowing death to reign in us. However, we now live in grace and are full of the gift of life. This gift issues in the effective reign of the divine life in us.

The Process of Reigning

Our experience in Adam is of death reigning, but our experience in Christ is of life reigning in us so that we can reign in life. Adam and Christ are two different realms with two different experiences, two different ways to grow, and two different results. The realm of Adam is according to sin; the realm of Christ is according to righteousness.

Praise the Lord for our great transfer (Col. 1:13)! We have been transferred from the kingdom of Satan to the kingdom of Christ; from the realm of condemnation to the divine and mystical realm of grace; from the reigning of death to the reigning of life; from the earthly domain to the heavenly domain; from being constituted with sin to being constituted with righteousness. Our being constituted with righteousness is the process of our reigning in life.

Sanctification begins with our being saved by life (Rom. 5:10) and ends with our conformation to the image of the Son of God (8:29). On the day we believed, the divine life entered us and began to save us. This is the beginning of sanctification. When the Lord returns, our whole being—inward and outward—will be conformed to the image of the Son of God. In that day, the sanctification process will be complete, and we will be fully constituted with righteousness. The process from our current position to that glorious one involves our reigning in life by allowing the divine life to reign in us day by day.

79

Justification of Life

Therefore, as through one man's offense judgment came to all men, resulting in condemnation, even so through one Man's righteous act the free gift came to all men, resulting in justification of life.
—Romans 5:18 (NKJV®)

WORD STUDY

This verse declares that it is through Jesus Christ's righteous act (*dikaiōma*) that the free gift came to all men. The Greek word *dikaiōma* can be translated "justification, righteousness" (Strong, #1345) or "a righteous act or deed" (Thayer, 151). Commentators generally refer to this righteous deed as the accomplished death of Christ on the cross (Alford, 2:364).

Through Christ's righteous act, the free gift came to all men, resulting in justification of life. The phrase "resulting in" is translated from one Greek preposition, *eis*, which literally means "to or into, indicating the point reached or entered of place, time, or purpose" (Strong, #1519). *Eis* could indicate that the free gift results in justification of life, that it is for the purpose of justification of life, or that it leads us into the realm of justification of life (Wallace, 741).

REVELATION AND APPLICATION

Sanctification is a lifelong experience and is never separate from justification. Justification is both judicial and, as the verse here says, of life. Every time Paul mentions justification in Romans, it is related to our experience.

Experiencing Justification

Paul summarizes justification in one verse, saying, "These whom He predestined, He also called; and these whom He called, He also justified; and these whom He justified, He also glorified" (Rom. 8:30). Justification is what connects God's calling to our glorification.

Justification not only deals with our status before God but is also a lifelong process. Our experience of sanctification is part of this process. If our understanding of justification is not adequate, we will find it difficult to experience sanctification. We must be sure of our justified status and of the operation and working of justification in life. Without such assurance, it is hard for sanctification to become experiential to us.

Justification in Resurrection Life

In Romans 3, Paul wrote that we are justified as a gift by the grace of God through the redemption in Christ Jesus (v. 24). In chapter 4, Paul further said that justification is related to the resurrection of Christ: "Who was delivered up because of our offenses, and was raised because of our justification" (v. 25, NKJV®).This verse is not easily understood by our natural mind. We would find it much easier to understand if Paul had written, "Jesus was delivered up because of our justification and was raised for our sanctification." It seems logical to think that we were justified because of the death of Jesus and are now sanctified because of His resurrection. However, the Bible tells us that the death of Jesus was because of our offenses, and His resurrection was for our justification. In other words, God's work of justification is totally related to and realized in the resurrection life of Christ. We are born again by the resurrection life, our growth is in the resurrection life, and our maturity comes from the resurrection life. Our entire Christian life, including our experience of sanctification, is related to our justification in the resurrection life.

The Greek word for justification in Romans 4:25 is *dikaiōsis*, a noun with the Greek suffix *sis*, which generally indicates an action or process (Robinson, 139–140). Therefore, *dikaiōsis* implies the process of justification. Jesus was delivered up because of our offenses and was raised for us to experience the process of justification. Paul uses this same Greek word, *dikaiōsis*, in Romans 5:18 for the "justification" of life. This justification of life is a result of our judicial justification before God and, in the resurrection life of Christ, is a process for us to experience lifelong.

Suppose we have been believers for fifty years, during which we loved the Lord, repeatedly consecrated ourselves to Him, paid a price for Him, and even gave up everything for Him. Behind all of these things was the working of the resurrection life within us to bring us through experiences of justification. Since this was the case over the last fifty years, it is still true today. No matter how long we have been believers, we must allow God's resurrection life to be transmitted and dispensed into us, for the purpose of our continual experience of the process of justification.

Unto the Reality of Justification

Paul wrote in Romans 5:

But the free gift (*charisma*) is not like the offense. For if by the one man's offense many died, much more the grace of God and the gift (*dōrea*) by the grace of the one Man, Jesus Christ, abounded to many. And the gift (*dōrēma*) is not like that which came through the one who sinned. For the judgment which came from one offense resulted in condemnation, but the free gift (*charisma*) which came from many offenses resulted in justification (*dikaiōma*). (vv. 15-16, NKJV®)

Notice that *charisma*, God's gift in outward operation, is mentioned at the beginning of verse 15 and at the end of verse 16. This gift eventually results in justification (*dikaiōma*). In a previous chapter, we called this aspect of justification the reality of everlasting justification.

The process which brings us from the *charisma* in verse 15 to justification in verse 16 is wonderful. In the realm of grace, the gift of life grows and produces many riches, and this growth of life in grace produces the *charisma*. Eventually, this *charisma* issues in the reality of everlasting justification.

One Righteous Act

Paul speaks of the righteous act of one Man (Rom. 5:18). The Greek word for "righteous act" is *dikaiōma*, the same word used in verse 16 for justification. This word contains the suffix *ma*, which typically refers to a completed action or the result of an action (Robinson, 139-140). Here it could indicate the act of Christ being crucified for our offenses. Yet it could also indicate the overall life of Christ—His birth, His human living, His crucifixion, and His resurrection. All these parts of the earthly life of Christ are together a completed righteous act that affects eternity. Because of this righteous act, we can now be brought into the experience of the justification of life.

The Justification of Life

As mentioned earlier, Paul uses the Greek word *dikaiōsis* in Romans 5:18 for the "justification" of life, which implies the process of justification. This justification is not only judicial but also of life. The process of the justification of life comes from the divine life within us. This life continually stirs within us to operate and become our subjective enjoyment, living, and satisfaction. Justification is not only an objective doctrine but is full of life, feeling, and application.

Justification is a continuous process. By the righteous act of the Lord Jesus (*dikaiōma*), we not only are justified judicially but also continuously receive the supply of the divine life. This supply is for the working of the justification of life (*dikaiōsis*).

A Wonderful Cycle

Romans 4 and 5 present a wonderful cycle to us. Romans 4:25 says that the resurrection of Christ is for our justification (*dikaiōsis*). Romans 5:16 says that the gift which came from many offenses resulted in justification (*dikaiōma*). In Romans 5:18, by the righteous act of Christ (*dikaiōma*), we experience the process of the justification of life (*dikaiōsis*).

In these verses, the process of justification (*dikaiōsis*) comes first in Romans (4:25), followed by the result of justification (*dikaiōma*) (5:18). This may seem logical to us, because the process should come before the result. However, in 5:18, the order of the words is reversed. The result of justification (*dikaiōma*) is mentioned before the process of justification (*dikaiōsis*). How can this be explained?

The answer is that we simultaneously live in both the process (*dikaiōsis*) and result (*dikaiōma*) of justification. Justification is not a linear experience; rather, these two experiences continually alternate. After experiencing the process of justification, we become more constituted with the reality of everlasting justification. The more we have the realization of this judicial justification, the further we are led into the process of justification.

For example, consider again those who, for fifty years, have believed into the Lord, loved Him, and been consecrated to Him. Have they experienced the result of justification—*dikaiōma*—or the process of justification—*dikaiōsis*? We have to say that they have had many experiences of the process of justification, and these experiences have given them more of a realization of justification. As their realization of justification increased, it brought them further into the process of justification.

We can never get away from either the process or result of justification. In our experience of resurrection life, we continually experience the process of justification and are constituted with the result of justification. This cycle continues for our whole life. No matter how old we are, we need to have more experiences of the result of justification in order that we would experience the full justification of life in greater measure.

Abraham: A Life of Justification

Abraham's life is a wonderful Old Testament example of the experience of both the process and result of justification.

Genesis 15 says that Abraham believed God and God accounted it to him as righteousness (v. 6). At that moment, Abraham had his initial experience of the result of justification. In chapter 16, the newly justified Abraham went his own way and begot Ishmael, laughed at God's promise in unbelief, and almost betrayed his own wife. We might wonder how God could still justify him. However, it was in Abraham's weakness, unbelief, laughter, and failure that he could experience more of the process of justification. By experiencing this process, Abraham could obtain a richer and more practical result of justification that would bring him on even further in the process of justification.

When Abraham offered up Isaac (Gen. 22:9-10), he experienced the God who gives life to the dead (Rom. 4:17). At that moment, the result of justification was richer in him than ever before. His first touch with the result of justification was according to God and involved little of his own experience. His second touch with the result of justification came from the richer experience of the God who gives life to the dead. The reality of justification had grown in him from the first experience to the second. Using the Greek words, we can say that he grew from the first *dikaiōma* to the second, and this growth was his experience of the process of justification, *dikaiōsis*.

Abraham's life gives us a picture of what following the Lord is like. When we believed into the Lord, we experienced within us the result of justification (*dikaiōma*). This caused us to be joyful, for we were justified and no longer condemned. However, God's desire is that no matter how much we enjoy this justification, we would begin to experience the process of justification.

The result of justification (*dikaiōma*) brings us into the process of justification (*dikaiōsis*), and our experiences of this process bring into us more *dikaiōma*. Every action of justification (*dikaiōsis*) is for a richer and more practical result of justification (*dikaiōma*) to be brought in, and every result of justification (*dikaiōma*) is for a deeper and richer experience of the process of justification (*dikaiōsis*). This cycle is for the purpose of sanctifying and maturing us in God's divine life.

The Life of Justification

Therefore, as through one man's offense judgment came to all men, resulting in condemnation, even so through one Man's righteous act the free gift came to all men, resulting in justification of life.
—*Romans 5:18 (NKJV®)*

WORD STUDY

Verse 18 ends with the result of the free gift to all men: "justification of life." The Greek word here for "life" is *zōē*, which is God's life, the divine and eternal life (Vine, 367). This is the same life mentioned in verse 17, "Those who receive abundance of grace and of the gift of righteousness will reign in life."

In 5:18, *zōē* is a genitive singular noun. The genitive case is typically used to qualify a noun. In this instance, God's divine life (*zōē*) qualifies justification. This relationship could indicate, among other things, that justification is characterized by life, possessed by life, or even destined for life. It could also mean that justification produces life or that justification is produced by life (Wallace, 727–728).

REVELATION AND APPLICATION

God's justification does not only deal with our judicial position. It is also a matter of life. We experience the divine life because of justification, and as we experience this life, the reality of justification is brought to us. Justification results in our experience of the divine life, and this life is a life of justification. This life is characterized by righteousness, and its operation and work produce righteousness.

The Foundation of Life

The twofold nature of justification is like the relationship between children and parents. Children and parents share a legal relationship, but children are also the reproduction, manifestation, and continuation of their parents' inward life. Their relationship has a foundation of life. The difference between the legal and life relationship is clearly seen in the relationship between orphans and their adoptive parents. This relationship has a judicial aspect, but not one of biological life. God's justification is both judicial and of life.

The moment we believed into Jesus Christ, the Son of God, we were justified judicially and also received God's divine life (*zōē*). This life caused us to become children of God in life (Gal. 3:26, 1 John 3:1) and brought us into a life relationship with Him. Now we have within us both our human life and God's divine life. We were justified both judicially and in life. We obtained the status of justification, and we also obtained the life that belongs to justification.

Because we possess the life brought in by justification, we will always be God's sons, whether He likes us or not. He must accept us as His sons because of the life relationship we have with Him. The life of justification is eternal and imperishable.

There was a child who did not attend to his proper duties and caused his father to be disappointed. His father said to him one day, "I am very unhappy with you, so I will cut you off. You are no longer my son!" Could this threat really be carried out? The answer is no. No matter how much the father openly condemned his son and insisted on disowning him, his son was still his son in life. The son could always say, "According to the law, you may not acknowledge me as your son, but according to life, I am your son forever. Since my life came from your life, my relationship with you is eternal and undeniable."

If we have such an understanding of justification, we will have a glorious feeling within when we consider how solid the foundation of life is within us, established by justification.

Experiencing the Life of Justification

This justification of life allows us to experience the things belonging to justification, including propitiation and redemption. Romans 3:25 tells us that Jesus was set forth as a propitiation by His blood. As we saw in chapter 49, this propitiation is Christ Himself, pictured in the mercy seat set over the ark. Those who live by the divine life live in the propitiation accomplished by Christ Jesus.

Within the ark, covered by the mercy seat, were three items: manna, typifying the supply of God, the two tablets of Law, typifying God's nature, and Aaron's budded rod, typifying the power and authority of resurrection. The inward experiences of the divine life also have these three aspects: God's supply, God's nature, and the power and authority of resurrection. The life of justification brings us into the experiences of these three aspects.

We usually experience God's supply more than God's nature. For example, a joyful feeling may fill us when we are among saints, singing together in church meetings. This experience has to do with the supply of God's life, yet it does not guarantee the experience of God's nature. Divine life is not only a matter of supply but also a matter of nature. Our experience of the divine life should not only include our enjoyment of God's supply as the manna but also our oneness with God through the tablets. God's supply satisfies us, and God's nature brings us into oneness with Him.

The divine life not only supplies us and brings the divine nature into us, but also causes us to experience the power and authority of the resurrection of Christ, typified by the budded rod of Aaron. This budded rod shows that even if we are short of enjoyment and supply in our following of the Lord, we can still survive. As we go through high mountains and deep valleys in our following of the Lord, the resurrection power will always operate in us to show us the authority of Christ's resurrection and bring us into the experience of Aaron's budded rod.

A Testimony of God's Righteousness

The life of justification in us testifies of God's supply, God's nature, and the power and authority of the resurrection of Christ. The operation and working of this life also testifies that God is righteous. After talking about the propitiation in Romans 3:25, Paul goes on to say, "For the demonstration, I say, of His righteousness at the present time, so that He would be just and the justifier of the one who has faith in Jesus" (v. 26). Although the Bible tells us that God is love (1 John 4:8), the life of justification also includes righteousness. For example, a brother was once promised a gift from a friend if he read the whole Bible. After he finished reading it, the friend's wife reminded him of that promise. Righteousness required that he buy a gift for that brother to fulfill his word. This is a simple example of the righteousness found in the life of justification.

The lesson of righteousness is not easy to learn. Love is one thing, but righteousness is another. In some churches, there is not a shortage of love or enjoyment, but there is a shortage of righteousness. Newly saved brothers and sisters who love the Lord and have a sincere heart toward Him should cause us to consider, "Can those whom the Lord has entrusted to us grow properly among us?" Our churches may be full of love, but if the relationships among the saints are not holy and if their fellowship is unrighteous, it becomes hard for these pure and sincere brothers and sisters to grow well.

Righteousness is related to both the inward operation of the life of justification and our outward living and testimony which issues from this operation. The Lord's leading in us is always righteous and our outward living should also be righteous. This allows the life of justification to grow and have a proper testimony.

There was a married couple who, in the words of their children, never argued. However, this couple admitted that they argued, yet never in the presence of their children. Why did they do this? They wanted to maintain a healthy atmosphere in their family so their children could grow in a healthy way. Similarly, within the church, we should guard every word our mouth speaks and every action our hands perform.

In summary, justification is of life, and this life is of justification. The two are inseparable. God's life is the eternal and imperishable foundation established by justification. This life allows us to inwardly experience the testimony of justification—the manna, the tablets, and the budded rod. This life of justification also testifies that God is righteous. May we always live in this life of justification and unceasingly experience the justification of life.

Unto Eternal Life through Jesus Christ

For as by one man's disobedience many were made sinners, so also by one Man's obedience many will be made righteous. ²⁰*Moreover the law entered that the offense might abound. But where sin abounded, grace abounded much more,* ²¹*so that as sin reigned in death, even so grace might reign through righteousness to eternal life through Jesus Christ our Lord.*
—Romans 5:19–21 (NKJV®)

WORD STUDY

In verse 19, the disobedience of Adam and the obedience of Christ are revealed as having profound effects on mankind—either making people sinners or righteous. The Greek word for "made" is *kathistēmi*, meaning "to permanently place down; to designate, constitute" (Strong, #2525). In other words, Adam's disobedience constituted people as sinners, while Christ's obedience will constitute people as righteous or with righteousness. H. Alford wrote, "Not by imputation merely...but 'shall be made really and actually righteous, as completely so as the others were made really and actually sinners'" (Alford, 2:365).

REVELATION AND APPLICATION

As we saw in chapter 74, our subjective experience of sanctification in Christ has five aspects, related to sanctification's source, our being, our realm, the effectiveness of sanctification, and our living. The source of our sanctification is grace and the gift of life, *dōrea*. In our being, the gift of life has grown, *dōrēma*, and become a gift in operation, *charisma* (Rom. 5:15–16); Additionally, the realm of sanctification is the realm of grace (5:18). Sanctification is effective in constituting us with righteousness (5:19), and our living allows grace to reign in us through righteousness to eternal life (5:21). In this chapter, we will consider the subjective experience of sanctification in Christ according to its effectiveness and our living.

According to Effectiveness: Constituting Us as Righteous

The goal, or outcome, of our experience of sanctification is eternal life (Rom. 6:22). Reaching this goal is totally related to our constitution. In Romans 5:19, the Greek phrase "will be made righteous" could also be translated "will be constituted as righteous." The obedience of Christ has an effective result—we will be constituted as righteous. This constituting process is our subjective experience of sanctification.

We are not only judicially justified, but we are also being constituted with righteousness. This constitution comes from obedience, specifically the obedience of one Man, Jesus Christ. To be justified judicially is different from being constituted as righteous. Simply put, a justified person may not yet have a righteous constitution. On the ground and status of justification, we must allow righteousness to grow and constitute us so that we might become righteous. In the past, we were only sinners who were dead in trespasses and sins, but today in Christ we can be constituted with righteousness. What a salvation we have!

According to Living: Grace Reigning through Righteousness

The Greek word for "righteousness" in Romans 5:21, *dikaiosunēs*, contains the suffix *sunē*, indicating the quality of righteousness (Robinson, 140). God's desire is to justify us first and then, in that justification, to constitute our nature with righteousness. This constituting is related to the effective result of being in Christ. In Him, a person continually being constituted with righteousness will have a living that allows grace to reign through righteousness (v. 21).

Before God gave the Law to Moses, people did not have a clear definition of what sin was. One day the Law entered to expose people's sin, and their offenses abounded. However, we can be thankful that where sin abounded, grace abounded much more. Grace now wants to reign through the renewed nature of man, a nature of righteousness, to bring us to eternal life through the Lord Jesus Christ. Sin used to reign in death, but grace reigns through righteousness unto eternal life.

Just as sin is personified in its reigning in death, grace is personified in its reigning through righteousness. The Lord Jesus Christ is the embodiment of the triune God as grace (John 1:14–17) and is now with our spirit as grace (Phil. 4:23). Sin reigns in death, but grace is more powerful than sin and reigns through righteousness. When we have been constituted with righteousness, grace reigns in us and through us.

In Adam, sin reigns, but in Christ, grace reigns. Grace is not only for our inward enjoyment and a realm in which we stand. It also becomes our person and reigns through our righteous living. Our subjective experience in Christ emphasizes not only our enjoyment of grace but also the person of grace. In this experience, we not only enjoy God but come to know His reigning grace.

Unto Eternal Life

In Romans 5:21, Paul used the Greek preposition *eis* within the phrase "to eternal life." *Eis* is a commonly used preposition that means "to or into (indicating the point reached or entered); also (figuratively) purpose (result)" (Strong, #1519). If it is translated "into," it could indicate the entering of a realm. With the thought of "result," it could be translated "unto," indicating the arrival at this realm by growth. We could say the phrase "to eternal life" means "to arrive at and enter into eternal life."

Our experience of sanctification begins and ends with the divine and eternal life. Over the course of our whole life, God measures to us many and various environments for one purpose—that we would grow unto this eternal life. Romans 8:28 says, "And we know that God causes all things to work together for good to those who love God, to those who are called according to His purpose." Notice that this verse says "all things." We will have many different experiences in our lives as things happen to us in our environments, but none of it is purposeless. Everything that happens to us is for us to obtain, enjoy, and be brought further unto the divine and eternal life.

For example, there was a brother who was in a car accident. This could have caused him to become bitter, or it could have caused him to turn to God. By cooperating with the Lord in this experience, the accident could serve to bring him into further experiences of the eternal life of God. Another example is a sister who suddenly became very sick one day. To her this experience was only a sickness, and it did not bring her unto the eternal life at all. In both of these examples, neither the accident nor the sickness was the real issue at hand.

Rather, it was a matter of whether these saints cooperated with the Lord in their experiences to be brought further unto eternal life. We should often ask the question, "Did I gain more of the eternal life in that experience?"

Our subjective experiences in Christ bring us through a full process, a process from the enjoyment of grace to the reigning of grace, from the gift of life to the gift in operation, from the justification of God to our constitution with righteousness, and from our gaining of eternal life to our full arrival at and entrance into eternal life. This full process of sanctification is so vast and so deep that it requires a lifetime to experience.

82

Dead to Sin

What shall we say then? Are we to continue in sin so that grace may increase? ²May it never be! How shall we who died to sin still live in it?
—*Romans 6:1-2*

WORD STUDY

In verse 1, the Greek word translated "continue," *epimenō*, is composed of two words: *epi*, meaning "over, upon" (Strong, #1909), and *menō*, meaning "to stay, abide, remain" (Strong, #3306). When used as a prefix, *epi* is often an intensifier of the word it is paired with. For example, *ginōskō* means "to know" (Strong, #1097), but *epiginōskō* means "to know well" (Strong, #1921) and can be translated "full knowledge" (see Col. 1:9). When *epi* is added to *menō*, it results in a stronger sense of "abiding" or "remaining," and denotes perseverance and persisting (Vincent, 3:65–66). Here, it could indicate that to "continue in sin" is to practice sin as a frequent habit (Rogers, 320).

REVELATION AND APPLICATION

Sanctification is a lifelong experience for a Christian—the

process of being saved in the life of Christ. In Romans 6, this process can be said to be that of our union and mingling with Christ. Romans 6 can be divided into three sections:

1. Verses 1–5: united and mingled with Christ in our being. This is covered in chapters 82–85 of this book.
2. Verses 6–11: united and mingled with Christ in our experience. This is covered in chapters 86–88 of this book.
3. Verses 12–23: united and mingled with Christ in our living. This is covered in chapters 89–92 of this book.

Having Died to Sin

In the opening of Romans 6, Paul describes how we experience the process of sanctification in our being. He wrote at the end of chapter 5, "Where sin increased, grace abounded all the more, so that, as sin reigned in death, even so grace would reign through righteousness to eternal life through Jesus Christ our Lord" (5:20–21). Consider the facts these verses provide: where sin increased, grace abounded all the more. This grace, which is so rich and abundant, reigns through righteousness, and we receive eternal life through the Lord Jesus Christ. In chapter 6, Paul addresses the obvious question that arises from such wonderful facts—should we dwell in sin in order for grace to abound even more?

Immediately, Paul strongly answers, "May it never be!" (6:2). His reasoning is that we have died to sin, and thus should no longer live in it. In other words, our very being has been changed. A Christian is someone who has died to sin. Paul also wrote in Galatians, "I have been crucified with Christ" (2:20). As Christians, we have died with Christ to sin, to the world, and to the flesh; therefore, we should no longer continue to live in sin.

The Bible's Warning

"To continue" can also be translated "to abide" or "to stay." This is the same word used in Acts 10:48, which says, "Then they asked [Peter] to stay on for a few days." Here, the word "stay" is used to indicate the dwelling of Peter in the house. In the same way, the phrase in Romans 6:1, "are we to continue in sin," carries the thought of remaining and dwelling in sin, indicating the power and place of sin. We should not remain under sin's power and should come out from under its authority. However, although we can come out from under the authority and power of sin, we may still find ourselves dwelling in it. We should not dwell in sin but should be watchful and come out from that place!

In both Romans 6:1 and 2, "sin" is singular, indicating our sinful nature. Here, Paul does not deny that Christians still have a sinful nature that can lead to committing sins. Yet he does not speak specifically against these acts here. Rather, Paul's word is that Christians should not consistently, habitually, and persistently abide in the sinful nature. We definitely should not abide in sin happily or boastfully, as we may have done before believing in the Lord. For example, lust may still operate in us, yet we must not be a lustful person, and we certainly should not persistently, habitually, or willingly abide in lust.

The matter of abiding is not small. The sinful nature operates in us, and this operation can come through many kinds of unlawful and improper things that tempt us to abide in sin. Because we are confined by the flesh, we undeniably fall into sin sometimes and may even temporarily experience abiding in sin. The authority and power of sin will not completely disappear until the second coming of Christ. However, the Bible warns us that we must not habitually and continually abide in sin today. We need to be reminded again and again that no matter how pure we are and how much we love the Lord, sin can tempt us and trap us at any time.

What does it mean to persistently and habitually abide in sin? It means that sinning becomes a lifestyle, even an addiction. For example, a Christian brother might gamble one day and feel guilty. If he goes to the Lord's presence and repents, he will be forgiven by the Lord (1 John 1:9). However, he may think in his heart, "It won't hurt if I gamble again, because as long as I pray after gambling, I will be forgiven again." With this unhealthy attitude, he may carelessly gamble day and night and gradually abide in the sin of gambling. If so, he not only committed the sin of gambling once, but also allowed this sin to become his habit.

Many people realize from experience that sin can grow and develop if it is not carefully guarded against. We must wake up, guard ourselves from abiding in sin, and not allow sin any opportunity to grow and develop in us. This becomes our testimony of having died to sin.

83

Baptized into Christ Jesus

May it never be! How shall we who died to sin still live in it? ³Or do you not know that all of us who have been baptized into Christ Jesus have been baptized into His death? ⁴Therefore we have been buried with Him through baptism into death, so that as Christ was raised from the dead through the glory of the Father, so we too might walk in newness of life.
—*Romans 6:2-4*

WORD STUDY

The Greek word used in verse 3 for "baptized" is *baptizō*, meaning "to make whelmed (i.e. fully wet)" (Strong, #907). The easiest explanation here is that Paul is referring to the common Christian practice of water baptism, in which a newly confirmed believer is fully immersed in water and then raised up from it. The past tense of this action shows that Paul is referring to an acknowledged fact and that he expects his readers to have passed through this experience already.

Paul uses the phrase "baptized into Christ Jesus." The word "into," translated from the Greek preposition *eis*, denotes inner union and participation (Vincent, 3:66). This thought is used again only a few words later in the phrase "baptized into His death," which also includes the word *eis*. The two phrases show us that baptism brings the believer into a state of union with Christ, a union that includes participation and conformity to Christ's death (Alford, 2:367).

In verse 4, participation in Christ and His death leads also to our burial with Him. Many commentators take this as a spiritual experience. Martin Luther wrote, "As the dead and buried Christ appeared in the eyes of the Jews, so also the spiritual person must appear in his own eyes and the eyes of others....[He] must be totally separated from and dead in his heart to all temporal things" (Luther, 101).

REVELATION AND APPLICATION

Romans 6:2 says that we have died to sin. All who are baptized into Christ Jesus have been baptized into His death (v. 3). Because we have been baptized into the death of Christ Jesus, we were also buried with Him (v. 4). Because we were buried with Him, we were also raised with Him, and our lives today are different, full of the newness of resurrection life. Now, just as Christ was raised from the dead through the glory of the Father, we live by the resurrection life and walk in newness of life (v. 4).

A Change of Realm through Baptism

To be baptized means to be immersed. Our baptism into Christ Jesus changes our realm of existence. We used to be in Adam and in the fallen realm of the old creation, but baptism transfers us from Adam into Christ Jesus, who is the divine and mystical realm of the new creation.

In this new realm, we have nothing to do with the world, with Satan, or with his authority and power. We are now in the realm of Christ! The way the Lord Jesus Christ lives is also the way we live—in newness of life (Rom. 6:4). The realm of our existence has changed. We no longer live in the natural realm but in the divine, mystical, and spiritual realm.

Baptized into Christ Jesus

We were baptized into Christ Jesus, who is, at the same time, both Christ and Jesus (1 John 2:22). Christ is His heavenly title and indicates His victorious resurrection. Jesus is His name given among men and indicates His incarnation. When Peter announced the gospel, he said, "Therefore let all the house of Israel know for certain that God has made Him both Lord and Christ—this Jesus whom you crucified" (Acts 2:36). Jesus was established as both Lord and Christ by God in resurrection. Now, in resurrection, this Christ has become a divine and mystical realm, which we enter through baptism into Christ Jesus. Through this baptism, we become related to the resurrected Christ in being, existence, and living.

When Jesus was given the title "Christ," which means "the anointed one," it showed that He was the One to accomplish God's will. Today, in resurrection, He is accomplishing and carrying out the eternal will of God. Therefore, a sense of purpose was generated in us when we were baptized into Christ Jesus, giving us a desire to live for the kingdom and will of God. Everyone on earth needs meaning, purpose, and motivation for living. When we were baptized into Christ Jesus, we were united with Him in His resurrection and His purpose to live for the eternal will of God.

To be baptized into Christ Jesus is also related to the living of Jesus on the earth, and thus relates directly to our living today. Jesus radiated all of God's divine attributes through His human virtues. Yet on the earth, He was despised, detested, misunderstood, and reviled. We who have been baptized into Christ Jesus will likewise experience being despised, detested, misunderstood, and reviled by others, and will even be considered a laughing stock (Matt. 10:25). To be baptized into Christ Jesus includes this kind of living.

However, no matter how much others misunderstand us or criticize us behind our backs, we can still rejoice. On the one hand, our baptism into Christ Jesus allows us to boast in victory, experience resurrection, and live for the eternal will of God. On the other hand, our baptism into Christ Jesus also allows us to live out His divine attributes through human virtues. Our baptism is not only into the heavenly Christ but also into the human Jesus. Do not think this is a small thing! The Lord Jesus said of Himself, "Take My yoke upon you and learn from Me, for I am gentle and humble in heart" (11:29). A person baptized into Christ Jesus will become a gentle and lowly person, who, although reviled by others, simply radiates divine attributes through human virtues.

Baptized into the Death of Christ Jesus

Paul strongly emphasized the fact that we who have been baptized into Christ Jesus were baptized into His death. Our baptism is not only outward but also indicates an inward union with the death of Christ Jesus. Our union with His death is for our being constituted with His death.

We must have a heavenly view of baptism. When we were baptized into Christ Jesus, our realm changed, and we were united with Christ Jesus and His death. Such a union brought us out from under all the negative authority and power in our lives, including the power of Satan, sin, our natural life, our self, and our flesh. Now we can enjoy a rest that is related to the eternal purpose of God.

However, we still often experience these negative authorities and powers. Satan will use all kinds of methods to attack and trouble us, but since we have been baptized into the death of Christ Jesus, we should experience an indescribable peace and rest. For example, a brother may become caught in a traffic jam on his way to a church meeting. As the meeting time approaches, he may murmur in his heart, "How irritating! I am in a hurry to get to the meeting, but Satan must be attacking me to keep me from arriving!" A complaint like this may really open the door for Satan's attack, and the brother will lose his peace.

Satan takes every opportunity to steal our restfulness away from us. We must remember that we have been baptized into the death of Christ Jesus—our natural life has died, our old nature has died, our flesh has died, and our self has died. Therefore, we who have been baptized into the death of Christ Jesus can be so restful and peaceful!

Three Aspects of Our Baptism

The meaning of baptism is very rich. Our baptism has three aspects: we are baptized into the heavenly aspect of Christ, into the human aspect of Jesus, and into His death. Our old life ended in the death of Christ Jesus, and our new life began in His resurrection. Additionally, because we were baptized into death, we have been freed from the authority of Satan.

According to experience, to be baptized into Christ is for our relationship with God, to be baptized into Jesus is for our relationship with people, and to be baptized into His death is for our relationship with Satan. Our life relationship with God and our healthy relationships with people are through our being in Christ Jesus. At the same time, the termination of our relationship with Satan, the world, the self, and our sinful nature is through our being in the death of Christ Jesus.

When we consider our relationships with God and with people, we should ask, "Is my relationship with Christ Jesus healthy?" When we consider the temptations and attacks of Satan, we should ask, "Is the death of Christ Jesus real to me?" A healthy Christian life must have all three of these aspects in healthy portions—the heavenly aspect of baptism into Christ, the human aspect of baptism into Jesus, and the reality of our baptism into His death.

For us to contact God, enjoy Him, and live before His presence, we must be in the resurrection of Christ Jesus. For our proper living in the midst of people, we must manifest His human virtues. For our handling of Satan's temptations and attacks, we must abide in His death. By abiding in His death, all the negative things in us will lose their authority and power.

The Termination of Self

The biggest frustration we can have in following the Lord is our "self" (Matt. 16:24). Self is the expression of the soul life. For example, if a brother is rebuked by an elder and as a result feels he has been treated unfairly, that feeling is his self. Whether he was mistreated or not is not the point. Rather, the fact that he feels mistreated indicates that his soul life is being expressed as the self. Those who do not know their self always feel misunderstood and mistreated.

Another example of the self is a brother who is told, "You are a really good brother. You have a great spiritual future and hope. The Lord will definitely use you in the future. May the Lord bless you!" This brother will be so happy that he almost forgets who he is! What is this? This is the self. On the contrary, if he is told, "You have no spiritual future. It will be very hard for the Lord to use you," his countenance will immediately change, and his whole heart will sink. What is this? This is also his self. When a person's soul life is touched, the reaction of self is often very strong.

Those who know their self do not often have rebukes for others but have much shining from the presence of the Lord. When Watchman Nee began to love the Lord, he received much help from an older sister, M. E. Barber. Among the young coworkers cultivated under her, the one she loved most was Watchman Nee, even giving all of her books to him before her departure from the world. She treasured Watchman Nee and spent a lot of time perfecting him. She cared for and cultivated him by helping him to know his self. She was sometimes very hard on him, even to an almost unreasonable point. She knew that if she did not treat Watchman Nee in such a way, this young man who greatly loved the Lord and strongly desired to serve Him would never know his self.

The manifestation of the flesh is always negative (Gal. 5:19-21). The expression of our flesh is clear and easy to identify in things like adultery, murder, and drunkenness. However, the expression of the self can look positive! When people's flesh is expressed, it is very easy for others to realize it. When people's self is expressed, even they may not know it and may consider their actions or thoughts as right, positive, and spiritual. We must learn how to discern between what is in resurrection and what is our self.

The manifestation of our self is most misidentified in the aspect of natural ability. Young brothers and sisters often have a hard time distinguishing it, because their natural ability is so strong. For this reason, many Christians actually serve and follow the Lord with their own ability and power. However, natural ability is consumed over time. A ninety-year-old man does not have much natural ability left! To be able to serve and follow the Lord even into our old age, we must learn to serve and follow Him not by our own natural ability but in His resurrection life.

Our following of the Lord must not be by our own nature, self, flesh, or anything else that is terminated in Christ's death. Learning to let our self die with Christ allows us to live in the powerful resurrection life of Christ. Even a ninety-year-old brother who experiences this power that cannot be consumed will be able to serve and follow the Lord in his old age. Oh, may we be those who can learn to die to our self and follow and serve the Lord in resurrection!

Hidden in Burial

Romans 6:4 adds that we who have been baptized into Christ were also buried with Him. We have not only died to Satan, the world, sin, our flesh, our self, and our corrupt human nature, but we have also been buried with Christ Jesus through baptism. Burial is the sign that our natural life, old nature, self, and flesh have been terminated in Christ so that we might enjoy the rest accomplished by His death.

Burial means that we have disappeared from the world and are restful before God. It means that people cannot find us anymore. After Jesus was buried, a large stone was rolled against the door of the tomb (Matt. 27:60). In burial, no one could find Him, and no one saw Him come out of the tomb. Only those who believed in Him, loved Him, and followed Him, like Mary, could find Him after He resurrected.

A brother said once, "For the sake of the saints in the church, I will leave work by 5:00 p.m. every day, and I will not work overtime on Saturdays. If my boss insists that I must work overtime, I will resign." This was a buried brother. He had disappeared from the world! If the world would try to find him, it would not be able to, because he had died with Christ and was buried. Only those who love the Lord and know God's heart's desire would understand him. However, if a person who does not know God's heart's desire can find us and understand us, it is not to our glory but to our shame.

Baptism into Christ Jesus is to be buried with Him into death. The testimony of baptism is only a moment in time, but the experience of baptism is lifelong. When Christians are baptized, they enter another realm in which their relationship with God is based on the resurrection of Christ Jesus, their relationships with people are based on His human virtues, and their relationship with the world is related to His death and burial. Even though we are still weak and many environments bother us, we have the resurrection and human virtues of Christ Jesus. Though we are overpowered and frustrated by our nature, flesh, and self, we are baptized into His death. Even if the world continually tries to attract us, we have been buried with Him through baptism.

Baptism is not only an outward testimony involving immersion in water, but it is also full of spiritual content and reality. A person who has been baptized into Christ Jesus can boast, "Now it is no longer I who live but Christ Jesus lives in me. His resurrection is my realm, His human virtues are my living, the effectiveness of His death is my experience, and His burial is my testimony. I am a dead and buried person, but I am also alive in the resurrection of Christ! I have been baptized into Christ Jesus and into His death, and I have been buried with Him!"

84

Newness of Life

Therefore we have been buried with Him through baptism into death, so that as Christ was raised from the dead through the glory of the Father, so we too might walk in newness of life.
—Romans 6:4

WORD STUDY

This verse compares the physical experience of Christ to our spiritual experience in Him. Just as Christ was buried and then raised from the dead, we are buried with Him through baptism and are raised to walk in newness of life. The phrase "newness of life" is a stronger expression than "new life," adding emphasis to the main idea of newness (Vincent, 3:67). The Greek word used here for newness, *kainotēs*, denotes "freshness" and carries the idea of a change (Rogers, 327). In other words, this life is different from our natural life.

In his many letters, Paul used several Greek words that are translated "walk." The word *stoicheō* signifies "to walk in line," similar to the marching of an army in which the soldiers keep step with one another (Rom. 4:12, Gal. 5:25, Phil. 3:16). The word *orthopodeō* means "to walk in a straight path," and signifies leaving a straight track for others to follow in (Gal. 2:14). However, the word Paul uses here in Romans 6:4

is *peripateō*, a word he always used figuratively to signify the total activities of the individual life. In other words, Paul used peripateō when discussing the general course of living (Vine, 664). This word means "to tread all around, walk about" (Strong, #4043). Thus, this walking in newness of life was meant by Paul to be applied to every portion of our living.

REVELATION AND APPLICATION

Romans 6:4 says that we are buried with Christ through being baptized into His death. This process terminates all the negative things in and around us, and it also leads to our entrance into a positive living and walking in newness of life. Thank the Lord! We have been buried with Christ, and just as Christ was raised from the dead through the glory of the Father, we too can walk in newness of life. The last phrase of this verse contains three important terms: life, newness, and walk.

The Divine Life Mingled with Man

In this verse, the life (*zōē*) is God's eternal and divine life. It is in this life that we are united to and mingled with the resurrected Christ. This uncreated life has existed from eternity past; however, mankind was very far from this life throughout the whole Old Testament. It was not until Christ was raised from the dead that this life could be united and mingled with us and become our subjective experience.

The divine life is the life of God, and it is God Himself (see 1 John 5:20). There is an urgent desire in God's heart to unite and mingle Himself with people through His life. This desire can be seen in the Old Testament, even though it could not yet be carried out. For example, the high peak of the book of Exodus is chapter 34 when Moses went up Mount Sinai.

The Lord descended in the cloud to stand with Moses and declared His own name in front of Moses (v. 5). At that moment, the Bible records this:

> *Then the Lord passed by in front of him and proclaimed, "The Lord, the Lord God, compassionate and gracious, slow to anger, and abounding in lovingkindness and truth; who keeps lovingkindness for thousands, who forgives iniquity, transgression and sin; yet He will by no means leave the guilty unpunished, visiting the iniquity of fathers on the children and on the grandchildren to the third and fourth generations." (Exo. 34:6-7)*

Moses was not the one praising, extolling, and declaring the Lord's name. Rather, the Lord Himself was declaring who He is. Moses had met with God many times, had received the Law and commandments, and had seen on the mountain the vision of the tabernacle, yet when he stood in the presence of the Lord, it was the Lord Himself declaring His own name. How earnestly the Lord desired to make Himself known to people! His heart's desire was to reveal Himself to man so that mankind could in turn know Him.

God, who is the divine life, stood beside Moses on top of the mountain with such eagerness and excitement. God so desired to reveal Himself that He declared who He is to Himself! At that moment, God was full of feeling. He was full of riches, desire, and hope for humanity, yet still He could not enter them to be united and mingled with them.

Today, we are much more blessed than Moses was. God could only stand outside of Moses, but today God can live inside of us. God could only stand beside Moses to declare His name, but today God can be united and mingled with us. This uniting and mingling is accomplished in the resurrection of Christ and in our experience and enjoyment of this resurrection. These experiences should cause us to live, walk, and serve in newness of life.

Living in Newness of Life

Paul uses the word "newness" to indicate a different nature. A person who is united and mingled with Christ has not only entered a new realm but has gained a new nature! When we believe into Christ, God's divine life enters us, bringing His divine nature. We not only receive life but also have a new nature by which we may live and walk.

What does it mean to walk in newness of life? We can compare this with a passage in Paul's letter to the Galatians: "If we live by the Spirit, let us also walk by the Spirit" (5:25). While both verses contain the English word "walk," they actually use two different Greek words. The Greek word used here in Galatians for "walk" is *stoicheō*, indicating a style of walking like that of an army marching together in oneness. However, the Greek word for "walk" in Romans 6:4 is not *stoicheō* but *peripateō*, which implies a daily walk that is free to go anywhere. When we examine these two types of walking, we see that Romans 6:4 tells us that no matter where we walk in the course of our day and no matter what we do or where we go, we can do it in newness of life. For example, even life's most common things, like eating and dressing, can be part of this walk in newness of life. This is really the miracle of miracles! We should be amazed by the fact that those who have been baptized into Christ Jesus and are buried with Him can have such newness of life in every aspect of their daily living in the resurrection of Christ.

Through the Supply of the Divine Life

The word "walk" in this verse is written in the subjunctive mood, which generally represents an action as uncertain, but probable (Wallace, 749). In other words, this walk is not an automatic thing once we are regenerated through faith. We must learn to take the supply of the divine life in many ways and forms to walk in newness of life. For example, a sister preparing for a church dinner may think, "When I bring my food out, it will make all the other sisters envious." This is not walking in newness of life but manifesting her old man. However, when she brings the food out she can still experience the operation of the divine life within her and cry inwardly, "Lord, save me from my pride!" This issues in a walking in newness of life; the divine life becomes a supply to her with its heavenly riches.

The divine and eternal life will continually supply us according to God's being. When we are enjoying a church meeting, He supplies us. Whether we are speaking for the Lord or listening to a message, He supplies us. After the meeting, He still supplies us. Even on our way home, we can experience the supply of the divine life in many portions and in many ways. No matter what situation we are in, this new and fresh life can supply us and operate in every aspect of our living. The dispensing, supply, and operation of this life should not be a doctrine to us, but a living experience!

Raised through the Glory of the Father

Romans 6:4 says that our walking in newness of life is just as Christ was raised from the dead through the glory of the Father. In this way, baptism is both a termination and a beginning. We were baptized into the death of Christ and buried with Him, yet we also walk in newness of life in the resurrection of Christ. Praise the Lord! Christ not only died but was raised, and this was through the glory of the Father. We died and were buried, yet we were resurrected and walk.

The glory of the Father is the manifestation of His being. In other words, when God is revealed to man, it is glory. Christ was crucified in weakness (2 Cor. 13:4), yet He was raised from the dead through the glory, or manifestation, of the Father. Likewise, if we know this eternal life and how to apply, enjoy, and be united to it, our every experience of weakness can be an opportunity for the glory of God to be manifested from us to resurrect us from the dead.

We should not despise our weaknesses. Usually, the more we want to overcome, the more we fail. The more we want to be strong, the weaker we find ourselves. The more we want to be one with God, the less we can match Him. However, our entire life involves experiencing our weaknesses in order that the glory of God would be manifested.

The apostle Paul testified that the Lord's strength is made perfect in man's weakness (2 Cor. 12:9). May our life be like the life of Paul, who continually experienced the death of Christ and was united together with Him in the likeness of His death (Rom. 6:5). If our life can match Paul's in this way, Christ's resurrection will be more of a reality in us. This reality of resurrection truly issues in our walking in newness of life.

85

United with Him

For if we have become united with Him in the likeness of His death, certainly we shall also be in the likeness of His resurrection.
—*Romans 6:5*

WORD STUDY

The Greek word used in this verse for "united," *sumphutos*, literally means "grown along with, that is, closely united to; planted together" (Strong, #4854). The word is a composition of two other Greek words: *sun*, denoting union, companionship, and resemblance (Strong, #4862), and *phuō*, meaning "to germinate or grow (sprout, produce)" (Strong, #5453). Bible translators have rendered this verse several ways, including the following:

"For if we have been planted together in the likeness of his death…" (*King James Version*)
"For, if we have become planted together to the likeness of his death…" (*Young's Literal Translation*)
"For if we are become identified with [him] in the likeness of his death…" (*Darby Translation*)

Commentators have written that "planted together" is a hard way to translate *sumphutos*, but that the word definitely denotes a growing together, an intimate and progressive union (Vincent, 3:67). It could also bear the idea of the process of grafting (Rogers, 327).

The Greek word translated "have become," *ginomai*, means, "to cause to be, to become" (Strong, #1096). The perfect tense of the verb in this verse indicates the abiding state or condition (Rogers, 327). In other words, this union and growth is not only a one-time event but an ongoing experience in the life of a Christian.

This verse also contains a conditional statement: if we have become united with Him in the likeness of His death, then we shall certainly be in the likeness of His resurrection. This uniting is accomplished through baptism, mentioned in the previous verse (Luther, 102). H. Alford wrote that the future tense is used—"we shall also be"—either because of the inference of the conditional statement or to indicate something deeper. He wrote, "The participation in His Resurrection, however partially and in the inner spiritual life, attained here, will only then be accomplished in our entire being when [the Lord returns, when] we 'shall wake up after his likeness'" (Alford, 2:368).

REVELATION AND APPLICATION

Union with Him

In Romans 6:5, Paul mentions the likeness of Christ's death and resurrection. The Greek word in this verse that joins us to these is *sumphutos*, indicating a union and growing together. Bible translators struggle with the translation of this verse, but the fact is, this union with Christ is a wonderful and mystical thing! We can rest in the wonderful fact that by baptism we have been united together with Christ in the likeness of His death.

The Greek verb used for "have become" is in the perfect tense. When considered in connection to the union mentioned, it unveils the heavenly fact that we not only have been united with Christ in this way but that we continue to experience this union with Him. This union is not only in the likeness of His death but also eventually in the likeness of His resurrection.

Growing and Bearing Fruit

The Greek word for "united with," *sumphutos*, is composed of *sun* and *phuō*. *Sun* is one of several Greek words that indicate a presence and companionship; yet of those several words, *sun* denotes the closest union (Strong, #4862). It not only indicates a presence and companionship but also implies an organic union, indicating it is a lifelong experience. While reading the Bible for many years, praying many times, and laboring and ministering in different ways, we should have cultivated this organic union with the Lord. This process requires much fellowship with the Lord and abiding in His presence; otherwise, the union produced will be very limited. This verse says that we have been united in the likeness of Christ's death, yet in the experiential process, we must diligently pursue Christ and properly labor for Him so our organic union can be healthy.

Phuō indicates an organic process of sprouting or growing (Strong, #5453). Thus, the organic union here issues from our being united, mingled, and incorporated with Christ's life. All Christians receive God's eternal life the moment they believe, and this life becomes the source of their lifelong following of the Lord. This life is like a seed that falls into the earth and then sprouts and grows. Eventually, its rich growth leads to its bearing the fruit of life. *Sumphutos* is truly a wonderful word to describe our union with Christ.

A. B. Simpson wrote a hymn with a line that reads, "A poor tree with better grafted, richer, sweeter life doth gain" (Martin, #328). We used to be poor trees, yet the Lord has grafted us into a better tree producing an organic union of life, the growth of life, and the bearing of the fruit of life. More specifically, *sumphutos* implies that our life is a grafted life, grafted into and united with the death of Christ.

When Romans 6:4–5 are read together, it seems that Paul was very confident that we have already been organically united with Christ. This is an accomplished fact, but it is also a fact for us to experience today. Yet when we pay attention to this experience, we often focus only on our union and not so much on our growth. For example, some sisters would wake up early to touch the Lord and be filled with His presence. They would sometimes be touched by the Lord to the point of tears. Yet later in the day, they would forget all about the Lord as they went shopping. They were indeed united with the Lord in the morning; however, not much growth was seen in their living.

Sometimes we go too far the other way and pay attention to our growth while ignoring our union with the Lord. For example, some brothers can preach the gospel very well, help others, lead a meeting, and arrange the services in the church. However, they may be unable to bring others the freshness of God's life, they may be short of anointing in their speaking, and they may not bring people to the presence of the Lord. Because they can do so many things, these brothers may feel that they have some growth in the Lord, yet their union with Him is lacking.

Paul uses a word that not only means union but also growth. Both are crucial. We are united with Christ in the likeness of His death and continually grow in this likeness. In the same way, we are united with Christ in the likeness of His resurrection and continually grow in this likeness.

The Likeness of His Death

Baptism indicates our union with the likeness of the death of Christ. Romans 6:4 says, "Therefore we have been buried with Him through baptism into death." Many people consider baptism only a singular event, but it should also result in a living in the reality of baptism, expressing our union with Christ.

Our union and growth with Christ is manifested in our conformation to the death of Christ. Paul said in Philippians, "That I may know Him and the power of His resurrection and the fellowship of His sufferings, being conformed to His death" (3:10). This conformation to His death is the result of our growth in the likeness of His death (Rom. 6:4).

The Greek word translated "conformed" in Philippians 3:10 is *summorphoō*, meaning, "to render like, that is, to assimilate" (Strong, #4833). Notice that this word contains the prefix *sun*, indicating a close organic relationship. This conforming is not like a factory producing identical cups that have no organic relationship to one another. Rather, it is the assimilating of both outward likeness and inward nature. It is organic, like two olive branches that not only share the same form but also life and nature.

Conformation is the result of our union and growth in the likeness of the death of Christ. It is both the result of the effective operation of the divine life within us and the fruit of the divine life manifesting itself out from us. As we grow, we will eventually bear the fruit of this conformity to the death of Christ. Consider our Lord Jesus, who lived His entire life under the principle of death. From the time He was born, He lived by this principle, culminating in His death on the cross.

The Lord Jesus never departed from the principle of death. He is "the Lamb slain from the foundation of the world" (Rev. 13:8, NKJV®). Jesus Himself understood this when He said, "Truly, truly, I say to you, unless a grain of wheat falls into the earth and dies, it remains alone; but if it dies, it bears much fruit" (John 12:24). Every part of Jesus's life pointed to His death. Consider that the God of the universe, who created all things, was willing to enter the womb of Mary and become a mortal man (Matt. 1:23). This was a kind of dying. When Nicodemus wanted to see Jesus, he came to Him in the middle of the night (John 3:1–2), typifying death. The woman of Samaria came to draw water and encountered Jesus in the scorching noontime heat (John 4:6–10), also typifying death. From the womb, Jesus began to live under the principle of death. His birth, life, and ministry were all under this principle. He continually treated Himself as if already dead, denying His soul life for the will of the Father. He became obedient, even unto the point of death, and that the death of a cross (Phil. 2:8).

Whatever Jesus did, He did according to the principle of death. At all times and in every environment, He denied Himself. No matter who came to Him or what He went through, He considered Himself as dead. He never said anything by Himself (John 12:49), nor did He do anything by Himself (5:19). He lived by the Father and was one with Him. This attitude and consideration was a major characteristic of Jesus. He never departed from the principle of death, which was the denial of His soul life, and in the end, He did not shrink back from the death of a cross.

A Deeper Experience of Death

Just as Jesus lived under the principle of death, so we who have been baptized into Him cannot help but live under the same principle. The experience of His death is lifelong, continuous, and continually deepens. This is our experience of union and growth in the likeness of the death of Christ.

We begin to experience this death from the moment we believe. However, our living now should allow the death of our Lord to work in us even deeper. This is not easily applied. All of us want to live, but few are willing to die. The church today is filled with people who love the Lord, but many who love the Lord refuse to die to themselves. If people only love the Lord yet are unwilling to die, unhealthy things can come in among them, such as strife, jealousy, rejection, and conflict. A person who is serious about following the Lord must be willing to die with Christ to all things.

Death is a sobering thing. Death would seem to be the opposite of growth. However, the healthiness of our growth in life and our usefulness in the hands of the Lord utterly depend on our choice of union and growth in the likeness of His death. For those who desire to live in Christ, their crucial lifelong experience does not lie in whether they can speak a message, receive praise from others, or have a manifested gift. Rather it lies in how much experience they have of the union and growth in the likeness of the Lord's death. When servants of the Lord serve in a church or go somewhere new to pioneer the work of the Lord, they are there to die. A blessed church is one in which there are many who are willing to die with Christ.

In the Likeness of His Resurrection

We will also have union and growth in the likeness of Christ's resurrection. The all-inclusive death of Christ not only rids us of all the negative elements within, but also issues in the operation of the divine life. In Christ's death, our old man was brought to the cross and the fallen, fleshly, and sinful portion of our being was crucified (Rom. 6:6). In His resurrection, we were recovered from the fall and regenerated to become a new man that is united with Christ and grows in the likeness of His resurrection.

When we eat food, our stomachs are satisfied; it is a natural consequence. In the same way, our experience of dying with Christ has a natural consequence—resurrection! Paul told the Corinthians, "We who live are constantly being delivered over to death for Jesus' sake, so that the life of Jesus also may be manifested in our mortal flesh" (2 Cor. 4:11). A person who grows in the likeness of the death of Christ must also grow in the likeness of His resurrection. Yet we do not need to struggle for this; it is a natural consequence! This is why Paul used the word "certainly" in Romans 6:5. Even more, the resurrection life can also operate in others, which is why Paul added in 2 Corinthians, "So death works in us, but life in you" (4:12).

The Reward of the Excellent Resurrection

Paul told the Philippians, "That I may know Him and the power of His resurrection and the fellowship of His sufferings, being conformed to His death; in order that I may attain to the resurrection from the dead" (Phil. 3:10-11). The common Greek word for "resurrection" is *anastasis*. However, in these Philippians verses, Paul used the Greek word *exanastasis*, found nowhere else in the Bible. It can be translated "the excellent resurrection," which is the reward the Lord will give to the overcomers (Rev. 20:4-6). How do we gain this reward? First, we must be united and grow with Christ in His death. Then, we must be united and grow with Him in the likeness of His resurrection. Eventually, this growth will issue in the excellent resurrection. What a hope this is!

Every believer will be resurrected (John 6:39; 1 Cor. 15:52) and participate in the New Jerusalem in the new heaven and new earth (2 Pet. 3:13; Rev. 21:1-2, 27). However, only those who are united and conformed to His death will receive an excellent resurrection in the day of the Lord's return. This is the reward the Lord reserves for the overcomers who are united with Him, who are conformed to His death, and who grow in His resurrection.

Our Crucified Old Man

Knowing this, that our old self was crucified with Him, in order that our body of sin might be done away with, so that we would no longer be slaves to sin; ⁷for he who has died is freed from sin.
—*Romans 6:6-7*

WORD STUDY

Romans 6:6 says that our "old self" was crucified with Christ. The Greek word used here for "self," *anthrōpos*, literally means "man" (Strong, #444). Thus, the phrase "old self" is sometimes translated "old man." The Greek word used here for "old" is *palaios*, meaning "of what belongs to the past" (Vine, 444). The old man could represent the believer's former self before conversion; thus Paul exhorts the Ephesians to "put off, concerning your former conduct, the old man which grows corrupt" (Eph. 4:22, NKJV®). The old man likely refers to the sinful corruption of the created nature of man. Martin Luther wrote, "The nature (in itself) is good, but the corruption of it is evil" (Luther, 102).

The purpose of the crucifixion of the old man—"in order that"—is so our body of sin might be done away with. The phrase "might be done away with" is one word in Greek—*katargeō*, which literally means "to render entirely idle (useless)"

(Strong, #2673). The word is composed of two Greek words: *kata*, a common preposition which in compounds intensifies the word it is paired with (Strong, #2596), and *argeō*, which means "to be idle" and carries with it the thought of inactivity due to unemployment (Strong, #692). This gives a humorous, yet encouraging, picture that the crucifixion of our old man has left the body of sin unemployed and without work.

Verse 7 says that one "who has died is freed from sin." The Greek word used here for "freed" is *dikaioō*. Also used in Romans 3:26 and 28, *dikaioō* is translated in those verses as "justified." It properly means "to render just or innocent" and could be translated "to free" (Strong, #1344). Here in Romans 6:7, it could mean to be declared free from sin or to be acquitted from sin (Rogers, 327).

REVELATION AND APPLICATION

In Romans 6:6, three negative things are mentioned: the old man, the body of sin, and slaves of sin. Verse 7 is very positive, mentioning freedom from sin. The bridge from the negative things in verse 6 to the positive freedom in verse 7 is an interesting fact: we have died!

The Bible shows us that we are composed of three parts: spirit, soul, and body (1 Thess. 5:23). When we believed into the Lord, the Spirit of God entered us and regenerated our spirit (John 3:4–6). However, sin still dwells in our body, and so our body is called the "body of sin." Our soul is caught between the two and serves whichever one prevails. When our spirit is strong, our soul is subject to our spirit. When our flesh operates, our soul is subject to our flesh.

The Old Man

When God created Adam, He breathed into his nostrils

the breath of life, and man became a living being (Gen. 2:7). In this way, man's soul—comprising emotion, mind, and will—was originally related to God and should have led man to God. People's emotion was originally for loving God, their mind was originally for thinking of God, and their will was originally for choosing God. When Adam ate the fruit of the tree of the knowledge of good and evil, however, man's soul lost its relation to God, became centered on the flesh and sin, and eventually became degraded by the effects of sin.

The old man has two aspects. The first aspect is our natural and God-created part, including our talents and abilities. The second aspect is our soul life, which is self-centered rather than God-centered. Adam's fall caused God's position as the head and husband to be usurped by the old man. People's natural talents and abilities are now directed toward themselves rather than toward God.

The Body of Sin

Since man's fall, our body has two aspects. On one hand, our body was created by God in His image and for our existence. On the other hand, sin has entered our body and dwells there (Rom. 7:17), tainting God's good creation and resulting in a sinful body. This sinful body is not only where sin dwells but has also become a tool through which sin can do many unhealthy things.

Many people commonly associate sin with specific practices, like lying, stealing, or gossiping. The Bible tells us that all unrighteousness and lawlessness is sin (1 John 3:4, 5:17). But sin is more than these practices. The Bible also tells us that anything done apart from faith is sin (Rom. 14:23). The Pharisees provide a good example of this. They believed in God, professed that they followed Him, and studied the Bible, but they did not have God Himself. They were outwardly related to God and the Jewish religion that promoted worship of Him, but they did not possess a faith in the living God who stood in their midst. The Lord Jesus told them, "[You] will die in your sin" (John 8:21). This shows that although they were seemingly so connected to God, they were sinners who were apart from God. Eventually, the Bible shows us that every person is a sinner and that all live and die in sin (Rom. 3:9–20, 23).

The Unemployment of the Body of Sin

Paul says that our body of sin has been "done away with, so that we would no longer be slaves of sin" (Rom. 6:6). In Greek, to be "done away with" means to be made inactive. It is like being fired and out of a job. There is a Chinese saying, "Without the head, hair has nothing to hold on to." The body of sin is like the hair, while the old man is like the head. Because our old man has been crucified and has died, the body of sin no longer has anything to hold on to. Without the old man, the body of sin loses its hold on people and is essentially out of a job!

When Adam fell, man's soul lost its relation to God, and man's body became a body of sin. The old man took over God's headship and became the boss that orders and directs the body—now the body of sin—into committing sins. But because our old man has been crucified with Christ, he can no longer use the body of sin as a tool.

When the Lord Jesus was crucified on the cross, our old man was also crucified with Him. No matter how good, broad, or strong a person's natural soul is, it is always related to the flesh and is hopeless in the eyes of God. However, we can thank and praise the Lord that, since our old man was crucified with Christ, our soul can again belong to our spirit, be united with God, and become an instrument useful to our regenerated spirit.

Freed from Sin

Paul also says that "he who has died is freed from sin" (Rom. 6:7). This is a fact for those who are saved and regenerated. However, this fact is only experienced by Christians who have the death of Christ working in them and causing a certain kind of self-awareness. Such believers realize that whether they overcome or fail, they are simply dead. When they feel very heavenly, they remember that they are dead. When they have a very humble and lowly living, they remember that they have died. Within them is the recognition, "I am a dead person."

The Greek phrase for "freed from sin" carries the thought of justification. In fact, some Bible translations render it, "justified from sin" (ASV, Darby). On one hand, to be freed from sin indicates a departure from sin. On the other hand, it indicates justification in Christ. Both of these are ours—we have been both freed from sin and justified before God. In this freedom, our past sinful deeds and history cannot catch us or stumble us anymore.

When we recognize that we have died and been justified and freed from sin, we should not look back at our previous sins. Neither should we focus on the power of sin pressing us today. We have died, we have been freed from sin, we have been released from the power of sin, and we have been set free from our sinful deeds and their history! Since we have been freed from sin, we are no longer bound by it! Because of our justification, we are no longer condemned by God. We no longer need to serve sin as slaves but can instead live as slaves of God (6:22).

Two Kinds of Knowing

Knowing this, that our old self was crucified with Him, in order that our body of sin might be done away with, so that we would no longer be slaves to sin; ⁷for he who has died is freed from sin. ⁸Now if we have died with Christ, we believe that we shall also live with Him, ⁹knowing that Christ, having been raised from the dead, is never to die again; death no longer is master over Him. ¹⁰For the death that He died, He died to sin once for all; but the life that He lives, He lives to God.
—Romans 6:6-10

WORD STUDY

Both verses 6 and 9 begin with the word "knowing," yet in Greek, they are two different words. In verse 6, the Greek word translated "knowing" is *ginōskō*. In verse 9, it is *oida*. Though distinctions between these words are not always clear-cut, there is often a difference in how the words are used. *Ginōskō* generally refers to knowledge gained by learning or experience, while *oida* often denotes an intuitive knowledge—an awareness or perception that comes from within (Thayer, 118, 172–174).

In his *New Translation* of the Bible, J. N. Darby remarked in a footnote on 1 Corinthians 8:4, "Two Greek words are used for 'to know' in the New Testament—*ginosko* and *oida*. The former signifies objective knowledge, what a man has learned or acquired. The English expression 'being acquainted with' perhaps conveys the meaning. *Oida* conveys the thought of what is inward, the inward consciousness in the mind, intuitive knowledge not immediately derived from what is external....The difference between the significance of the two words is often slight; the objective knowledge may pass into conscious knowledge, but not vice versa."

The Greek word used in verse 6 for "self," *anthrōpos*, literally means "man" (Strong, #444). Thus, the phrase "old self" is sometimes translated "old man."

REVELATION AND APPLICATION

In Romans 6:6–11, Paul talks about our being united and mingled with Christ in our experience. These verses are filled with divine and heavenly descriptions of this process, which is sanctification. A crucial matter in these verses is that of knowing. Two different Greek words are used in this passage for "knowing"—ginōskō (v. 6) and oida (v. 9). The secret to understanding these verses lies in understanding the differences between these two words.

Two Kinds of Knowing

Knowledge is important because it changes our view. We need a view of what has been accomplished by Christ. The first knowing in these verses, *ginōskō*, is to know that our old man was crucified with Christ, that our body of sin has been done away with, and that we should no longer be slaves of sin (Rom. 6:6).

It is very hard to understand this verse because it is difficult to define some of the terms Paul uses. For example, what is the old man? What does it mean to be crucified with Christ? What is the body of sin, and what does it mean that it is done away with? Furthermore, what does it mean to be a slave of sin? Without revelation from the Lord, we cannot easily understand what Paul says here. To make matters more difficult, our experience does not match Paul's description of the body of sin being done away with. Even after regeneration, we still seem to experience the power of sin within us, and we still commit sins.

Many Christians have struggled to understand this portion of the Bible. This struggle shows that we need not only the ginōskō knowledge of verse 6, but also another kind of knowledge. Paul uses a second knowing, *oida*, when he speaks of knowing that Christ is raised from the dead, that He will never die again, and that death is no longer master over Him (6:9).

In general, *ginōskō* indicates an objective knowledge gained by learning or experience. *Oida* generally refers to an inward knowledge or intuition. By these general definitions, we would think *ginōskō* would deal with all facts and events around us while *oida* would deal with the subjective experiences within us. It would seem logical for the crucifixion of our old man to be an inward subjective revelation (*oida*), while Christ's resurrection would be an objective fact to learn (*ginōskō*). However, Paul wrote in the exact opposite way! He wrote that we must *ginōskō* our old man's crucifixion and *oida* Christ's resurrection.

Knowing the Resurrected Christ

Our inward spiritual knowledge and intuition expressed by the Greek word *oida* is related to our subjective experience, and Paul reveals in these verses that this knowledge and experience can never be apart from Christ. When we consider ourselves, we must learn an objective fact (*ginōskō*). When we turn our attention to Christ, however, we will subjectively and inwardly come to another kind of knowledge (*oida*).

All the inward experiences and realizations of spiritual things involve Christ Himself. If we want to move from the realm of outward learning and experiencing (*ginōskō*) to the realm of inward knowledge and application (*oida*), we must forget about us and lay ourselves aside. Every profound, inner, and spiritual experience or realization is related not to knowing ourselves better, but to knowing Christ Himself.

Objectively, we can see our old man crucified with Christ. Inwardly, we can see the resurrected Christ and realize all He has accomplished. When all that Christ has accomplished is realized in us, our self will vanish, leaving only Christ, the knowledge of Christ, and the vision of this resurrected Christ.

Hiding in Christ

If we desire to subjectively experience our old man's crucifixion with Christ and the unemployment of the body of sin, we must take our eyes off ourselves and focus on Christ. The body of sin is completely dependent on the old man, which is mankind's self-focused fallen nature. Whenever we focus on ourselves, funny questions begin to come out of us. We may wonder, "Did I really die? Am I still alive? Did I sin? Did I overcome? Was my behavior good?" Our old man's focus on self causes the body of sin to spring into action and become employed. The fact in the Bible, however, is that the body of sin is out of a job and has been done away with. For this fact to move into our subjective experience, our eyes need to focus on Christ.

The Bible tells us clearly that Christ, having been raised from the dead, will never die again and that death is no longer His master (Rom. 6:9). Since we have died with Christ, we will also live with Him (6:8). The Christ we died with is resurrected, and we are raised with Him from the dead! Death no longer has dominion over Him or over us! The experience of this wonderful fact lies in our inward knowledge of Christ, in whom we are hidden and in whom there is no self-focus. Whenever our self emerges, we lose our focus on Christ, and thus lose the subjective reality of being dead and alive with Him. We must focus on Christ alone, abide in Him, and hide ourselves in Him.

Christians should be more afraid of victory than failure. This may sound strange to some people. Surely, Christians ought to be victorious, and victory should be a normal part of the Christian life. Yet we should be afraid of victory, because our victories often make it difficult to remain hidden. Those who are hidden in Christ should be careful with their accomplishments. If they boast about their accomplishments or victories, it can become a stumbling block for them.

For example, there was a brother who preached the gospel every day. This was very good, but one day he said, "Thank the Lord! I have preached the gospel daily for the past three months!" Right after he said this, he failed to go out to preach the gospel the next week. A sister I knew spent time to revive her spirit before the Lord every morning. This was a sweet experience for her, but one day she testified, "Praise the Lord! I was so victorious these three months in keeping my morning revival every day!" Right after she said this, she failed to keep this morning time over the course of the next week. If someone says, "Thank the Lord, I have not lost my temper for half a year!" their temper will surely burst out tomorrow, because they are no longer hidden in Christ.

The most normal life is to be hidden in Christ. If we watch, observe, enjoy, and abide in Christ Himself and Christ alone, our self will disappear. Many victories will become very normal to those who are hidden in Christ. If we are these hidden ones, our morning revival and gospel preaching will be very natural to us. Church meetings, loving the saints, and pursuing and serving the Lord will all become normal and ordinary parts of our lives. By the Lord's mercy, there are many servants of the Lord who can speak for Him, yet to them, this should be somewhat unexceptional. If a brother begins to consider when he wakes up, "I will do my best to give an outstanding message that will astonish the congregation," then he is finished, because he has become self-focused, and he unconsciously lives out his old man.

Objective Facts Becoming Subjective Reality

After looking so much at the importance of inwardly seeing Christ in resurrection, we should remember that objective knowledge and experience are still very important. In fact, *ginōskō* and *oida* are linked together. *Ginōskō* deals with our understanding and revelation, while *oida* is the subjective realization in our spirits of such revelation.

This matter of the spirit is crucial. After Christ was raised from the dead, He became the life-giving Spirit (1 Cor. 15:45) so that He might enter our spirit and become united and mingled with us (6:17). Christ's resurrection is realized in our regenerated spirit. This realization leads to believing that we will live with Him (Rom. 6:8) and issues in subjective experiences of His death, of His life, and of the life we live with Him (6:8–10).

Even though *ginōskō* deals with outward and objective knowing, it can still lead to inward knowledge and realization (*oida*). For example, many people who have immigrated to the United States heard about the country before they moved. This was their objective knowing of outward facts. Gradually, this knowledge produced a desire within them to leave their homes. Their desire was a subjective inner realization based on their knowledge of objective facts. After immigrating, their knowledge of the United States was no longer secondhand but personally real and substantial. Their outward learning produced inward desire, which motivated them to take action, and in time, substantiated their outward knowledge. This is the relationship between *ginōskō* and *oida*. Knowing spiritual facts, even in an objective way, should bring us into an inner realization of them in our spirit.

Here in Romans, our old man's crucifixion with Christ is a fact accomplished by the Lord Jesus and now revealed in our spirit. Objectively, we have died with Christ. The revelation that our old man has been crucified with Christ brings us into many subjective experiences, and in this way our crucifixion with Christ is realized and substantiated in our spirit. Whenever we touch the Lord, enjoy His presence, and have intimate fellowship with Him in our spirit, within us is the reality of our old man's crucifixion with Christ. Our experience of sanctification is totally related to our knowledge of this revelation and to our being filled with its reality in our spirit.

88

Considering Ourselves to be Dead

Even so consider yourselves to be dead to sin, but alive to God in Christ Jesus.
—*Romans 6:11*

WORD STUDY

The words "even so" link this verse with the previous passage, which covered the death and resurrection of Christ (Rom. 6:9–10). He died to sin and lives to God, and death is no longer His master. Now, because of our union with Him in death and life (vv. 4–8) we have a responsibility: we must consider ourselves dead to sin and alive to God in Christ Jesus.

The Greek word used here for "consider," *logizomai*, literally means "to take an inventory, that is, estimate" and can be translated "conclude, count, account, impute, reckon, suppose" (Strong, #3049). It is a form of the Greek word *logos*. The present imperfect tense of the word could mean "do this continuously" (Rogers, 327). It is also written in the middle voice, which emphasizes the subject's participation in the action, whether by performing it or experiencing it (Wallace, 746).

In this verse, *logizomai* (from *logos*) is used as a verb. *Logos* can simply be translated "word, saying" (Strong, #3056), yet it often denotes the expression of thought or the embodiment of a conception or idea (Vine, 683). In the New Testament, it is used by the apostle John for the preexisting Christ, the *logos* who was both with God and was God (John 1:2). Other writers of the Bible use *logos* to describe a Christian's responsibility to give an account (*logos*) to men and God (1 Pet. 3:15, Matt. 12:36). In general, the word *logos* has profound implications throughout the Bible (Kittel, 4:103-110).

REVELATION AND APPLICATION

The Crucial Word of God

The Greek word translated "consider," *logizomai*, is the verb form of the word *logos* and is written in the middle voice, emphasizing our participation in the working of the *logos*. The conclusion we must reach in Romans 6:11—considering ourselves dead to sin—must be a result of the operation of the *logos* within us. The apostle John attached great significance to the *logos*, calling it the Word which was "in the beginning" (John 1:1) and the "Word of Life" (1 John 1:1). When this Word operates in us in life, it results in the consideration mentioned here in Romans.

Considering ourselves dead to sin is totally related to the Word (*logos*). When people believe into the Lord, He comes in as the Word to abide in them. Not every Christian chooses to live Christ, but very few Christians can deny Him, because they have an awareness of Christ within them through the Word. Many Christians can testify that even when they feel weak and defeated, the Word in them issues in an unexplainable recognition of who Christ is.

The apostle Peter had such experiences. Even though he denied Jesus three times, he still believed in the Lord. We know this because he bitterly wept when he realized what he had done (Matt. 26:75). He would not have had such a strong reaction if he did not believe. Though he denied the Lord with his mouth, Peter's spirit never denied Christ. We too have such inner realizations produced by the indwelling Word.

The Word Operating Within

The most crucial step in the process of sanctification is to have the consideration that we are dead to sin. All Christians who desire to pursue the Lord and please God must account, or reckon, themselves dead to sin in order to escape from the slavery and bondage of sin and to live an overcoming life. Many Christians have read and been helped by Watchman Nee's book, The Normal Christian Life. In it, he says that the way of victory for a Christian lies in this consideration, which is the natural accounting and realization of faith. Another older brother said that this consideration lies in the faith that comes from seeing. These statements by very spiritual men show that this consideration is related to faith, and that it cannot be generated within ourselves by our own effort.

When people begin to love the Lord, they may make many resolutions. A man may resolve never to lose his temper again. However, the result of such a resolution is only more anger when it cannot be kept. Even this man's relatives may be fed up after a while. He may try to consider himself dead to anger, but he will only find himself angry again. His effort will not work if the operation of the *logos* is lacking in him. This consideration in Romans 6 is produced by the *logos* operating in us.

Paul says that we should consider ourselves dead to sin. The longer we are in the Lord, the more we will find that we cannot have such an accounting by our own strength. The more we want to count ourselves dead to sin, the more we cannot! In order to count ourselves dead, we must first see the fact that we have already died with Christ (Rom. 6:8). This is only brought about by the operation of the *logos* within us. When the *logos* causes us to truly see and recognize the fact of our death with Christ, the consideration in verse 11 will come about spontaneously.

Knowing and Considering

This consideration is related to the knowledge in Romans 6:9, which is the inward intuition and knowing (*oida*) of our spirit. As we saw in the previous chapter, this knowing is totally related to Christ Himself and to our hiding in Him. We spontaneously consider ourselves dead to sin when we focus on Christ and hide ourselves in Him. However, we are unable to have such a reckoning of ourselves, despite our best efforts, whenever we become distracted from Christ.

Returning to the previous example, the more the man tries to consider himself dead to anger, the more he will become angry because he cannot succeed. Until he recognizes the outward facts (*ginōskō*), and until these become inwardly recognized in his spirit (*oida*), he will be unable to come to the reality of this consideration. This is why the operating Word of God is so sweet. It is by the inward operation of the *logos* in him that he can inwardly see and know that Christ was raised from the dead, that death is no longer His master, and that He lives to God! As his focus turns to Christ, he will be able to count himself dead to sin and alive to God in Christ Jesus.

All the divine and heavenly facts in this section of Romans become applicable to us when we know them subjectively in our spirit. The operation of the *logos* in us issues in this inward knowledge and focuses us on Christ. In Him, we spontaneously consider ourselves dead to all things apart from God and alive to God in Christ Jesus!

The True Nature of Believers

The true nature of believers is manifested when they consider themselves dead to sin but alive to God in Christ Jesus. What is the true nature of a believer? A man can learn to make sounds like a cat or dog, but that does not change the fact that he is a man. No matter what animal sounds he makes, they are fake, because his true nature is that of a man. Similarly, believers can act in many fake ways, but their true nature is found in Christ and in His death and resurrection. This true nature becomes manifested in the experience of dying to sin and living to God in Christ Jesus.

It is very easy in a church to confuse what is true with what is fake and what is temporary with what is eternal. Once regenerated, a believer's nature is changed, and the reality of this new nature is wholly related to God, while everything related to sin and the flesh is fake. We all have shortcomings and problems, but we should learn to count one another's failings as fake. It is better to quickly leave an angry brother alone, because his anger is fake. In reality, he has died to sin and lives to God. A few hours later, he might praise God in a church meeting or read the Bible and pray in his home. It can seem like he has two personalities, but which one should we believe is true? We must recognize the true nature of a believer so that we can see the brothers and sisters in our churches in a healthy way.

In the Realm of Christ Jesus

We are alive to God "in Christ Jesus" (Rom. 6:11), denoting that Christ Jesus is a realm. This is the divine and mystical realm, the realm of the Spirit. It is in this realm that we live to God, and it is in this realm that Christ's accomplishments affect us.

Only by being in this realm can we consider ourselves dead to sin and alive to God. It is only in this realm that we can experience our organic union and mingling with Christ Jesus. By our own effort, we cannot die to sin or live to God. Only by living in the realm of Christ Jesus and hiding in Him can such consideration become reality within us.

89
Not Letting Sin Reign

Therefore do not let sin reign in your mortal body so that you obey its lusts.
—Romans 6:12

WORD STUDY

Here, as in previous verses, Paul personifies sin and exhorts believers to "not let sin reign" in their mortal bodies. The Greek phrase translated, "not let sin reign," is *mē oun basileutō*. The word *basileutō* means "to rule as king" (Strong, #936), while *mē* is a primary particle of qualified negation (Strong, #3361). Written in the present tense and imperative mood, the phrase could be translated, "do not continue to let sin reign," or even, "do not make it your habit to let sin reign" (Rogers, 327). In other words, this is an ongoing process for the believer to participate in actively.

According to the Greek text, "sin" is feminine while "body" and "its" are both neuter. This indicates that these lusts belong to the mortal body, and that when sin reigns within our body, it causes us to obey the body's lusts. The Greek word used here for "lusts," *epithumia*, means "a longing, especially for what is forbidden" (Strong, #1939). The Greek word is composed of two other words: *epi*, meaning "upon, over" (Strong, #1909) and *thumos*, meaning "passion" (Strong, #2372). More than small feelings, lusts are strong desires, cravings, or longings (Vine, 161, 384).

REVELATION AND APPLICATION

Not Letting the Body of Sin Work

In Romans 6:12, Paul again introduces the personified sin, this time as reigning in our mortal bodies. In 6:6, our old man was crucified with Christ in order that the body of sin might be done away with. This being "done away with" indicated an unemployment or a lack of activity. We may have expected the complete destruction of the body of sin. However, it still exists, and although it is ineffective, it has not been cut off or destroyed yet.

What does it mean for sin to reign? According to the Greek language, the base of the word for "reign" is *bainō*, the same Greek word that is translated "to walk" (Strong, #939). For sin to reign indicates that it is not lying motionless within us, but that it is "walking," active, and always seeking opportunities to make us obey the lusts of our body. Once sin is so operative, it will surely rule and reign in our mortal bodies.

In this verse, the Greek word for "reign" is written in the active voice, while the word for "obey" is written in the passive voice. This indicates that when sin is actively ruling, we become passively obedient. From morning to evening, sin looks for ways to become active in us and to make us passive sinners. However, if we live in Christ and give sin no opportunity to be active, we become the active ones and sin becomes passive. In other words, we must take the initiative to not allow sin to reign in our mortal bodies.

Paul never denies the existence of the power of sin in Christians, but his words show that it is possible for us to actively limit the opportunities sin has in us. Our old man has been crucified with Christ and the body of sin has been done away with (6:6); the body of sin is out of work and has nothing to do! Based on this, why would we ever assign the body of sin a job to do? This is a problem for many Christians. Even though the body of sin has been done away with, for some reason we help it find work to do. We do this because although we may understand the facts (*ginōskō*), we do not inwardly see in our spirit (*oida*) that our old man has been crucified with Christ.

Not Letting Sinful Desires Accumulate

The Bible is so good and simple—"do not let sin reign"! If we become lax in this matter, sin will become active, will reign, and will cause us to passively obey the lusts of the body. In the beginning, we may only have simple feelings regarding something. As these feelings accumulate, however, they become powerful lusts. Do not think feelings are insignificant; the scope of our passions is unlimited, and these feelings can visit us at any time. When sinful feelings rise up in us, we should learn to hide in our union with Christ so that we can ignore them. The more we pay attention to these feelings, the more they accumulate. Once enough of these feelings accumulate, they become powerful lusts.

Lusts are actually quite weak initially, but if they are not put to death by the subjective realization of Christ in the spirit, they accumulate, strengthen, and grow into a powerful force that people cannot help but obey. Here is an illustration to show this principle: A man could be traveling across the country and stop in Las Vegas to see the beautiful hotels. The beauty may attract him and provoke a small desire to visit further. After entering a hotel and seeing many people gambling, the man may feel like trying a little gambling. This is the beginning of his desires accumulating and strengthening. If the man has never gambled before, it might be easy for him to reject such a desire. However, if he tries gambling, it will become harder to resist in the future. It would be even more serious if he unfortunately won some money, because the desire in him would flare up and accumulate even more. Eventually, gambling becomes a lust that many people are unable to resist. In all of our living, it is important to have discernment so that we can reject sinful desires in their initial stages to prevent them from growing into powerful lusts.

Knowing the Death and Life of Christ

Refusing to let sin reign means not giving any opportunity for sin to be active and not allowing our sinful feelings and passions any opportunity to accumulate. The secret to this lies in Romans 6:9–10: knowing that Christ has been raised from the dead, that He is never to die again, that He died to sin once for all, and that the life He lives is unto God.

Our old man's crucifixion with Christ is a revelation for us to learn and experience, while the subjective recognition of Christ's resurrection is produced in us from our spirit (see chapter 87). The "knowing" in verses 9 and 10 is this subjective recognition. When our spirit has this recognition, our experience will match Christ's experience. Just as death no longer rules over Him, it will not rule over us. Just as Christ died to sin, we can consider ourselves dead to sin through faith and baptism. Finally, just as Christ lives unto God, we too can live unto God in Christ.

90

Presenting Ourselves to God

And do not go on presenting the members of your body to sin as instruments of unrighteousness; but present yourselves to God as those alive from the dead, and your members as instruments of righteousness to God. [14]For sin shall not be master over you, for you are not under law but under grace. [15]What then? Shall we sin because we are not under law but under grace? May it never be! [16]Do you not know that when you present yourselves to someone as slaves for obedience, you are slaves of the one whom you obey, either of sin resulting in death, or of obedience resulting in righteousness?

—*Romans 6:13-16*

WORD STUDY

This passage deals with a believer's complete surrender, whether to God or to sin. Several Greek words in this passage merit notice. The Greek word for "present" is *paristēmi*, which can also mean "to stand beside" (Strong, #3936). It is used twice in verse 13, first in a present imperative form—"do not go on presenting the members of your body to sin as instruments of unrighteousness." The present imperative here denotes the daily habit of giving our members to the service of sin. When "present" is used again in verse 13—"but present yourselves to

God"—it appears in the aorist form, indicting the act of self-devotion to God once for all (Vincent, 3:70–71).

The Greek word used in verse 13 for "instruments," *hoplon*, comes from the Greek word *hepō*, meaning "to be busy with" (Strong, #3696). *Hoplon* means an implement, utensil, or tool, especially for offensive use in war (Strong, #3696). M. R. Vincent wrote, "The conception being that of sin and righteousness as respectively rulers of opposing sovereignties and enlisting men in their armies. Hence the exhortation is, do not offer your members as weapons with which the rule of unrighteousness may be maintained, but offer them to God in the service of righteousness" (Vincent, 3:70).

This passage not only deals with our soldiership, but also our servitude (Alford, 2:370). Verse 16 tells us that our presenting, or standing, determines whom we serve. Yet the verse gives only two options for our service—to sin, or to obedience (presumably to God). H. Alford wrote, "You are the servants either of God or of sin, there is no third choice" (Alford, 2:371).

REVELATION AND APPLICATION

Presenting Ourselves

One of the strongest parts of this passage deals with presenting ourselves to God, which means standing with God. In verse 13, we are told to present ourselves to God and to present our members as instruments of righteousness. Then verse 16 says we are slaves of the one whom we obey. Presenting ourselves to God means standing with God and righteousness and becoming slaves of God. If we present ourselves to sin, we are standing with sin.

When we think of presenting ourselves to God, we usually think of an act of consecration. Presenting ourselves to God, however, is actually the application of an accomplished fact. For example, many people migrate to the United States from China, yet very few of them really present themselves to their new country. To present ourselves to the United States means to experience the country's bountiful riches, to enjoy its abundant production, and to live in its exquisite culture. If Chinese people come to America but move to Chinatown and live a Chinese lifestyle, they have not properly presented themselves to America and are not applying the fact that they now live in another country.

Similarly, since we are in Christ, we should present ourselves to Christ. When we believed into the Lord Jesus, we experienced a great and divine migration. We migrated from the kingdom of sin, of the world, and of Satan to the heavenly, divine, and mysterious kingdom of Christ. In this kingdom is the triune God Himself, as well as everything He has accomplished and experienced. All of these riches become applicable to us through the act of presenting ourselves to God.

Presenting ourselves is not only an outward action; it also involves our inner will. It is the presentation of our whole person, not just small portions of our lives. The aorist tense of the Greek word "present" shows that it is a firm decision that we will stand with the Lord lifelong. This standing is positional and becomes experiential as the riches of our triune God are applied and enjoyed by us.

Unfortunately, many Christians have never presented themselves to God. They believe into the Lord and have Him within, yet they still live their original old life. Paul's word here is that we should not live our old life in which we presented our members to sin as instruments of unrighteousness. Rather, we should present ourselves to God and our members as instruments of righteousness to God.

Instruments of Righteousness

The Greek word for "instrument" can be translated "tool" or "weapon" and comes from a root word meaning "to be busy with." Both tools and weapons are created for specific purposes. Similarly, our existence is for a purpose with which we are to be busy. Paul exhorts us not to present ourselves to sin, becoming instruments busy with unrighteousness. Rather we should present ourselves to God as alive from the dead, instruments busy with righteousness.

Becoming an instrument of righteousness means to be busy with righteousness. It means that our lives become busy with all the things that God initiates in our spirit. Many believers share a common problem of always changing what they think they ought to be busy with. When we do not serve in our spirit, we become busy with many things, but when we serve in our spirit (Rom. 1:9), we become busy with righteousness. Those who have presented themselves to God have very busy lives. Yet there is only one focus of their busyness—the righteous God who dwells in their spirit.

Sin No Longer Reigning

Presenting ourselves to God is for our whole life. When we present ourselves to God, stand with Him and His accomplishments, and present our members as instruments of righteousness, we become busy with the things of our righteous God and experience wonderful results. As righteousness operates in us, sin is unable to reign over us, for we are not under law but under grace (Rom. 6:14).

To be under grace means to stand in grace, the realm where we have peace with God (5:1–2). It also means to dwell in Christ, the divine and mystical realm, and to abide in Him, grow in Him, and walk in Him. We exist in this realm where there is peace with God, and our living is produced by the operation and working of the divine life. When we are in this realm, sin no longer rules or reigns over us.

We will stand with whomever we present ourselves to. Romans 6:15–16 tells us that we obey and become slaves to whomever we present ourselves. If we stand with sin, we will obey sin and become slaves of sin unto death. If we stand with God, we will obey God and become slaves of obedience unto righteousness.

91

The Form of Teaching

But thanks be to God that though you were slaves of sin, you became obedient from the heart to that form of teaching to which you were committed.

—Romans 6:17

WORD STUDY

In this verse, Paul thanks God for the believers' obedience from the heart to the form of teaching to which they were committed. Several Greek words in the New Testament are translated "form," including *morphōsis* (translated "embodiment" in Romans 2:20), *morphē* (as in Phil. 2:6–7), and the word used in this verse—*tupos*.

The word *tupos* means "a stamp or scar; a shape, i.e. a statue; specifically a model for imitation" (Strong, #5179). W. E. Vine explains that the metaphor here is of metalworking, when molten material is poured into a cast or frame in order to take its shape (Vine, 251). *Tupos* is derived from the Greek word *tuptō*, which means "to thump or strike" (Strong, #5180) and indicates violent beating, blows, or wounding (Vine, 54).

REVELATION AND APPLICATION

A Form Produced by God's Work

This is the second time in Romans Paul has used a word that can be translated "form," but the two instances are actually different Greek words. The first instance is found in Romans 2:20, which reads: "An instructor of the foolish, a teacher of babes, having the form (*morphōsis*) of knowledge and truth in the law" (NKJV®). In Romans 6:17, the word translated "form" is *tupos*. Although both *morphōsis* and *tupos* can be translated "example" or "form," their meanings are not the same.

Morphōsis (Strong, #3446) and its related word, *morphē* (Strong, #3444), both emphasize the appearance of something, whether inward or outward. *Morphōsis* is used in 2 Timothy 3:5 of sinners who outwardly appear godly yet deny the inward power of godliness. *Morphē* is the word used in Romans 8:29 (along with the prefix *sun*) for our conformation (*summorphos*) to the image of the Son of God. This conforming is not only to an outward form but also to an inner nature. The verb form of *morphē*—*morphoō*—is found in Galatians 4:19: "My children, with whom I am again in labor until Christ is formed (*morphoō*) in you." This usage indicates an inner working. *Morphoō* is also used in 2 Corinthians 3:18 for an outward and inward transformation: "But we all, with unveiled face, beholding as in a mirror the glory of the Lord, are being transformed (*morphoō*) into the same image from glory to glory, just as from the Lord, the Spirit."

Why didn't Paul use any of these words here in Romans 6:17? Instead, he chose to use the word *tupos*, which emphasizes God's work on a person in life. Consider those with great intelligence and vast talent. No matter how smart they are, their talent will not develop properly if it is not cultivated or worked upon. A person's talent can easily become an outward display without much reality or substance. However, when those who cultivate their talent grow into master writers, scientists, or artists, they no longer have merely an outward form of talent. Rather, their talent is who they are, and they have a form that has been worked upon both inwardly and outwardly. This is *tupos*.

Paul emphasized obedience from the heart to the form (*tupos*) of teaching to which the Romans were committed. In other words, their obedience was not simply to an outward form but to a teaching wrought by God in Paul. God worked on Paul to a point that obedience was produced in the hearts of the Roman believers. The form (*tupos*) of teaching was not merely doctrine alone but was the result of God's work in Paul for many years.

Scarred by Striking and Pressure

Tupos, which can be translated "scar" or "stamp," comes from a Greek word meaning "to strike." Thus *tupos* is a form or mark produced by striking or heavy pressure. To be a proper organic form in life, we need to experience God's work upon us. This process involves striking and heavy pressure which leaves a mark or scar upon us.

This is where *morphōsis* can be very different from *tupos*. We do not merely obey the form of teaching with our mouths but with our hearts also. An authoritative figure can make people obedient with their mouths but not their hearts. This would be a morphōsis. However, a person with real authority, like the apostle Paul, has been dealt with and stricken by God, heavily pressured, and left with a scar, a mark, or a sign within, becoming an organic form (*tupos*) for others to obey. This is the narrow way of conformation unto the death of the Son of God (Phil. 3:10).

We should not look for a way to live but for a way to die in the church life. Few people consider, "How can I die for the church? How can I die for the saints? How can I die for Christ?

How can I die for the testimony of Christ?" Only a person who is willing to die, who is conformed to the death of the Son of God, and who has a mark left by this death, can be a real form of teaching.

A Pattern for the Believers

Paul encouraged his genuine son Timothy to be an example (*tupos*) to the believers "in speech, conduct, love, faith and purity" (1 Tim. 4:12). He also encouraged Titus to show himself to be a pattern (*tupos*) of good deeds (Titus 2:7). Paul even said of himself that he was a pattern (*hupotuposis*) to all who would believe, as one to whom Jesus Christ had given mercy and displayed patience (1 Tim. 1:16). Paul was strongly resolute that a servant of the Lord must be a tupos to all the saints.

This word Paul used for himself in 1 Timothy (*hupotuposis*) is composed of two Greek words: *hupo*, meaning "under" (Strong, #5259), and *tupos*. Paul became a pattern under the mighty working of God. God struck him and applied pressure again and again; Paul lived under the constant striking of God. The inward marks left by this work upon him made him a pattern to the believers. He was not a passive or dead pattern but an active and living one.

A real pattern needs to be continually struck by God. Whether we can become patterns or not is based upon our willingness to accept God's striking. Are we willing to allow God to strike us? Or will we shy away from even the light touch of God? However, even if we cannot bear His touch, God will continue to work in us until we are one day made into patterns.

God's striking includes both His hand upon us outwardly and the work of the word of God inwardly. We need the word of God operating within us to strike and affect us and to form our constitution (Heb. 4:12). The hand of God leads us, strikes us, and heavily pressures us through outward environments. A true *tupos* is formed by the inward impact of the word of God and by the shaping of God's hand through outward environments.

The word of God also supplies and strengthens us inwardly, even as the hand of God strikes us and pressures us outwardly. The cooperation between God's words and hand produces a form of teaching within us that is a pattern to those we are with, even causing them to obey this teaching from the heart.

May the Lord have mercy so that we could be worked upon by Him to become healthy patterns for the sake of all the believers around us!

92

Unto Sanctification

And having been freed from sin, you became slaves of righteousness. ¹⁹I am speaking in human terms because of the weakness of your flesh. For just as you presented your members as slaves to impurity and to lawlessness, resulting in further lawlessness, so now present your members as slaves to righteousness, resulting in sanctification. ²⁰For when you were slaves of sin, you were free in regard to righteousness. ²¹Therefore what benefit were you then deriving from the things of which you are now ashamed? For the outcome of those things is death. ²²But now having been freed from sin and enslaved to God, you derive your benefit, resulting in sanctification, and the outcome, eternal life. ²³For the wages of sin is death, but the free gift of God is eternal life in Christ Jesus our Lord.
—Romans 6:18-23

WORD STUDY

In this last passage of chapter 6, Paul concludes his writing on serving and presenting. He writes in verse 19, "So now present your members as slaves to righteousness, resulting in sanctification." The words "resulting in" are translated from the Greek word *eis*, which means "unto." It denotes what the presentation of our members as slaves of righteousness is leading to or having as its result (Alford, 2:373). According to the verse, the result of this presenting is sanctification.

The Greek word translated "sanctification" in both verses 19 and 22 is *hagiasmon*, meaning "consecration, purification" (Thayer, 6). It is derived from the word *hagios*, which is translated "saints" in Romans 1:7. Sanctification refers to the process or state of being set apart for God's service and the development and display of His characteristics (Rogers, 328). In 6:19 and 22, it is probably better understood as the process of sanctification (Vincent, 3:72).

In verses 21 and 22, the word "benefit" is translated from the Greek word *karpon*, which literally means "fruit" (Strong, #2590). When we were slaves of sin, our fruit was unto death. When slaves of God, our fruit is unto sanctification (*eis hagiasmon*) and eternal life (*zōē*). The term "wages," found in verse 23, implies working; fruit, however, implies growth.

REVELATION AND APPLICATION

Presenting unto Sanctification

The freedom from sin in Romans 6:18 is the result of our having died to sin in 6:7. This freedom is the release from sin and its power. We have died with Christ, we have been buried with Him, and our past has been terminated. The power of sin is no longer effective in us. Now that we have been set free from sin, we can become slaves of righteousness.

Verse 19 ends with the phrase, "so now present your members as slaves to righteousness, resulting in sanctification." The word "resulting" is better translated "unto." The presenting to righteousness is unto sanctification. Sanctification has a process, an effectiveness, and a final product. It changes both our status and our nature. As the righteous God works in us, we experience this process of being saturated with His divine life and holy nature, leading us unto our sanctification.

This verse also talks about righteousness. God is holy and His work is righteous. God leads us in righteousness so that we might serve Him, follow Him, become His slaves, and eventually be unto His holiness. According to His holy being, He reveals Himself to us. According to His righteous work, He leads us so that we might partake of His righteousness and eventually become sanctified.

The process of sanctification is totally related to righteousness. As we experience the inward working and leading of our righteous God, the reality of His righteousness in us is manifested in the living of a righteous life. This is what Paul meant when he said we should present our members as slaves to righteousness unto sanctification (v. 19).

Honor Based on God's Righteousness

Our God is not only holy but also righteous. Because of this, He must honor Himself and everything He does. God is not like us; very few people honor themselves today, and very few people even know how to honor themselves. For example, we may pray to God, saying, "I am willing to love You, to follow You, and to serve You." Immediately after praying this, we may forget our words and become busy with the affairs of this age, laying aside the things of God. This is an example of dishonoring ourselves and our prayer.

God honors Himself much more than we honor ourselves. Though we forget, fail, and disregard God, He never forgets, fails, or disregards us. He honors Himself and He honors whatever desire is in us toward Him. Because He is working in us according to His righteousness, He honors our prayers and has promised that He will complete what He has begun in us (Phil. 1:6). To accomplish His heart's desire in us, He must continue to work in us. To not do so would be unrighteous. His righteousness demands that He honor Himself and all of His work.

Consider an example of respectable parents whose children are very sloppy. Will the parents give up on their children because of their sloppiness? They will not, but will do their best to cultivate honor and respectability in their children so they can eventually live a normal and healthy life. The parents would say, "Our children do not honor themselves, but we honor ourselves, so we must take care of them, raise them up, and nurture them." God treats us the same way. No matter what our situation is, God will accomplish His work in us according to His righteousness.

Assurance Based on God's Righteousness

As we follow the Lord, God's righteousness provides assurance for us. Many Christians who have followed the Lord for years may ask, "How is it that I still love the Lord? By nature it is impossible for me to love Him or follow Him, yet I have loved Him, pursued Him, served Him, and followed Him for so many years." God's righteousness is the reason we are able. Once He has begun a work in us, He cannot righteously let us go. Because of His righteousness, He will walk with us so that we can have a persistent faith in His economy, in His divine being, and in all of His accomplishments.

Even when we are weak and fail or stumble, we can still come back to God's presence. He must accept us because of His righteousness. He has become our Savior, put us into the realm of grace, and in His righteousness has given us eternal life. According to His righteousness, He must accept, receive, lead, and bless us, and He cannot help but be responsible for us. Oh, what a blessing that He is a righteous God!

Bearing Fruit unto Sanctification

According to Romans 6, if we present ourselves to God

and our members as instruments of righteousness (v. 13) we will become slaves of righteousness (v. 18) and of God (v. 22), and will bear fruit unto sanctification and eternal life (v. 23). This life is dispensed into us by God according to the operation and working of the gift of God in His righteousness. This life is not only our enjoyment and reality in Christ today but also in eternity.

The phrase in verse 22, "you derive your benefit, resulting in sanctification," can also be translated "you have fruit unto sanctification." Fruit cannot be produced by work; rather, it takes a growing process. Likewise, the fruit of sanctification does not come from work but from spiritual growth. Our growth in life involves many things, like praying, reading the Bible, preaching the gospel, and repenting and confessing. However, when these things become religious works, they do not result in the fruit that is unto sanctification. The true fruit comes from our growth in life, step by step, and is not dependent on performing certain works. The fruit of sanctification comes from growth, the result of which is eternal life.

We may see a man searching for food in a garbage can and buy lunch for him out of compassion. Is this fruit borne unto sanctification, or is it just a benevolent act for a poor man? There is a big difference between these two. If it is for satisfying a desire to do a good deed, this is an act any human being can perform. If it is out of the merciful inward parts of God to bring His love to the poor, we have fruit unto sanctification.

Reading the Bible, praying, bringing people to salvation, manifesting a gift, or giving money to the poor as religious works do not issue in the fruit unto sanctification. It does not matter how much we do outwardly. What matters is the inward growth of the divine life. It is not an outcome of doing but of growing. The fruit unto sanctification is not a result of our own efforts; it only comes from the growth of the divine life.

The Gift of God

The end of chapter 6 reads, "For the wages of sin is death, but the free gift of God is eternal life in Christ Jesus our Lord" (v. 23). The "gift" in this verse is not *dōrea*, the initial gift of life, but *charisma*, the gift in operation. Why did Paul use *charisma* here instead of *dōrea*? According to our understanding, *dōrea* would seem to fit this verse much better. However, in both chapters 5 and 6, all the operation and working of the divine life is realized as the gift in operation (*charisma*).

Upon regeneration, we received the initial gift of eternal life and began to live and walk in this life. However, if we are not able to operate in the divine life, it will remain abstract and will not be easily applied in our living. It is through the gift in operation (*charisma*) that we can be brought to eternal life, constituted in eternal life, and be unto eternal life.

The gift in operation allows us to serve God, become slaves of righteousness, and bear fruit unto sanctification and eternal life. With this gift in operation, we are no longer slaves of sin but slaves of righteousness.

93

Married to Christ

Or do you not know, brethren (for I am speaking to those who know the law), that the law has jurisdiction over a person as long as he lives? ²For the married woman is bound by law to her husband while he is living; but if her husband dies, she is released from the law concerning the husband. ³So then, if while her husband is living she is joined to another man, she shall be called an adulteress; but if her husband dies, she is free from the law, so that she is not an adulteress though she is joined to another man. ⁴Therefore, my brethren, you also were made to die to the Law through the body of Christ, so that you might be joined to another, to Him who was raised from the dead, in order that we might bear fruit for God.
—Romans 7:1-4

WORD STUDY

In verse 2, the Greek word for the adjective "married," *hupandros*, means "under (i.e. subject to) a man; married, and therefore, according to Roman law under the legal authority of the husband" (Vine, 315). It is this metaphor of marriage that Paul chooses to use in order to demonstrate our freedom from the old husband and our new union with Christ.

The difficulty of these verses lies in the attempt to keep the metaphor consistent. Although in verses 2 and 3 the survivor is the liberated one, in verse 4 it is the one who has died who is freed. This difficulty, along with several others, causes some scholars and commentators to abandon the analogy and look rather at the principles behind it (see Alford, 2:375). However, we can maintain the consistency of Paul's metaphor through all the verses by viewing the husband in Romans 7:3 as our "old man" in Romans 6:6. This is how Martin Luther interpreted these verses (Luther, 109).

REVELATION AND APPLICATION

In Romans 7, Paul talks about what believers should know concerning Christ's work and how they struggle in the process of sanctification. The entire chapter seems to be an expansion of 6:14: "For sin shall not be master over you, for you are not under law but under grace." The first six verses of chapter 7 stress the importance of a believer's recognition of the process of sanctification. Verses 7 through 25 then depict a believer's struggle within this process. In our experience of the process of sanctification, it is important to first recognize our freedom from the old man and our being joined as a wife to Christ.

Husband or Wife?

In a healthy marriage, the husband is the head of the wife and loves her, while the wife is subject to the husband and respects him (Eph. 5:22–33). After creating man, God held the position of the husband and mankind was in the position of the wife. Isaiah 54:5 says, "For your husband is your Maker, whose name is the Lord of hosts." The end of the Bible also shows the New Jerusalem as a bride prepared for her husband, who is Christ (Rev. 19:7-8, 21:2). Unfortunately, the fall of man resulted in people leaving their position as God's wife and taking the place of the husband.

What does it mean for us to take the position of husband from God? It means acting independent of God and walking by our own will. This was what happened in the garden of Eden when Eve acted independently of her husband, Adam (Gen. 3:6). In our own experience, it means we no longer subject ourselves to God as our Head. Before our redemption, we were all our own husbands; we had all left God, acted independently of Him, and walked by our own will. Upon receiving salvation, we became related to God. By relying on Him and obeying Him, we returned to the status of a wife.

Living as a Husband or a Wife

The Bible declares that before receiving salvation, we each acted independently of God. Isaiah 53:6 says, "All of us like sheep have gone astray, each of us has turned to his own way." Only after receiving salvation do we become dependent on God. We were husbands before salvation and became wives after salvation. In experience, however, many believers still inwardly struggle between these two positions. Even after believing into the Lord and being justified, we may still act as a husband in our relationship with God.

When we live according to ourselves, we are standing in the husband's place. Our healthy living before God according to His heart's desire requires our standing as His wife. When we walk by our own will and live according to our own desires, we stand as a husband. When we walk by the Spirit, live a life of union and mingling with God, and totally rely on Him, we stand as His wife.

Whenever we leave God to walk and live according to ourselves, we become a husband rather than a wife. This is the principle of the old man, who desires only to live for himself.

In the old man, we are under the demand of the Law, ruled by the Law, and try to satisfy the demands of the Law. In this condition, sin dwells and reigns in our flesh; yet because of the regulating by our conscience, we attempt to satisfy the Law. This living under the Law is a confinement for all people. When a person stands as the husband, God will give the Law. Once the person stands as the wife, God will give life.

Our New Husband

Our husband, which was the old man, died by being crucified with Christ (Rom. 6:6). Martin Luther had a very good utterance about this section. He said that the old man revives when we recognize the Law, and as we understand the Law, we recognize the old man (Luther, 109). In our experience, the old man (our old husband) dies whenever we take the status of wife, and in that standing, we are freed from the old man and the Law. In this condition, we can finally experience the reality of being married to Christ, the One who was raised from the dead (7:4). This marriage is not only a change in our status but a union in life with Christ. Our being married to Christ unites us to Him and enables us to live by Him and hold Him as our Head.

Through the fall, our husband became the old man. But "I" am no longer the husband (Gal. 2:20), rather Christ is! Originally "I" was the head, but now Christ is the Head! Our old man has died, we are freed from him, and we are married and united to Christ in life. In this union, Christ is our new husband, and God's life can overflow from us to bear fruit and glorify God (Rom. 7:4). How wonderful it is to be married to Christ!

God's View of Our Body

For while we were in the flesh, the sinful passions, which were aroused by the Law, were at work in the members of our body to bear fruit for death.
—Romans 7:5

WORD STUDY

The Greek word for "flesh," *sarx*, is used over 140 times in the New Testament (Brown, 1:674). Generally, it is used to designate the sphere of earthly man as opposed to the spiritual sphere of God (Kittel, 7:124–126). Man is "flesh in his natural state apart from Christ; it is the human nature without the divine Spirit" (Vincent, 3:76). In Romans, the term "flesh" is used by Paul not only for the nature of man, but also for the dwelling place of sin; the flesh is the place in which nothing good dwells (Rom. 7:17–18).

The Greek word for "member," *melos*, means "a limb or part of the body" (Strong, #3196). This could include the eyes and hands (Matthew 5:29–30), feet and ears (1 Cor. 12:14–20), the tongue (James 3:6), or other various body parts. Although Paul writes in Romans 7:17–18 that sin dwells in the flesh, verse 5 shows that "the sinister power of sin uses the members as an instrument to express itself in actions" (Kittel, 4:562).

REVELATION AND APPLICATION

Our Subjective Feeling toward Sin

Those who are "in the flesh" experience lives marked by the operation of sinful passions in their members. This is despite living under the Law! The passions of sin are the power of sin and lead to the manifestation of sin in sinful deeds.

Why did Paul bring up sinful passions here? He does so because of our subjective organic union of life with Christ (Rom. 7:4). Our feeling and recognition of sin is not only an issue of our conscience but also the result of our union with the Lord. The deeper and more profound our subjective union with Christ is, the deeper and stronger our feeling toward sin will be.

Everyone's subjective definition of sin is different. For example, is it sinful for parents to read their children's diaries? The parents might say, "Our kids were born to us and raised by us; they owe their very life to us. Why shouldn't we read their diaries?" The children may have a very different feeling. In another example, should we give our seat to others on the bus? If we don't, is that a sin? The question of sin is very hard to answer. Besides man's general recognition of sin, our subjective definition of sin is related to the feelings and realizations that are produced by our union with Christ in life.

Committing Sin through Our Members

Romans 7:5 mentions both flesh and members, indicating a distinction between the two. When we are in the flesh, we assume the status of husband. In this state, our passion for sin is aroused by the Law and is at work in our members to bear fruit for death.

Without Christ, we are only flesh and our members inevitably commit sins. "Flesh" is our being and "members" are related to our living. Stealing, lying, cursing, and many unhealthy things are done by our members, and the person who commits such things is flesh. When we are in the flesh, we do many sinful things through our members.

Whenever Paul mentions "members" in chapters 6 and 7, he always speaks of plural members, never a singular member (see Rom. 6:13, 19, and 7:5). The operation of sin in the flesh never comes through one member alone but rather through many. When sin operates it looks for the cooperation of many members, and thus the operation of sin involves our whole person.

For example, a woman may steal lipstick from a grocery store—a sinful action is done with her hand, which is one of her members. However, for sin to operate in her flesh, it needed her eyes to see, her feet to walk around, and her ears to hear if anyone was nearby. Although it was her hand that opened her pocket and put the lipstick in, the theft involved her whole body. Even more, it began from a simple feeling to commit sin that was not dealt with, and so it eventually became a lust she could not overcome (James 1:15). This is how sin operates—our whole person is involved!

The Body of Sin, Death, and Mortality

In Romans, Paul describes our body using three different Greek words. These words are translated as body (*sōma*, 6:12), flesh (*sarx*, 7:18), and member(s) (*melos*, 6:13). Every human being has a body with many members. The fallen body is the flesh, in which there is nothing good (7:18) and in which sin and the law of sin dwell (7:17, 21, 23). The sin dwelling in our body operates through our members when we live according to the flesh. When the flesh develops to its fullest extent, we become "of flesh" or fleshly (7:14). Fleshly is the opposite of spiritual (see 1 Cor. 3:1) and not only indicates one who commits fallen deeds but the fallen self as well.

Paul uses three phrases in Romans 6–7 to describe our body (*sōma*): the body of sin (Rom. 6:6), the body of death (7:24), and the mortal body (6:12). Our body is of sin because sin dwells in our body. The fruit of sin is death (6:21, 23), thus our body is the body of death. Furthermore, though we have been saved through Jesus Christ, our bodies remain perishable—a mortal body. Ultimately, only the overcomers who are raptured alive at the coming of the Lord will not face a physical death.

These three descriptions of the body in Romans focus on the existence of our body rather than on our person. Though our body is of sin, death, and mortality, who will reign over it? The answer to this question is dependent on what status we take, resulting in us becoming either spiritual or fleshly. When we stand in the place of the husband, our body is independent of God and ruled by sin and Satan, and our person—the old man—is fleshly. When we stand as the wife, our body becomes reliant on God, ruled by the Holy Spirit, and our person is spiritual.

God's Complete Redeeming Work

Although "flesh" is often used negatively in the Bible, "body" is not necessarily negative. Romans 7:4 mentions Christ's physical body, which is sinless and through which we have died to the Law. Today our mortal body is of sin and of death. However, through the sinless body of Christ, we died to the Law so that we might belong to the One who was raised from the dead, Christ, who is our new and real husband.

The redemptive work of God is wonderful! Christ accomplished redemption with His physical body, and God's work on us today is not apart from our physical bodies. For example, church meetings involve both spirit and body. Living before the Lord healthily is a matter of both spirit and body. We are even told in the Bible to present our bodies to God as a living and holy sacrifice, which is our spiritual service (12:1).

The fact is that God pays great attention to our physical body. Even though our body is perishable, is called the body of sin and death, has sin dwelling in it, and is mortal, all the work of God on us is still related to our body. In fact, He even desires to "give life to your mortal bodies through His Spirit who dwells in you" (8:11).

God truly regards our body as important. Eventually, His work will result in the redemption of our body, which will no longer be fallen, fleshly, and mortal, but glorified as a redeemed, glorious, and spiritual body (8:23; 1 Cor. 15:43–44). God's complete salvation involves our spirit, soul, and body (1 Thess. 5:23)!

95

Released from the Law

But now we have been released from the Law, having died to that by which we were bound, so that we serve in newness of the Spirit and not in oldness of the letter.
—Romans 7:6

WORD STUDY

This verse begins with the statement that "we have been released from the Law." The Greek word used here for "released" is *katargeō*, which can also be translated "delivered, loosed, made of no effect" (Strong, #2673). This same word is used in Romans 6:6 to indicate that the body of sin has been rendered useless, or has been made unemployed (see chapter 86). Here in 7:6, it is followed by the Greek preposition *apo*, rendering the meaning "separated from" or "discharged from" (Rogers, 328). In other words, the phrase could be translated, "we have been discharged from the Law."

The second half of this verse, begun by the phrase "so that," explains the purpose of deliverance from the Law—service in newness of the Spirit. The Greek word for "newness," *kainotēs*, does not emphasize newness in respect to time but rather renewal or freshness (Strong, #2537, #2538). The genitive phrase "of the Spirit" describes the newness; however, it is unclear in the Greek whether this refers to the human spirit or the Holy Spirit. First Corinthians 6:17 may offer a bridge between the two: "But the one who joins himself to the Lord is one spirit with Him." W. E. Vine says, "While the phrase [in Romans 7:6] stands for the new life of the quickened spirit of the believer, it is impossible to dissociate this from the operation of the Holy Spirit, by whose power the service is rendered" (Vine, 431).

REVELATION AND APPLICATION

Released from the Ordinances of the Law

In this verse, "released" denotes the thought of deliverance from or having nothing to do with the Law. We have been released from the demands of the Law, which means that now we have nothing to do with it. We are no longer held by the Law and are no longer responsible for its demands. This is echoed in Ephesians 2:15, which says of Christ, "By abolishing in His flesh the enmity, which is the Law of commandments contained in ordinances."

This release from the ordinances of the Law is a result of our dying to the Law. An ordinance is based on the Law. For example, a young boy was brought by his parents when they visited their friends. This child saw a piece of candy on the table, took it, and ate it. He did not know this was wrong; to him it was perfectly normal to take and eat candy. He had no law regarding this candy. However, his parents viewed this act very differently. They told him, "You cannot just take this candy. You must ask first." Here were two new ordinances for the child: "You cannot randomly take others' things" and "You cannot eat candy before asking."

Ordinances are different from the Law. It was not the Law itself that Christ abolished in His body; it was the Law as contained in ordinances (Eph. 2:15; Col. 2:14). The Law itself is holy, good, and righteous (Rom. 7:12), and it is unchangeable and cannot be abolished (Matt. 5:18). God gave the Law to man, and based on the Law many commandments, statutes, and judgments followed. These commandments, statutes, and judgments marked the entire Old Testament age. The Law itself cannot be abolished, yet here in Romans we are told that in Christ we have died to the Law that held us. Therefore, we are no longer responsible for the ordinances produced by the Law.

Ordinances say things like, "Do not handle, do not taste, do not touch" (Col. 2:21). It is easy for such things to come in and control our lives. Yet when we live in ordinances, we leave our status as a wife, dependent on Christ, and take the place of the husband, independent of God and determined to live out these ordinances by our own effort. In these ordinances, sin finds opportunities to operate and produces desires that unconsciously draw us into all kinds of temptations.

In Newness of the Spirit

It is wonderful that we have been released from the Law, but we may wonder what this release is for. What is the purpose of such an action? This verse tells us that our release from the Law is so that we might serve the Lord in newness of the Spirit and not in oldness of the letter.

The problem of sin was addressed and answered in Romans 6—we have died to it! In chapter 7, the problem of the ordinances of the Law is solved. In chapter 6, our old man was crucified with Christ so that the body of sin might be done away with, that we should no longer be slaves of sin (v. 6). Because our old man has died, Paul says that we have been released from the law (7:2) unto Christ who was raised from the dead (v. 4). Now we can serve our new husband, Christ, in newness of the Spirit and not in oldness of the letter.

Newness is a major characteristic of regeneration. To serve in newness of the Spirit is the result of our inward realization (*oida*) that Christ was raised from the dead and will never die again, and that the life He lives is unto God (6:9–10). When we apply the reality of the resurrection of Christ in our spirit, it becomes a source of fresh, new life. In this fresh, new life, we can serve the Lord joyfully!

When we see and begin to comprehend the resurrected Christ, ordinances lose their hold on us. Through the body of Christ, we have died to the Law (7:4), we have been released from the Law (v. 6), we are joined unto the One who was raised from the dead (v. 4), and now we can serve in newness of the Spirit (v. 6). When the reality of these verses is realized in us, we return to our intended status as the wife of Christ, taking Him as everything and being responsible only unto Him.

96

Sin's Opportunity

What shall we say then? Is the Law sin? May it never be! On the contrary, I would not have come to know sin except through the Law; for I would not have known about coveting if the Law had not said, "You shall not covet." ⁸But sin, taking opportunity through the commandment, produced in me coveting of every kind; for apart from the Law sin is dead. ⁹I was once alive apart from the Law; but when the commandment came, sin became alive and I died; ¹⁰and this commandment, which was to result in life, proved to result in death for me; ¹¹for sin, taking an opportunity through the commandment, deceived me and through it killed me.

—Romans 7:7–11

WORD STUDY

Romans 7:7–11 begins a section (vv. 7–25) that has been called a "most important and difficult passage" (Alford, 2:376). In it, Paul explains the role of the Law in bringing out sin, using his own personal experience as an illustration. In verse 8, Paul writes that sin takes, or seizes (Strong, #2983), opportunity through the commandment. The Greek word here for "opportunity," *aphormē*, means "a starting point" (Strong, #874). The word means more than a mere opportunity or occasion; it also denotes a base of operations for an expedition and the resources needed to carry through that expedition (Rogers, 329). Somehow, the commandment provides sin with both the opportunity and the materials needed to produce evil desire.

The sentence, "For apart from the Law sin is dead," must not be taken to mean that sin was absent apart from the Law. Rather, it means that sin was powerless (Alford, 2:379) and inactive (Vincent, 3:78). Overall, this section should not be understood solely to show that the commandment brought about recognition of sin. It also displays the weakness of the commandment in dealing with our sin and sin's ability to use the commandment as a snare for us.

REVELATION AND APPLICATION

Romans 7:9 says, "I was once alive apart from the Law." There is a question among Bible scholars regarding what period of history Paul is referring to. Many scholars believe this was Paul's experience as a child or as a Pharisee (Alford, 2:379). Although the passage may be referring to Paul's life in Judaism before believing into the Lord, it describes a principle every believer experiences.

The Opportunity for Sin to Operate

Paul had the Law of God before he believed into the Lord Jesus, yet the sin in his flesh still seized an opportunity to operate. Incredibly, Romans 7:8 tells us that it was the commandment of the Law that gave sin this opportunity! A spiritual brother once said, "In our experience, sin utilizes the commandment, and the commandment helps sin to continually operate in us." The holy, good, and righteous Law should have nothing to do with sin, yet in our experience, sin utilizes the commandments of the Law to operate in us.

Sin is dormant before the commandment comes, and it is not until the commandment appears that sin is revived. Sin operates forcefully wherever the commandment is. In other words, the commandment of the Law does not help us overcome sin at all. The clearer the commandment is, the more opportunities sin finds to operate. The more complete the commandment appears, the more deceitfully, violently, and vigorously sin operates (vv. 11, 23). Sin utilizes the commandment, and in doing so produces in us all manner of evil desires.

Struggling with God's Law

Many Christians today are what the Bible calls Gentiles— people who are not Jewish by birth. The Jewish people had been given the Law of God on tablets of stone. The Gentiles did not have the Law in the same way, but Romans 2:14– 15 indicates Gentiles have the Law inscribed in their hearts, and their consciences bear witness to that Law within them. Our experience is different from Paul's because, as a Jew, he had received the teaching of the Law of God from his youth. Though we who are Gentiles did not receive such teaching, our consciences still bear witness to the Law that has been inscribed in our hearts.

Before believing into the Lord, we may have experienced a period of struggle similar to Paul's experience. We may have strongly desired to do good deeds because of the Law written within us. We would have found, however, that we were unable to fulfill the Law by our own strength. We were like naughty children who know they ought to be good and that they should not grieve their parents, but they are totally unable to behave well. Before salvation, to one degree or another, every person experiences the struggle Paul writes of in these verses.

Struggling Because We Are Complicated

This experience of struggling not only occurred before we were saved but also occurs after our regeneration. After believing into the Lord and loving Him, many of us begin to appreciate the Law of God and desire to live a life that satisfies the demands of the Law. Yet in this desire, we often forget that the most important thing is to be a wife to the Lord.

We knew that we should do good, and not evil, even before believing into the Lord. This feeling to do good continues after believing, and once we love the Lord, we become even more eager to live a righteous life. Yet amazingly, the more we desire to live a righteous life, the more we cannot! This is because we do not know how to apply our status as a wife. After believing into the Lord and loving Him, every Christian has a period of time during which they fall into this struggle.

Our life as believers is not simple. Before our regeneration, we had our natural life in our soul and sin in our flesh. After salvation, another life was added within us—God's eternal life. We now have the life of God in our regenerated spirit, our natural life in our soul, and sin in our fleshly body. All three exist simultaneously. According to the objective facts in Romans, sin does not control us any longer; God's life is reigning, and our natural life has become the wife of Christ, relying on the divine life and serving her husband.

Learning to Be a Wife to Christ

A wife has the most joyful position in the universe, because her husband is in charge of all things and she only needs to enjoy. A husband needs to feed his family and struggle and toil (Gen. 3:17–19). A wife has only to enjoy all her husband possesses and has nothing to worry about. A wife in a household should tell her husband, "You are the lord of this household. You are my head; all the responsibility falls on you, and

I only need to enjoy your rich supply." This ought to be true in our physical life, and it is true in our spiritual life. Unfortunately, our human nature is often unwilling to take the position of a wife and only wants to be a husband.

Paul makes it quite clear in Romans that after we believe into the Lord, we are freed from our old man and are married to Christ, who is our true husband, our leader, and the One responsible for our whole life. What a sweet thing this is! Unfortunately, we usually like to act as the head and husband, and we attempt to please God by our own effort. We are often unwilling to be a wife and refuse to take Christ as our true husband. When we leave the status of a wife, however, we surely experience the power of sin in us.

Every Christian who desires to grow will have this experience. We who have become married to Christ often do not want to accept His supply and instead try to serve Him by our own strength. Whenever we do this, however, we come back disappointed and discouraged. How miserable! A brother once gave a good message, and many saints were very touched by it. He thought in his heart, "My message was so impressive and everyone was so moved. Next time I speak, I will bring everyone to tears!" At this point, he left his status as a wife. Originally, he spoke for the Lord out of a simple heart. He constantly prayed, called on the Lord, looked unto the Lord, was one with the Lord, and kept his spirit awake and aroused. He was like a wife closely attached to her husband. But after speaking so well and giving such a touching message, he was not willing to be a wife the next time. At that moment, sin found an opportunity to operate in him.

Nothing is more important for a Christian than learning to be a wife to Christ. Once we are a wife, we are dead to the Law, the commandments, and the ordinances. As a wife, we are alive only to our husband, Christ, who was raised from the dead.

The Commandment and Life

And this commandment, which was to result in life, proved to result in death for me; ¹¹for sin, taking an opportunity through the commandment, deceived me and through it killed me.
—Romans 7:10-11

WORD STUDY

The phrase in Romans 7:10, "to result in life," is rendered from the Greek words *eis zōēn*. The word *eis* is a preposition that can be translated "to or into" for movement, or "unto" to indicate a purpose or result (Strong, #1519). In other words, the commandment's purpose was to bring men unto eternal life (*zōē*).

Paul found that the commandment, which was meant to bring him unto life, was actually unto death (*eis thanaton*). Paul's surprise at this unexpected result is expressed by the word at the end of verse 10, "proved" (Vincent, 3:79). The reason for this result is revealed in verse 11 (the word "for" indicating the coming explanation of verse 10): Paul's sinful nature was able to use the commandment to deceive, beguile, and kill him. The same is true for all mankind. This death may be an allusion to physical death, but it can also indicate our inward spiritual death before God (Alford, 2:380).

REVELATION AND APPLICATION

The phrase in Romans 7:10, "this commandment, which was to result in life," shows that the commandment's purpose was to bring people into the enjoyment of the reality of the divine life. If our relationship with God is unhealthy, the outward commandments become horrible for us and will result in death. If our relationship with God is healthy, however, the outward commandments will become sweet and will bring us into the enjoyment of the divine life.

The Healthy Operation of Life

The divine life and the commandments of God match each other. In fact, the reason God gave so many outward commandments was for us to obtain and enjoy the divine life. However, Paul says here that the commandment which was to result in life was found to result in death. If God's commandments were originally intended for people to obtain life, why did they become commandments unto death? They became like this because people are unwilling to allow the divine life to operate in a healthy manner within them.

To illustrate, when we are with our family members, there is an unexplainable comfort and satisfaction. This is because there is a life of love within us. This life has a law that makes us happy to be with family members and talk with them. If our family members call us and we do not want to pick up the phone, it shows that there is unhealthiness in the operation of the life within us. Spiritually speaking, if we are willing to allow the divine life to have a healthy operation in us, the commandments of God become commandments unto life. Without life operating in us, the commandments are unto death.

Serving by the Law of Life

The commandments were not meant for death, but for life. The Bible commands us to not forsake assembling ourselves together, but to exhort one another (Heb. 10:25). According to this, it is biblical to exhort others to come to church meetings. Many Christians find church meetings undesirable and only another pressure. However, those who have a healthy relationship with God will not only be willing to come to church meetings but will also be desirous and joyful! The life within them matches the commandment to assemble, so assembling is not a burden. In some people, the commandment to assemble is unto death. In others, it is unto life. This difference exists because the result of the commandment matches the operation of life within us. When we are dead to sin and alive unto God, the commandments are not a burden but are unto life.

Those who serve the saints must learn to serve by the law of the divine life. Every life has its law. Human life has a law, animal life has a law, plant life has a law, and God's life also has a law. When we serve others, we should learn to serve by the law of God's divine life. We should not force people to come to church meetings, nor should we simply ask them to serve in the church. Instead, we must help them one by one to live by the law of the divine life.

Knowing how to serve the saints is a matter of learning how to cooperate with the law of life. The law of God's life involves loving the brothers; loving the church; and loving, pursuing, and serving the Lord. Those who have learned to cooperate with the law of life should visit the saints, especially the ones who have not come to church meetings for a while. Additionally, they are able to touch the law of life within others, and they never allow this life to lose its effectiveness in the saints.

The Outward Commandments and Inward Life

Again, the divine life and the commandments of God match each other. Inwardly, we have the divine life. Outwardly, we have the Law of God and the commandments that match the divine being of God. The inward law of the divine life matches the outward commandments of God.

The more of God's commandments we have outwardly, the more joyful we ought to be inwardly. We can rejoice in all of God's commandments! He commanded us not to forsake the assembling together of ourselves with other believers (Heb. 10:25). He also commanded, "Rejoice always" (1 Thess. 5:16), "Pray without ceasing" (v. 17), and "In everything give thanks" (v. 18). We would outwardly agree with all of these biblical commandments, which also match the law of the divine life already within us. The more we live in the law of the divine life, the more we spontaneously fulfill the demands of the commandments of God, and the more we experience sanctification.

The commandments of God bring us into the enjoyment of the divine life, and the divine life echoes the commandments of God. Without the divine life in us, the commandments will merely cause us to die. With the inward divine life operating in us according to its law, the commandments will not cause us to die but rather will cause us to live, obtain eternal life, and enjoy this life.

98

Three Laws

So then, the Law is holy, and the commandment is holy and righteous and good. [13]Therefore did that which is good become a cause of death for me? May it never be! Rather it was sin, in order that it might be shown to be sin by effecting my death through that which is good, so that through the commandment sin would become utterly sinful. [14]For we know that the Law is spiritual, but I am of flesh, sold into bondage to sin. [15]For what I am doing, I do not understand; for I am not practicing what I would like to do, but I am doing the very thing I hate. [16]But if I do the very thing I do not want to do, I agree with the Law, confessing that the Law is good. [17]So now, no longer am I the one doing it, but sin which dwells in me. [18]For I know that nothing good dwells in me, that is, in my flesh; for the willing is present in me, but the doing of the good is not. [19]For the good that I want, I do not do, but I practice the very evil that I do not want. [20]But if I am doing the very thing I do not want, I am no longer the one doing it, but sin which dwells in me.

[21]I find then the principle that evil is present in me, the one who wants to do good. [22]For I joyfully concur with the law of God in the inner man, [23]but I see a different law in the members of my body, waging war against the law of my mind and making me a prisoner of the law of sin which is in my members.

—*Romans 7:12–23*

WORD STUDY

The Greek word for "law," *nomos*, can mean a general regulation, specific command, or a figurative principle (Strong, #3551). Romans 7:12-23 contains references to at least three different laws. They are

1. The Law of God (v. 22). Paul says, "I joyfully concur with the Law of God in the inner man"; he "rejoices in...i.e. feels satisfaction concerning" this law (Strong, #4913). This law is also holy (v. 12) and spiritual (v. 14). M. R. Vincent explains "spiritual" as indicating that this law is the expression of the Holy Spirit (Vincent, 3:80). The Law of God is an expression of God, who is spirit (John 4:24).
2. The law of the mind (Rom. 7:23). This is not the Law of God itself, but the consent of man to the Law of God (Alford, 2:384). Thus, it is the law of the mind that wants to do good (v. 19), hates to do evil (vv. 15, 19), and joyfully concurs with the Law of God (v. 22).
3. The law of sin (v. 23). This law is in our members (v. 23), wars against the law of the mind (v. 23), and brings us into captivity (v. 23). It is this law of sin that causes us to do what we do not want to do (vv. 15, 17).

G. Campbell Morgan wrote of this passage, "It is an almost startling revelation of the experience of all those who come honestly to the measurement of the law. It is a double experience, that of a man doing hated things and by his very hatred of them consenting to the goodness of the law which forbids them. The will to do the good is with him, but not the power. He even experiences delight in the Law of God, but because of the principle of sin which masters him, he is unable to obey" (Morgan, 105).

REVELATION AND APPLICATION

Three Laws

Within this section, Paul mentions three laws: the Law of God, the law of the mind, and the law of sin. The Law of God was given to us outwardly, the law of the mind is within our minds, and the law of sin is in our flesh (or in our members). Each of these laws is related to a different life.

Paul first talks about the Law of God. This Law testifies of who God is, and it is also the rule or principle by which God operates. It is totally according to God's life and being. Therefore, the Law is holy, righteous, and good (Rom. 7:12), and because God is spirit, the Law is spiritual (v. 14). This is extremely profound. Because the Law is spiritual, we are unable to attain to it by our natural being. Only by being born again, living in the reality of the Spirit, and enjoying the divine life within us can we match, display, and enjoy the Law of God. Since God's Law is spiritual, His Spirit is necessary to fulfill it.

Next, Paul talks about the law of the mind. This law is according to the natural life within us. Because of the law of this life, we joyfully concur with the Law of God (v. 22) and want to do good (v. 21). This is why every person wants to do good; even those who do not have God's life desire to be good and charitable people. We too, who possess God's life, desire to be approved by God by satisfying the demands of His holy Law. We may pray, "Lord, I desire to be one with You. I want nothing more than to please You and be according to Your heart's desire." When our mind is in fellowship with our conscience, we will find that our natural being is readily willing to answer the request of the Law, to please God, and to live out His Law.

Finally, Paul talks about the law of sin, which is in our members (v. 23). This law is according to the fallen life and nature of Satan himself. The law of sin holds the power of the sinful nature, found first in Satan, which now dwells in our flesh. Our natural life may be fully willing to fulfill the request of the Law, but this is ultimately only wishful thinking. The law of sin dwells in our flesh, in our members, and wars against the law of our mind, which desires to do good. The law of sin always overcomes the law of our mind and thus brings us into captivity.

Captured by the Law of Sin

Nothing good is in our flesh; in fact, it is sin that dwells there (Rom. 7:17–18). Sin actively lives in our flesh and powerfully operates from there. For this reason, Paul called it the "law of sin" in our members. A law, according to life, is a principle that cannot be overcome. For example, we must eat to live. This is a law people cannot overcome. Similarly, when sin operates in our members, we cannot conquer it. The law of sin is so powerful that it will bring us again and again into captivity.

There is a song with a good description of the power of sin:

Can blood so precious, so strong sustain
This foremost sinner of all?
While Satan blames and accuses oft
My impotence and fall.
I tremble, fearing the pow'r of sin,
Besieged by fear I am lost,
Though sense of sin often swallows me,
Redemption paid the cost. (Martin, #143)

This song talks about the power of sin overwhelming us, causing us to fear and tremble. Sin is very powerful in us, and its overwhelming force is an experience every Christian faces. Sometimes we feel victorious and heavenly, but other times we feel the power of sin as it operates in our flesh, even to the point that we would cry out, "Lord, save me!" When sin operates, it produces an unspeakable fear in us as we find that we can do nothing in ourselves to deal with it.

The Battlefield within Us

Why is the power of the law of sin able to bring us into captivity so easily? It is because we always feel that we can do good on our own, so we try to satisfy the demands of the Law by our own effort. If we insist on trying to do good by ourselves and do not know how to be the proper wife of Christ, yielding to Him the first place in our beings and lives, we will never overcome the law of sin, and we will surely be captured by it. This is the result of the law of our mind desiring to do good by overcoming the law of sin but being completely unable to do so.

In fact, within us is a battlefield. The law of sin is always present with us and is always warring against the law of our mind to bring us into captivity. The most intense and tiring battlefield is not around us but in us. This war is waged from morning to evening, to the point we would exclaim like Paul, "Wretched man that I am!" (Rom. 7:24).

Defeated While Trying to Do Good

Nothing in the human life is more fierce than this inward battle. The law of our mind always hopes to fulfill the Law of God, yet the evil in our flesh is always present with us, controlling us, and bringing us into captivity. We have never won on this battlefield, nor will we ever win. No matter how much hope we have and how great an effort we make, we always fail. Even if we overcome sin on one occasion, we will surely fail another time. We may experience temporary minor victories, but whenever the law of sin wages war against the law of our mind, we end up defeated.

For example, there was a brother who had a bad temper. After enduring in much prayer, the Lord empowered him for a period of time during which he overcame his temper. He became happy and satisfied, yet this victory also caused him to become unconsciously proud. This pride became an even bigger problem. It caused him to rely on himself more and more. He no longer relied on God but sinned in acting independent of God. On one hand, this brother overcame his temper for a short time; on the other hand, this experience only led him to another failure. The law of our mind never overcomes the law of sin, and we are always captured by the law of sin in our members.

Our experiences tell us that when we focus on being victorious and doing good, all we get is failure, failure, and more failure. Whenever people want to do good, there is a power in their members that captures them and causes them to do what they are not willing to do. They clearly know something is not right and that it offends God, the church, and the saints, but they can do nothing to resist the power of sin. This is our experience. The more we want to do good, the more we cannot. The more we want to overcome, the more we cannot. Paul said, "Wretched man that I am! Who will set me free from the body of this death?" (Rom. 7:24). However, he also said, "Thanks be to God through Jesus Christ our Lord!" (v. 25).

99

Sold into Bondage to Sin

For we know that the Law is spiritual, but I am of flesh, sold into bondage to sin.
—Romans 7:14

Wretched man that I am! Who will set me free from the body of this death? ²⁵Thanks be to God through Jesus Christ our Lord! So then, on the one hand I myself with my mind am serving the law of God, but on the other, with my flesh the law of sin.
—Romans 7:24-25

WORD STUDY

In Romans 7:14, Paul says that he is two things:

1. Of flesh
2. Sold into bondage to sin

The Greek word used here for "sold," *peraō*, means "to traffic, i.e. dispose of as merchandise or into slavery" (Strong, #4097). According to W. E. Vine, Paul uses it in verse 14 to metaphorically express being fully under the dominion of sin, as slaves are under their masters (Vine, 559).

The desperate cry of Paul in verse 24, "Wretched man that I am!" is the result of the terrible condition experienced as a slave of sin (Morgan, 105). The Greek word for "wretched," *talaipōros*, can also mean "miserable, distressed, unhappy" and is an expression of despair or condemnation of man that can also be used to describe the state of being pulled in two directions (Rogers, 329).

REVELATION AND APPLICATION

Sold to Sin

We know the Law is spiritual, yet we are fleshly and sold to sin (Rom. 7:14). To be sold to sin is to be under the power and authority of sin. This is our experience today if we are not in the reality of being in Christ.

What does it mean to be sold? First, it means that we are disposed of as merchandise. We were originally meant to be the property of God; however, we can sell ourselves into bondage to sin, becoming merchandise under sin's control. When brothers resolve to go to the casino to gamble, even saying "We would choose to die in the casino," we can be sure that they are far from God and sold into bondage under sin.

The second thing selling denotes is the exchange of value for a product or service. Sin provides many things and services in the world that people can obtain only by exchanging their own value for what sin provides. People unconsciously make this transaction without realizing that they are exchanging their godly value for what sin offers.

Mankind was created to belong to God, to live for God, to manifest God, and to accomplish the will of God. What value a person has in God's eyes! However, Satan schemes and provides many sinful goods and services that cause people to unconsciously exchange and lose their value. What makes these things even more horrible is that in many cases people find them enjoyable, reasonable, and even honorable in the sight of others. Yet no matter how happy or satisfied these things seem to make us, our value before God is lost when we are sold into bondage under sin.

For example, suppose there is a man who loves to travel. This week he will go to New York, next week to Beijing, and to London the following week. All he wants to do in his life is travel! Is this a sin? Honestly speaking, it is not; it is only his hobby of traveling. However, in his hobby is "the lust of the flesh and the lust of the eyes and the boastful pride of life" (1 John 2:16). This hobby does not come out of sin, but out of his love for the world. By his immense love of traveling, this man loses his value before God. His life should be extremely valuable, with an existence for God and a life lived in the will of God. Through the "service" of traveling, however, he exchanges his value and is purchased by sin.

Be watchful! We can unconsciously be sold to sin. When we face the many things of the world, we should not be overly concerned with whether they are good or bad. Rather, we should ask, "Am I maintaining my value before God?" If we really understand what it means to be sold into bondage under sin, we will realize how high a value we have before God. If we did not have such value, Satan would not put so much effort into developing things that cause us to lose our value. When we understand what it means to be sold into bondage under sin, we will recognize that many things can cause us to turn from what is on God's heart, rendering us incapable of accomplishing His will. These things are traps that lead us into slavery.

A Cry of Hopelessness

Paul admitted that he was fleshly and sold under sin (Rom. 7:14). He felt the warring between the law of sin in his members and the law of his mind, a war that brought him into captivity and forced him to obey the law of sin (v. 23). In such a state of failure, helplessness, and despair, he could only cry out, "Wretched man that I am!"

What does it mean to be wretched? The Greek word for "wretched" is composed of two words—*piera*, meaning "a test" (Strong, #3984), and *talanton*, indicating a balance or weight of measurement (Strong, #5007). To be wretched is the state brought by being tested and found unable to balance the weights on the scale. In this case, to be wretched was the state of hopelessness brought by being utterly unable to measure up to the standard of the Law.

Paul was a wretched man. He was like a man standing on a balance, measuring himself against the standard of the Law, and finding himself lacking. He desired to meet this standard before God by improving himself, but the weight of sin always prevented him. This caused him to become a wretched man.

We are very complicated people, and rarely are we balanced. On one hand, our nature desires to do good. We honor the Lord in our spirit, and we know how sweet and glorious it is to live a holy, heavenly, righteous, and spiritual life. On the other hand, the power of sin is continually stirred up in us by the people and things around us, causing us to become unbalanced, unable to measure up to the standard of the Law. Even if we restrain and suppress ourselves in the hope of diminishing the power of sin even a little, we still cannot measure up. The more we try to deal with the power of sin and the law of sin, the stronger it becomes. Eventually, we cannot help but cry out, "Wretched man that I am!"

Deliverance

Part of Paul's wretchedness was related to his body. The law of sin occupies the body of fleshly people and forces them to serve this law with their flesh. Their body becomes a "body of death" (Rom. 7:24). According to verse 25, we want to serve the Law of God with our mind, but eventually we serve the law of sin with our flesh. It does not matter what we want. The law of sin becomes our master, taking us prisoner and making us wretched people.

Therefore, Paul's cry was not only for deliverance from the power of sin but also for deliverance from the body of death. It is called the "body of death" because death operates in us by sin, which causes us to be weak, paralyzed, and dead. Whenever sin operates in our members, it brings the element of death into our body. In this state, we are unable to please God, and we find ourselves becoming weaker and weaker. Our body is not only of sin (6:6) but also of death. In this body of death, which is part of the old man, sin is able to dwell in us, occupy us, and take us over. What a pitiful situation we are in.

But we should thank and praise the Lord! Our old man has been crucified with Christ, so that this body of sin and death has been made ineffective and unemployed. If we liken the old man to an employer, the body is like an employee. Now that the old man has died, the body of sin has become unemployed. Since our old man has been crucified with Christ and the body of sin has been nullified and made ineffective, we should no longer live to serve the law of sin in this body of death. Instead, we should live in newness of the Spirit with our new husband, Christ, who was raised from the dead. What a deliverance this is!

100

The Law of the Spirit of Life

Therefore there is now no condemnation for those who are in Christ Jesus. ²For the law of the Spirit of life in Christ Jesus has set you free from the law of sin and of death.
—*Romans 8:1-2*

WORD STUDY

Romans 7 ended with Paul's cry, "Wretched man that I am! Who will set me free from the body of this death?" (v. 24). The Greek word translated "set me free," *rhyomai*, implies a rushing to aid or rescue (Strong, #4506). It was used to denote the act of a soldier who runs at his comrade's cry to rescue him from the hands of the enemy (Rogers, 329). In other words, Paul ceased looking within himself and turned his eyes outward for a savior to free him.

Romans 8:2 clearly states the agent that frees from the law of sin and of death: the law of the Spirit of life in Christ Jesus. The Greek word translated here as "set you free" is *eleutheroō*, meaning "to liberate, i.e. to exempt" (Strong, #1659), or "freedom to go wherever one likes (Vine, 255). This word was used in chapter 6 for our freedom from sin (vv. 18, 22) and in chapter 7 for the freedom of a woman from the law concerning her husband (v. 3). It indicates a triumphant solution to the condition described by Paul in chapter 7. H. Alford writes, "This 'law of the Spirit of life' having freed him from the law of sin and death, so that he serves another master, all claim of sin on him is at an end—he is acquitted, and there is no condemnation for him" (Alford, 2:386).

REVELATION AND APPLICATION

Romans 8 is the final chapter covering the topic of sanctification and is one of the finest sections in the Bible. This chapter can be divided into two sections. The first section, verses 1–13, covers sanctification. The second section, verses 14–39, covers glorification. The first section, regarding sanctification, explains our relationship with the Spirit in the sanctifying process and can be broken further into three main points: our recognition (vv. 1–4), our experience (vv. 5–6), and our living (vv. 7–13).

Freed in Christ Jesus

The end of Romans 7 flows directly into the beginning of chapter 8. Paul was a wretched man, having realized that his body was a body of death. Yet he hoped to be set free from this body. In fact, there is only one way to be set free—through death. However, our liberation from the law of sin is not through our own physical death but through the death of Christ Jesus on the cross. Therefore, Paul said, "Thanks be to God through Jesus Christ our Lord!" (7:25).

Paul's expression of gratitude was through Jesus Christ our Lord. Now, at the beginning of chapter 8, it is in Christ Jesus that there is no condemnation. Jesus Christ our Lord saved us, freed us from slavery to the body of death, and in resurrection has become united with us in life. Christ is a living person in whom we can experience organic salvation according to the law of the Spirit of life. If we desire to know this freedom subjectively, we must first see that there is a living person, Christ Jesus, who is our Lord. He is with us, saves us, and liberates us so that in Him we might have freedom from the law of sin and of death.

Fulfilling the Law by God Himself

Romans 8 begins with a person—Christ Jesus—but also talks about a law—the law of the Spirit of life. This is important when considering Paul's conclusion in chapter 7. By the end of chapter 7, a wretched Paul concluded that he could never satisfy the demands of the Law of God. Paul would say to us, "No matter how determined we are and no matter how much we want to do good, we are fleshly and can never fulfill God's Law."

The law of the mind can never fulfill the Law of God. No matter how strongly our mind echoes the Law of God, we cannot keep it. Even if we hate all the things that oppose the Law of God, these are the things we find ourselves doing. Even if we are willing to serve the Law of God with our mind, its realization is always beyond us. This is because we are of flesh, while the Law of God is spiritual in essence, nature, and substance, and is completely in one accord with the Spirit of God.

The Law reveals God, but the Law itself does not produce God's operation in us. For that, we need the Spirit of God Himself. Thank the Lord that His divine and eternal life is within all believers today. When we were regenerated, God's divine life entered into us. This life operates in us, and by this operating life, the law of the Spirit of life is produced in us. This inner law of the Spirit of life is echoed in the outward Law of God, and it is only through God's life that the Law of God can be realized in us.

The Law of God is an echo of the law of the Spirit of life, and only the law of the Spirit of life can fully match the Law of God. We have said before that every law is according to a certain life. Hunger is a result of the law of natural human life. The matching of the divine law to the divine life is very normal. Only when God Himself enters into us and by His life in our spirit produces the law of the Spirit of life can He satisfy in us the demands of the law.

The Demands of Different Laws

The end of chapter 7 presented us with three different laws: the Law of God is outside of us, the law of our mind is in our soul, and the law of sin is in our body. Now, a fourth law is introduced: the law of the Spirit of life, which is in our regenerated spirit. The law of sin in our members makes our body the body of sin and of death. The law of our mind desires to do good and is inclined to keep the Law of God. However, we are weak and the result is always captivity to the law of sin, which allows sin to reign in our mortal bodies. When the law of the Spirit of life operates in us, however, Christ, the real Lord, reigns in us. As our true husband, He is responsible for us and supplies us with His divine and heavenly riches.

All three laws within us—the law of sin, the law of our mind, and the law of the Spirit of life—have a different operation and work associated with them. The law of the Spirit of life in our spirit is a spiritual, heavenly, and divine law with the divine characteristics and the power of resurrection. In this resurrection life, the Spirit of life operates and works according to His law.

A helpful analogy is the law of natural human life. According to this law, people need to eat when they grow hungry. This is the operation of the law of natural life. According to the law of the Spirit of life, Christians meet together, read the Bible, and pray. If a man does not eat food, he grows weak according to the law of natural life. Likewise, if Christians do not go to church meetings, read the Bible, or pray, they will not grow closer to God, and they will surely become inwardly withered and discouraged. The law of the Spirit of life operates according to the inner demand of God's life. All of God's operation and work is wrapped up in this law of the Spirit of life. The Law of God perfectly echoes the law of the Spirit of life, and the demands of the Law of God are the same demands found in the law of the Spirit of life.

When we disobey a demand of the law of the Spirit of life, the sense of this law will gradually grow dim in us. For example, if we do not go to a church meeting once, the life within us may generate a strong feeling. If we do not go to a church meeting twice, the feeling of life will grow dimmer. If we do not go to a church meeting three or four times, the effectiveness of the operation of the law of the Spirit of life will seem non-existent. If this situation continues, we will gradually lose the sense of life and will fall away from the reality of sanctification.

We must understand that the law of the Spirit of life has demands. The healthier a Christian's spiritual life is, the more this life will operate and work, and the greater the demands of its law will be. Medical doctors often ask patients about their appetites. If the patient's appetite is good, the doctor will feel reassured that the law of the human body is operating adequately. It is possible to judge the health of the law of the human body by analyzing the appetite. The law of the Spirit of life can manifest itself in certain ways, such as through sorrow, joy, strength, and power. A healthier spiritual life is reflected in more strength, more joy, and more power, which are all indicators of a greater oneness with God. The more we live according to the law of the Spirit of life, the stronger it operates and the healthier our spiritual life will be.

The Highest Life and the Highest Law

The divine life is the highest life; thus, the law of the Spirit of life is the highest law. The divine life is eternal; thus, this law is characterized by eternity. The divine life is powerful; thus, this law is powerful. The divine life is in resurrection; thus, the operation of this law can overcome all death and limitation.

It is marvelous that on the day we believed into the Lord, His divine life was mingled with us. At that moment, God's eternality, power, and resurrection were all mingled within us. These characteristics of the divine life also became a law operating in us. This is truly a wonderful thing!

A believer may ignore or despise this law, and may even discredit and spoil its operation after being saved. However, the salvation a person obtains is once for all. This is because the law of the Spirit of life is within every Christian and is always waiting to operate with its eternal and divine characteristics. Yes, it is possible for a believer to be separated from the operation of this law by sin and the world. But whenever other saints come to spiritually nourish this one, or when outward environments cause a crying out to the Lord, the eternality, power, and resurrection of the law of the Spirit of life will spring into operation. This law is the highest law in the universe, unable to be suppressed by any other law. It easily overpowers the law of sin and of death.

Freed into a New Realm

Paul was a wretched man at the end of Romans 7, but he realized that those who are dead in Christ Jesus have been freed. Romans 7:6 says, "But now we have been released from the Law, having died to that by which we were bound, so that we serve in newness of the Spirit and not in oldness of the letter." Romans 8:2 says, "For the law of the Spirit of life in Christ Jesus has set you free from the law of sin and of death." What an echo these two verses are to each other!

According to the Greek text, *eleutheroō* (to free) indicates freedom of movement. However, the liberation in Romans 8 is not simply a departure from one place and an arrival at another. This liberation is the leaving of a whole realm for another, and indicates a new status, identity, and living.

Praise the Lord for our freedom! We have been released from the realm of the flesh and have entered the realm of the Spirit. We have been released from the realm of weakness and have entered the realm in which we can walk by the Spirit. We have been set free from all the negative, fleshly, deadly, worldly, and satanic things and have entered the divine and mystical realm. We were also set free for freedom (Gal. 5:1). The law of the Spirit of life has freed us, so we no longer have anything to do with the power and results of sin.

Paul's cry for deliverance in Romans 7:24 was a cry for salvation. This cry has been answered! We have been brought out from under the law of sin by the work of the Holy Spirit, the dispensing of the divine life, the effectiveness of Christ's death on the cross, and the power of resurrection. We are like a fish that used to be in a small pond, yet a flood came and washed it into a large river beyond the pond. Just like that fish, we were limited in our previous realm. We were limited by the law of sin, by death, and by our body of death. Yet like that fish, we have been delivered from limitation! We have been delivered by Christ Jesus, by the operation of the law of the Spirit of life, and by our experience of the flood of divine life. We can declare, "Praise God! I have been released from all my limitations by the Lord Jesus Christ, because the law of the Spirit of life has released me and made me free in Christ Jesus! Hallelujah!"

101

No Condemnation in Christ Jesus

Therefore there is now no condemnation for those who are in Christ Jesus. ²For the law of the Spirit of life in Christ Jesus has set you free from the law of sin and of death.
—Romans 8:1-2

WORD STUDY

The Greek word in Romans 8:1 for "condemnation" is *katakrima*, meaning "an adverse sentence" (Strong, #2631). The root word, *krinō*, means "judgment, i.e. condemnation of wrong"; it is the decision one passes on the faults of others (Thayer, 360). *Katakrima* is the sentence pronounced, with a suggestion of the punishment following (Vine, 119).

Katakrima is the same word found in Romans 5:16 and 18. Verse 16 says, "For the judgment which came from one offense resulted in condemnation" (NKJV®), and verse 18 says, "Through one man's offense, judgment came to all men, resulting in condemnation" (NKJV®). The end of chapter 7 is filled with the expressions of a man suffering from the feeling of condemnation, or the depression and agony caused by the sense of sin through the Law (Morgan, 113). Chapter 8 offers a marvelous release—"Therefore there is now no condemnation for those who are in Christ Jesus."

REVELATION AND APPLICATION

Objective and Subjective Condemnation

Paul told us in Romans 7 that there is a law of our mind; it desires to do good and wishfully wants to satisfy the Law of God. Our minds hope to live good, holy, and righteous lives according to God's desire. However, we can never succeed. Under our own power, we always fail, stumble, offend the Lord, and do what does not please God. From such a pattern of failure, a hopeless feeling is produced, and we fall into the feeling of condemnation.

In Romans 2 and 3, Paul talked about condemnation. This condemnation was objective, before the throne of God, and according to the Law of God. Now Paul talks about condemnation again in chapter 8, but this time it is subjective, within us, and according to our conscience.

Chapter 8 does not begin with "overcoming" or "victory" but with "no condemnation." How can we escape condemnation? It is by the law of the Spirit of life which, in Christ Jesus, has released us from the law of sin and of death (v. 2). According to God's objective condemnation of mankind, we are justified freely only by the redemption accomplished by the Lord Jesus. When dealing with the subjective condemnation, we are freed by the law of the Spirit of life. This law causes us to realize God's response to our failures based on Christ's redemption, and this realization releases us from subjective condemnation.

God's Response to Our Failures

We condemn ourselves whenever we fail. However, if we do not live in the realm of victory or defeat, success or failure, we will not experience this kind of condemnation. We tend to emphasize doing good and overcoming, just as Romans 7:18

says, "the willing [to do good] is present in me." However, the verse goes on to say, "but the doing of the good is not." The fact is, the more we try to overcome sin and the more we try to live an overcoming life by our natural strength, the stronger the feeling of condemnation will be within us as we fail again and again.

We want to overcome sin and failure, but the result is always failure. However, God would tell us, "I do not condemn you! Why are you condemning yourself?" We want to walk with God in holiness, but we often walk our own way in impurity. Still, God would tell us, "I do not condemn you!" It is marvelous that we who were once condemned by God can now be without condemnation. This is more profound than we can ever comprehend.

God does not pay attention to what we focus on. We think that we can pray more if we do good things today, and that we should pray less if we do something bad. However, God never changes. If we do well, He honors the redemption He has accomplished. If we do not do well, He still honors His redemption. His desire is that we would abide in such a heavenly and divine fact, and that we would simply live Him out. Neither our momentary overcoming nor our failure is important; God does not notice either. He only honors what He has accomplished.

The experiences of many people indicate they are hoping and striving to overcome, yet there is always a power that cannot be overcome—the law of sin (7:23). Oh, how wretched man is! How terrible our situation is! Yet God would calmly tell us, "Therefore there is now no condemnation for those who are in Christ Jesus." In other words, neither overcoming nor failing is the issue, for both are negative when they come out of ourselves. It is in Christ Jesus that God does not condemn us at all, for in Christ, all the negative things have been dealt with.

"No condemnation" is the only answer God would give to those who are struggling to overcome. We might say, "Lord, I am very bad. I have utterly failed. Lord, I cannot believe that I am like this, and confess to You that I have fallen to the uttermost. I am pitiful to the uttermost. You must save me!" To such a "confession" the Lord will always say, "I do not even understand what you said. Don't you know that whenever I see you I have unspeakable joy and satisfaction?"

The Lord likes when we come to Him; He likes to see us. He loves us so much that He died for us and lives for us today. We often do not understand that He never expected us to do well. Such expectation comes from us, not from Him. His expectation is different. We want to do well, but He wants us to abide in His accomplished fact of redemption. There is surely "no condemnation" at all to those who are in Christ Jesus.

No Condemnation Organically

We have not only been freed from the body of death by the Lord Jesus Christ, but in Him, we are also freed from condemnation. Our status is "not condemned," yet this has nothing to do with our being good or bad, or our overcoming or failing. As soon as we are in Christ Jesus, we are not condemned. Only when we realize this can we subjectively and organically experience what Romans 8:2 says: "For the law of the Spirit of life in Christ Jesus has set you free from the law of sin and of death."

Oh, how rich the Bible is! Condemnation was taken away through the redemption of the Lord Jesus. Though we may think this is only a judicial matter, in our experience it is also an organic matter. Paul not only talked about the Spirit of life but also the law of the Spirit of life. The Spirit of life is a person, and His law is operating and working in us organically to free us from the law of sin and of death. By His law, we can subjectively and organically experience "no condemnation."

102 | Condemning Sin in the Flesh

For what the Law could not do, weak as it was through the flesh, God did: sending His own Son in the likeness of sinful flesh and as an offering for sin, He condemned sin in the flesh.
—*Romans 8:3*

WORD STUDY

The Greek word used here for "likeness," *homoiōma*, can also mean a form or abstract resemblance (Strong, #3667). It is important that Paul used the term "likeness of sinful flesh." It means that the Son of God, Jesus Christ, had a nature like sinful human nature, but did not Himself possess such a sinful nature (Alford, 2:387). M. R. Vincent explains the many phrases Paul could have used, but did not, in this passage. To say "He came in flesh" would not have expressed the bond between Christ's humanity and sin. "In the flesh of sin" would have represented Him as partaking of sin. "In the likeness of flesh" would have implied He was not really and entirely human. The full phrase, "in the likeness of sinful flesh," perfectly illustrates that Christ was genuinely human, conformed in appearance to the flesh, yet He was sinless (Vincent, 3:85).

REVELATION AND APPLICATION

The Likeness of Sinful Flesh

The chief characteristic of flesh is weakness. We like to stress our victories, but what we usually experience is failure. We desire to do good, yet we do the evil that we do not will to do. However, God's focus today is not on our victories or failures but rather on the salvation He has accomplished in Christ Jesus. Because the law of sin is in our flesh (Rom. 7:17-18), the Law of God is weak through the flesh. But what the Law could not do, God did by sending His own Son in the likeness of sinful flesh.

We must be clear that the Lord Jesus came in the likeness of sinful flesh; there was no sin within Him. Jesus compared Himself to the bronze serpent raised up by Moses in the wilderness, which had the likeness of a serpent but not its poison (John 3:14). Similarly, the Lord Jesus only had the likeness of sinful flesh and did not have its nature. Sin was always following the Lord Jesus, yet it could not enter Him (Heb. 4:15). This does not mean that sin never tried. The temptation to sin was always near the Lord Jesus, and sin greatly desired to enter Him, but it could not find a way. The ruler of the world had no place in Jesus (John 14:30). When the Lord Jesus died on the cross, He was crucified together with sin and all that is related to it, and thus the problem of sin was solved. We used to be the condemned ones, but now sin is the one that has become condemned!

The Condemnation of Sin

Though the same Greek word is used, the condemnation in Romans 8:3 is not the same condemnation that was mentioned in chapter 5, which had come to all men (5:18). Romans 8:3 does not speak of the condemnation of people, but of sin. "Sin" here is singular, indicating the sinful nature. When Adam fell, his body became flesh, the dwelling place of sin, and its members began living out this nature in many sins. There is ultimately only one source of this sinful nature—Satan, who is the ruler of this world (Matt. 4:8-9, John 14:30).

Today, the world's system is a workshop for sin. This system echoes people's sinful nature and nurtures any sinful desire within them. The world is the realm in which our flesh exists, and our flesh is weak in resisting the world. God's solution is both outward and inward. Outwardly, God has condemned sin in the flesh so that we who are in Christ Jesus might not be condemned. Inwardly, the Spirit of life dwells in us, and His law operates to cause us to live Him out.

The Greek word for "to condemn," *katakrinō*, comes from the words *kata* and *krinō* (to judge). In compound words, the preposition *kata* frequently denotes intensity (Strong, #2596). The two words together could indicate an enhanced or intensified judgment. *Katakrinō* not only implies the judgment but also the sentence given (Vine, 119). Sin has been both judged and sentenced! God has given the sinful nature in us a sentence of death, yet it is sin He has condemned, not those in Christ Jesus. He judged and sentenced sin "so that the requirement of the Law might be fulfilled in us, who do not walk according to the flesh but according to the Spirit" (Rom. 8:4).

103 | Fulfilling the Requirement of the Law (1)

So that the requirement of the Law might be fulfilled in us, who do not walk according to the flesh but according to the Spirit.
—Romans 8:4

WORD STUDY

The Greek word translated "requirement" is *dikaiōma*. Although it can be simply translated "righteousness" (Strong, #1345), *dikaiōma* is better thought of as a legal claim or judicial sentence. The Greek suffix *ma* is often used to denote the result of an action (Robinson, 139). Thus, *dikaiōma* is the consequence of God's action of establishing righteousness. One way to think of this phrase is, "the righteous requirement of the whole Law."

The Greek word Paul uses here for "walk," *peripateō*, means "to walk about, to conduct one's life" (Rogers, 330). It is used to indicate a person's daily walk in the habits of life.

REVELATION AND APPLICATION

The Fulfillment of the Righteousness of the Law

Why does Paul mention the fulfillment of the righteousness

of the Law? He does this because the Law cannot just be set aside. God did not forsake the Law (Matt. 5:18), and the Lord Jesus came to the world to fulfill it (v. 17). The nature, manifestation, and operation of the Law are good, holy, and righteous. The Law is not an insignificant thing!

The fulfillment of the righteousness of the Law was accomplished judicially by the redemptive work of the Lord Jesus on the cross. But we experience this fulfillment organically as we walk according to the Spirit and as the law of the Spirit of life operates and works in us.

Our Mingled Spirit

It is often hard to tell in Greek whether the word "spirit" is referring to God's Spirit or our human spirit. It is possible that in Romans 8:4, "Spirit" does not refer exclusively to either but rather to our mingled spirit—the union of the Holy Spirit with our regenerated spirit (1 Cor. 6:17). The fulfillment of the righteousness of the Law is not only related to the judicial fulfillment of the Law's requirements by Christ; it also indicates that we can live out the reality of the Law through the organic operation of the law of the Spirit of life in us!

The righteousness of the Law is realized in the Spirit of life. We should be less concerned with trying to overcome sin and instead allow the righteousness of the Law to be realized through the Spirit in our spirit. In this way, our life and walk according to our mingled spirit will actually fulfill the righteousness of the Law.

Walking according to the Indwelling Spirit

The fulfillment of the righteousness of the Law has an outward, judicial aspect related to the death of Jesus and an inward, organic aspect related to the indwelling of the divine life. The righteousness of the Law is a requirement. This requirement has been satisfied judicially by the death of Jesus and can now be fulfilled in us organically through the Spirit of life dwelling in us.

In the Old Testament, the Law of God was given as an outward declaration and testimony of who God is. All of the commandments reflect who God is, from "You shall have no other gods before Me" (Exo. 20:3) to "You shall not covet... anything that belongs to your neighbor" (v. 17). Today, God is not revealed only in an outward way, but He is also dwelling in our spirit as the Spirit of life. When we live and walk according to His Spirit in our spirit, we automatically live out the righteousness of God and fulfill the requirements of the Law.

Since the righteousness of the Law is fulfilled in those who do not walk according to the flesh but according to the Spirit, there is no condemnation from God. Even more, as we walk according to the Spirit, our conscience has no reason to condemn us. Our conscience is a function of our spirit. When we live according to our mingled spirit and thus fulfill the righteousness of the Law, there is no condemnation by our spirit.

The Shining and Leading of the Spirit

What does it mean to live according to the Spirit? It means to follow the Spirit of God by means of the mingled spirit within us. This following of the Spirit of God has two aspects: shining and leading. The Spirit shines on us so we would see our true condition, and He leads us to meet God in our present situation. Yet whether He is shining or leading, He never brings us into condemnation.

In our experiences, we often feel a lack of the Spirit's shining and leading, and our consciences are full of condemnation. Real shining and leading from the Spirit never involves condemnation. Rather, these two aspects only involve termination. For example, when the Spirit shines on us regarding a certain matter, we see our natural being and this seeing brings in the killing element of the cross. When the Spirit leads us out of an issue that enslaved us, we meet God, and this issue loses its power in us.

For example, one brother overly indulged in movies. He knew he watched movies too much, and even other saints told him it was wrong. However, he still had a strong attraction to movies. He struggled to overcome his bondage to them, yet the more he struggled, the harder it was for him to overcome. It was not until the day the Spirit shined on him and led him to meet God in this matter that movies lost their effective hold on him. When that light came, what he once indulged in, he now loathed and lost all interest in. At that moment, he was released from the bondage of movies and obtained freedom.

The reality of "no condemnation" in Romans 8:1 is in our meeting God. Someone may say, "My conscience really bothers me because I know I should not be drunk, but I cannot overcome it." Our answer to them should be, "It is impossible for you to overcome alcohol. It is not a matter of overcoming but of meeting God in this matter. Until you meet God in this matter, it will be impossible for you to stop drinking, and you will never overcome it." If we are caught by our bad temper, we must meet God in that matter. If we are caught by novels, we must meet God in that matter. Anything can bind us, and unless we meet God in these matters, we will never be free and without condemnation from our conscience.

Living in Light

The Christian life is sweet. No matter how many years we have been saved, we should appreciate the sweetness that comes because the Lord never condemns us. This does not mean we are never weak. We can be weak to the uttermost, but the Lord still never condemns us. On one hand, the Lord continually feeds us; on the other hand, He continually shines on us. Whenever His light dawns on us, it produces a release and a freedom for us.

True freedom never involves condemnation, and for there to be no condemnation, there must be redemption. The source of freedom is redemption. Because of the redemption accomplished by Christ, we can never be condemned by God. He can shine and lead us through many issues, yet because of the redemption of Christ, He will never condemn us. We should tell the Lord, "Thank You for not condemning me. I want to meet You in many more situations and in deeper ways so I can experience freedom in all things." The more we meet God in the Spirit, the more we are released. The more His light shines on us, the more freedom we have.

All of the Lord's shining on us happens within the realm of His light. Psalm 36:9 says, "In Your light we see light." In the light of Christ, healthy Christians should continually experience being shone upon. They should see, touch, and enjoy this "light in the light." By this experience, we grow in Christ. Light causes us to properly see both ourselves and the way to follow the Lord. If we learn to abide in the light and be led by the Spirit in the light, we will be brought into ever deeper experiences of meeting God.

How marvelously complete, wonderful, and sweet the salvation of God is in us. Others may condemn us, and we may many times even condemn ourselves, but God does not condemn us. May we be willing to live in the Spirit, live in the light, and meet God in the Spirit. By this we can live before God in a healthy manner, and the righteousness of the Law can be fulfilled in us as we walk according to our mingled spirit.

104 Fulfilling the Requirement of the Law (2)

So that the requirement of the Law might be fulfilled in us, who do not walk according to the flesh but according to the Spirit.
—Romans 8:4

WORD STUDY

The Greek word translated "requirement" is *dikaiōma*. Although it can be simply translated "righteousness" (Strong, #1345), *dikaiōma* is better thought of as a legal claim or judicial sentence. The Greek suffix *ma* is often used to denote the result of an action (Robinson, 139). Thus, *dikaiōma* is the consequence of God's action of establishing righteousness. One way to think of this phrase is, "the righteous requirement of the whole Law."

Paul writes that by walking according to the Spirit, the righteousness "of the Law might be fulfilled in us." This is a much deeper thought than if Paul had written, "might be performed by us." The very aim of God in giving the Law, that is, our sanctification, is fully accomplished in us by our walking according to the Spirit (Alford, 2:388). The Greek word used here for "fulfill," *plēroō*, literally means "to cram a net," or figuratively "to furnish, satisfy, execute." It can also be translated "accomplish...complete...fill (up), fulfill...perfect, supply" (Strong, #4137).

The Greek word Paul uses here for "walk," *peripateō*, means "to walk about, to conduct one's life" (Rogers, 330). It is used to indicate a person's daily walk in the habits of life.

REVELATION AND APPLICATION

Fulfilled in Jesus

Romans 8:4 contains the wonderful phrase, "so that the requirement of the Law might be fulfilled." Paul uses *dikaiosunē* many times in Romans for "righteousness," but here he uses *dikaiōma*. Generally, the Greek suffix *sune* indicates quality, while *ma* indicates the result of a process (Robinson, 139). *Dikaiōma* is an active word that indicates God established righteousness through the Law. This righteousness was fulfilled in the Lord Jesus. He is righteous, His living was righteous, and His accomplishment was righteous. The Lord's very being is the manifestation of righteousness. He is the incarnation of our righteous God. His act of righteousness accomplished the requirement of God's righteous Law (Rom. 5:18).

The Law of God has a requirement. In the Lord Jesus, our righteous God came to satisfy His own requirement of righteousness. Because the Law is a description of God Himself, He is its reality. As the incarnated God, Jesus was righteous. God required in the Law, "You shall have no other gods before Me" (Exo. 20:3). This requirement demands a righteous living according to it. Jesus was the reality of the Law itself, and His living testified of and accomplished all of its requirements.

Fulfilled in Us

Romans 5:18 talks about the righteous act of the Lord and uses the same Greek word found in 8:4—*dikaiōma*. Our

Lord, the manifestation of righteousness, accomplished this righteous act, allowing people today to be justified unto life. Through this act, the reality of righteousness is brought into us. Righteousness is therefore no longer only objective, theoretical, and distant. It is in us as our life, experience, application, and testimony.

The righteous requirement of the Law was fulfilled in the Son of God and is now fulfilled in those who walk according to the Spirit. We would be totally unable to fulfill this righteousness today if it was not fulfilled in the Son of God first. The reason we can fully realize this righteousness is that it has already been fulfilled. The Lord Jesus is a model for us to follow by walking according to the Spirit.

As our model, the Lord Jesus is actually very close to us. He is not outward and distant but is inside of us for our subjective application, enjoyment, and experience. How? The Bible is very clear that the Lord is the Spirit (2 Cor. 3:17). When we allow Christ to have the first place in our hearts and lives, and when we allow Him to lead us, live out of us, and reveal Himself through us, we walk "according to the Spirit" (Rom. 8:4). In this walk, the righteousness of the Law will automatically be fulfilled in us.

Walking by the Indwelling Spirit

We may think that "walking according to the Spirit" involves a special feeling within us. However, this walking is not according to our feelings; it is according to the extent we take Christ as our person, for He is our model. The righteous requirement of the Law has already been fulfilled in Him, and this righteousness will be realized in us too. For this, He not only died on the cross but also became the life-giving Spirit in resurrection. As the Spirit, our Lord is united and mingled with our spirit (1 Cor. 6:17). Whenever we live and walk in this mingled spirit, the righteous requirement of the

Law is fulfilled in us and in our living by the operation and working of the law of the Spirit of life.

We need the revelation that the Lord Jesus has already fulfilled the righteous requirement of the Law. This revelation should change our manner of living to one which radiates Christ and fulfills the righteous requirement of the Law. The apostle Paul was a good example of this. He not only had rich revelations about Christ but also allowed Christ to become his living (Eph. 3:3-4; Phil. 1:21).

The Fulfilling of Righteousness in Us

"To fulfill" (*plēroō*) could be translated "to complete" or "to perfect." The noun form, *plērōma*, "stands for the result of the action expressed in *plēroō*" (Vine, 258). To fulfill something is to bring it unto its fullness or completion. The Lord Jesus did not come to destroy the Law or the Prophets but to fulfill them (Matt. 5:17). In other words, He brought them unto their completion. Here in Romans, we can say that fulfilling the requirement of the Law in our living is to bring this righteousness unto its fullness in us.

The Lord Jesus was righteous and lived righteously. However, this living was confined to Him alone. It was not until He became the life-giving Spirit in resurrection and entered into us that the righteous requirement of the Law could be completed in us unto its fullness. This is a process. The righteous requirement of the Law has been fulfilled in the Lord Jesus, and now this righteousness will be perfected and will grow unto its fullness in those who walk according to the Spirit.

Plēroō implies the organic process of growth. Righteousness is fulfilled in us by growing in us until it is expressed through us, and it will continue to grow until it reaches its fullness. What is emphasized here is not our victory but the manifestation of the fullness of righteousness. This does not mean that we can complete the righteousness of the Law by our own strength. The righteousness of the Law was already fulfilled in the Lord Jesus; now in us it will grow unto its fullness. The process began by the fulfillment of the Law by Jesus, and this righteousness is growing in us today until it reaches its fullness.

An Illustration of Fullness

The noun *plērōma*, "fullness," can be thought of as a cargo ship fully loaded with cargo. Such a ship can be said to have reached its fullness. This fullness is not the cargo itself, nor is it the cargo ship alone. Both the cargo ship and the cargo are needed for this fullness. If the cargo ship does not have cargo, it is empty. No matter how large a cargo ship is—forty thousand, fifty thousand, or even a hundred thousand tons—it is empty without cargo. Without some heavy objects placed in its hold, it will not even be able to go out to sea. At the same time, if the cargo sits on the dock with no cargo ship to be loaded into, it will never arrive at the place it is supposed to go. The purpose for the cargo will not be carried out.

In this way, we are like the cargo ship and Christ is like the cargo. Our fullness is only reached when we are filled with Christ. As we are filled with Him, the righteous fact accomplished by Christ will become applicable and experiential for us. This is the process by which the righteous requirement of the Law becomes fulfilled in us.

The Ultimate Fullness

Every aspect of our daily life is part of this process which will result in a fullness. Each time we walk according to the Spirit, it is a one-time realization of the righteousness of the Law within us. When we live in the Spirit today, we live in the reality of the righteousness of the Law and become more constituted with this righteousness. This is an initial fullness in us, which is precious and honorable. However, the ultimate fullness of the righteousness of the Law will only be realized in the New Jerusalem, when God and man are fully united and mingled together.

There are twelve gates in the New Jerusalem, upon which are the names of twelve tribes of Israel (Rev. 21:12). Israel relates to the Law, showing that these twelve gates are the guarantee that all the fellowship, living, and walking in the holy city are according to the righteous requirement of the Law. The fact that there are twelve means that the righteousness of the Law has obtained its ultimate fullness. Praise God! What a fullness! This fullness can be experienced in our living today and will be the testimony of God in eternity.

105

Walking according to the Spirit

So that the requirement of the Law might be fulfilled in us, who do not walk according to the flesh but according to the Spirit.
—*Romans 8:4*

WORD STUDY

The Greek word Paul uses here for "walk," *peripateō*, means "to walk about, to conduct one's life" (Rogers, 330). It is used to indicate a person's daily walk in the habits of life.

REVELATION AND APPLICATION

The process by which the righteousness of the Law is fulfilled in us has both judicial and organic aspects. The judicial aspect has been fulfilled by Christ's condemnation of sin in His flesh (Rom. 8:3). The organic aspect is part of the sanctification process and is fulfilled as we walk according to our mingled spirit (1 Cor. 6:17).

Challenges in Walking according to the Spirit

What does it look like to walk according to the Spirit?

This walk involves attention to the inner leading of the Spirit. For example, a brother may have a feeling to visit a certain brother. When he obeys this feeling, he is walking according to the Spirit. However, this is only the first step; walking according to the Spirit does not end after traveling to see that brother. He must still follow the Spirit to know what to say to that brother and how to get along with him. Even to make the decision to read the Bible or pray with this brother requires careful walking according to the Spirit.

Recall the example of a brother who was held in bondage by movies until he met God in that matter. By walking according to the Spirit, he lost all desire to watch movies. The Spirit of God freed him from wasting so much time, and now this brother could follow the Lord in a more devoted way. However, he could have discounted the leading of the Spirit and reasoned in his heart, "Now that I do not watch movies anymore, it will be okay for me to watch television." Such discounting of the leading and feeling within us from the Spirit is our common problem.

Additionally, when we walk according to the Spirit, we will always face the problem of self-exaltation. Consider the previous example of the brother who overcame movies. After his overcoming, it was possible for him to testify to the saints that by walking according to the Spirit he had overcome his problem. However, it was also possible that even while giving such a good testimony, he could admire himself in his heart, saying, "I cannot believe how good, victorious, and spiritual I am!" He could have even rebuked other saints, saying, "I do not watch movies anymore; why are you still watching them?" If this had happened, we would have to say that he had truly walked according to the Spirit in the matter of movies, yet later, he exalted himself and his flesh began to operate. Though he overcame in one aspect of his life, he still experienced failure.

Walking according to the Spirit means to walk in one accord with the Spirit of God. It means God's Spirit is the standard, principle, and model for our daily walk. This relationship requires a close union in life. When we walk according to the Spirit, we walk according to how the Spirit works in us. There is no outward form to fit ourselves into; rather, there is the living Spirit of God actively dwelling in us so that we can walk according to Him all our lives. Those who walk in this way learn to not look at themselves, but at the Spirit. They do not consider who they were the previous hour but ask how the Spirit is moving inside of them right now. The Spirit is always their standard, principle, and model at the current moment.

Walking in Oneness with the Spirit of Life

Walking according to the Spirit is simply walking in one accord with the Spirit of life. The operation of the Spirit brings life to us, enabling us to have such a walk. However, even after we have been saved, we still often walk according to our flesh, meaning that we are in one accord with it. However, since we have been born again and the Spirit of life dwells in us, we should walk according to the Spirit and be one with the Spirit.

The apostle John wrote, "We know that no one who is born of God sins" (1 John 5:18). The phrase "born of God" indicates those who have been born again, meaning those who have a regenerated spirit. The regenerated spirit does not sin, so those who walk according to their mingled spirit do not sin. Christians are people who have regenerated spirits indwelt by the Spirit of God and who enjoy the resurrection life. The Spirit of God is a Spirit of supply, power, direction, and support, who enables us to live in newness of life.

To walk according to the Spirit of life is God's desire for us. Such a living is not by a demand or a commandment, but the result of a life and life-supply. This kind of living and walking according to the Spirit should be so normal and common in our lives.

106

The Mind of the Flesh or the Spirit

For those who are according to the flesh set their minds on the things of the flesh, but those who are according to the Spirit, the things of the Spirit. ⁶For the mind set on the flesh is death, but the mind set on the Spirit is life and peace.
—Romans 8:5–6

WORD STUDY

In Romans 8:5–6, Paul turns his focus to the mindset of believers. From the Greek word *phraō*, meaning the mind (Strong, #5424), comes the verb *phroneō* ("set their minds") in verse 5, and the noun *phronēma* ("mind set") in verse 6. "*Phroneō* [means] to think, to set one's mind or heart upon something, to employ one's faculty for thoughtful planning, with the emphasis upon the underlying disposition or attitude. It denotes the whole action of the affections and will as well as of the reason. *Phronēma* is a way of thinking, mindset, aim, aspiration, striving" (Rogers, 330). Thus, the phrase "set their minds on the things of the flesh" could be translated, "to concentrate their attention on the things of the flesh." The same pattern of translation can be applied to the phrase concerning the Spirit.

In verse 6, the phrase "mind set on the flesh" could also be translated "the mind of the flesh." Similarly, the phrase "mind set on the Spirit" could be translated "the mind of the Spirit" (Vincent, 3:90). These verbs in verse 5 and the nouns in verse 6 go together. A mind set on the things of the Spirit is the mind of the Spirit. A mind set on the things of the flesh is the mind of the flesh (Alford, 2:388).

REVELATION AND APPLICATION

A Difficult Phrase to Understand

In this section on sanctification, Romans 8:4–6 may be the hardest passage to understand. A person who experiences sanctification has a mind set on the Spirit (v. 6), fulfills the righteousness of the Law (v. 4), and obtains life and peace (v. 6). These all sound wonderful, but the hardest part to understand in these verses is what it actually means to have a "mind set on the Spirit," or to be "spiritually minded" (KJV).

We can somewhat comprehend many spiritual topics, such as God, the Holy Spirit, the indwelling life of God, and the church. However, when we talk about being spiritually minded (v. 6) and setting our minds on the things of the Spirit (v. 5) for the sake of life and peace, many of us are utterly unable to comprehend this concept.

Experientially, it seems the more we make an effort to set our minds on the things of the Spirit and to be spiritually minded, the less we have life and peace. When we feel like we are the most spiritually minded, we often experience the most powerful operation of our flesh. When we feel the most spiritual, it is very possible that we are actually in our flesh. Quite honestly, we just do not understand what it is to be spiritually minded, nor do we know what it means to set our minds on the things of the Spirit. In our lack of understanding, it seems like such phrases are impossible to experience in our Christian lives, and that they are ideals that we occasionally stumble close to experiencing without knowing how.

Setting the Mind on the Spirit

A brother once testified, "Praise the Lord! I was spiritually minded yesterday!" This was surely very good. However, this good experience from the previous day brought in a bad experience for him the next day. This brother realized that he was spiritually minded yesterday but was fleshly minded today. Why was this? He had thoroughly enjoyed his morning time with the Lord the day before, spending it in the Lord's presence, contacting the Lord with a pure heart, and having sweet fellowship with Him. This whole experience was spiritual—the fruit of his living according to the Spirit. Because of such a good experience, he had repeated the same method the next morning in order to have the same enjoyment. However, simply repeating yesterday's practice is living according to a method, not living according to the Spirit. Living by methods, not by the Spirit, will only lead us to be fleshly minded.

The mind is very important. Actually, Romans 8:5-6 is entirely related to our mind. If we have the mind of the flesh, we set our mind on the things of the flesh and the result is death. If we have the mind of the Spirit, we set our mind on the things of the Spirit and the result is life and peace. Understanding the place of our mind is crucial to understanding this passage. Although our mind is part of our soul, Paul did not mention the soul here, only the mind. This is because our mind truly represents our person. The center of the soul is the mind. What we love, what we think, and what we want are all related to our mind.

For example, when an emotional brother sees another person loving the Lord, a lot of feelings get stirred up within him. When he sees another person who does not love the Lord, there are also a lot of feelings generated. Although this brother may be considered an emotional person, the expression of his emotion is through his mind. When he remembers certain saints in his heart, it is not only his emotions at work but also his mind. Our mind is our person. No matter how rich our emotions are and no matter how strong our will is, the expression and operation of the soul is always through our mind.

We will always follow our mind. We will be where our mind is set, because our mind is what truly represents who we are. Thus, when Paul talked about the relationships among the mind, flesh, Spirit, and divine life, he said, "The mind set on the flesh is death, but the mind set on the Spirit is life and peace" (8:6).

The Lord of Our Mind

In Romans 8:6, the phrase "the mind set on the flesh" could also be translated "the mind of the flesh." Similarly, the phrase "the mind set on the Spirit" could be translated "the mind of the Spirit." What is the difference between these translations, and why does it matter? The phrases "the mind set on the flesh" and "the mind set on the Spirit" imply that we have control over our mind; in other words, we can choose to have our mind set on the flesh or on the Spirit. The phrases "the mind of the flesh" and "the mind of the Spirit" imply that the flesh or the Spirit controls our mind. Although the Bible translation we are using says, "the mind set," the more literal translation of these phrases indicates that our flesh or the Spirit controls our mind. If we have the mind of the flesh, the result is death. If we have the mind of the Spirit, the result is life and peace.

The phrase "the mind of the flesh" indicates that the flesh is the lord of our mind, becoming the constitution, the nature, and the director of our mind. Likewise, "the mind of the Spirit" indicates that the Spirit is the Lord of our mind, becoming the constitution, nature, and director of our mind.

This thought can be related to Romans 7:23: "I see a different law in the members of my body, waging war against the law of my mind and making me a prisoner of the law of sin which is in my members." Since the law of sin in our members has captured us, we have the mind of the flesh. However, the law of the Spirit of life has set us free from the law of sin and of death (8:2). Now we can have the mind of the Spirit, be filled with the Spirit of life, and enjoy Christ as life and peace. Therefore, it is not only a matter of setting our mind but also a matter of who the lord of our mind is. If our flesh is our lord, we have the mind of the flesh. If the Spirit is our Lord, we have the mind of the Spirit.

The Instinct of the Indwelling Divine Life

The divine life within us instinctively turns us to the mind of the Spirit. The test of what mind we are currently under is the sense of life. Whenever the mind of the flesh operates in us, it brings death. This involves the feelings of weakness, darkness, emptiness, oppressiveness, dryness, distress, and dissatisfaction. However, at such times we instinctively turn to the mind of the Spirit to obtain life and peace.

In the flesh there is death. In the Spirit there is life. At times, we may unconsciously say, "Lord Jesus, have mercy on me!" What causes us to have such a marvelous prayer? When we feel dead inside, the divine life instinctively turns us to the mind of the Spirit to obtain life and peace.

The Key to Sanctification

The key to sanctification is the mind of the Spirit. The experience of sanctification is enjoyed through the mind of the Spirit. In order to apply, enjoy, and experience the reality of sanctification, we must have the mind of the Spirit. We do not need to struggle in self-effort, nor do we need to abide in the feeling of failure. We only need to actively abide in the Spirit. By this abiding, the mind of the Spirit firmly and organically operates in us, bringing us into life and peace and the reality of sanctification.

107

The Flesh Being Hostile toward God

Because the mind set on the flesh is hostile toward God; for it does not subject itself to the law of God, for it is not even able to do so, ⁸and those who are in the flesh cannot please God.
—Romans 8:7-8

WORD STUDY

In Romans 8:7, the phrase "the mind set on the flesh" may be more accurately translated, "the mind of the flesh" (Vincent, 3:90). This mind is hostile toward God because it does not subject itself to the Law of God. The Greek word translated here as "hostile," *echthra*, is another form of the word used in Romans 5:10 to call us "enemies" of God. *Echthra* means "hostility" and can be translated "enmity, hatred" (Strong, #2189). The mind of the flesh has this reaction toward God because it cannot "subject itself to" or arrange itself under the Law of God. This statement may have a shade of military meaning behind it, due to the use of the word "hostile." The thought would be that the mind of the flesh is "marshalled under a hostile banner" to God (Vincent, 3:90).

The end of 8:7 then displays the utter hopelessness of the situation—the mind of the flesh is not even able to subject itself to the Law of God. It does not have the power to do so, and thus, such subjection is simply impossible (see Strong, #1410).

REVELATION AND APPLICATION

The Hopelessness of the Flesh

Although chapter 8 is the last chapter Paul uses to cover sanctification in Romans, it contains two disappointing verses—verses 7 and 8. Both deal with the flesh and its relationship with God.

Anyone who experiences sanctification in the divine life will have the experience described by these verses. They will desire to please God but will find out that the mind of the flesh is hostile toward God. In fact, the flesh has no hope before God. Those in the flesh cannot please God, because they are not subject to the Law of God, nor are they even able to be! As we pass through this experience of sanctification, it produces an unexplainable sighing and groaning within us.

Hostility toward God

Romans 8:7 says that "the mind set on the flesh is hostile toward God." In Greek, "hostile" involves the thought of hatred. The mind of the flesh is not only hostile toward God but also hates Him.

According to our nature, we desire to do good, to please God, and to obey His Law (7:21, 25). Additionally, our inner man agrees with and likes the Law of God (v. 22). However, there is nothing good in our flesh (v. 18). There is another law in our members, warring against the law of our mind and bringing us into captivity to the law of sin in our members (v. 23). This causes us to walk according to the flesh, set our mind on the things of the flesh, and have the mind of the flesh (8:5-6).

Once people have the mind of the flesh, they cannot be subject to the Law of God, nor can they possibly be (v. 7). Thus, the demand of the Law cannot be fulfilled in them. In response, the mind of the flesh becomes angry and hostile toward God.

Once we cannot be subject to God, our inward parts will easily become hostile toward Him. Our thoughts and our hearts will quickly turn against Him. The more we try to please God by our own efforts, the easier it is to have the mind of the flesh, and the more easily we become hostile toward God. In these moments, we must learn to compose ourselves and tell the Lord, "I know that the mind of the flesh is not subject to Your Law, nor can it be. You know that I love You, Lord, so I beg You to have mercy on me so that I do not have the mind of the flesh which hates You."

The Relationship between the Flesh and God

Those who are experiencing the process of sanctification must recognize their flesh. The mind of the flesh is not subject to the Law of God. The result is hatred and hostility toward God. People of the flesh and in the flesh will find it impossible to please God (Rom. 8:8). There is no difference between good or bad flesh. Flesh can never match God, and its efforts will never please Him.

Though our flesh is so hostile toward God, we often find ourselves living according to it. Dear brothers and sisters, our last name is "Flesh," our occupation is to live in the flesh, and our relationship with God is one of hostility. We do not match God at all. It is like comparing dogs with humans. Dogs are dogs and people are people—they never match! Similarly, flesh is flesh, God is God, and there is no association between them. They never match each other.

The Only Way Out

After saying so much about sanctification, it seems like Paul is telling us in Romans 8:7-8 to give up on the idea of being sanctified. He lists these discouraging facts: we are fleshly, we are hostile toward God, and there is no possibility that we could be subject to His Law. We cannot please God at all! In this situation, what can we say? There is a hymn by A. B. Simpson that reads,

> *I am crucified with Jesus,*
> *And He lives and dwells with me;*
> *I have ceased from all my struggling,*
> *'Tis no longer I, but He.*
> *All my will is yielding to Him,*
> *And His Spirit reigns within;*
> *And His precious blood each moment*
> *Keeps me cleansed and free from sin.* (Martin, #405)

Actually, we should not hope in ourselves at all! Rather, we should give up all our effort, cease from our struggling, live according to the mingled spirit, and allow the Spirit of life to operate freely. When we give up, God is able to transform and sanctify us.

Another hymn reads,

> *Jesus! I am resting, resting*
> *In the joy of what Thou art;*
> *I am finding out the greatness*
> *Of Thy loving heart.*
> *Thou hast bid me gaze upon Thee,*
> *And Thy beauty fills my soul,*
> *For, by Thy transforming power,*
> *Thou hast made me whole.* (Martin, #402)

And another,

Yes, 'tis sweet to trust in Jesus,
Just from sin and self to cease;
Just from Jesus simply taking
Life and rest, and joy and peace. (Martin, #407)

When we read Romans 5–8, we realize that we have died with Christ and now live with Him. We should give up the efforts of our flesh. We should no longer walk according to the flesh, set our mind on the things of the flesh, or have the mind of the flesh. Rather, we should walk according to the Holy Spirit, set our mind on the things of the Holy Spirit, and allow the mind of the Spirit to lead us. By following the Spirit's leading, we live in the newness of life and experience the reality of sanctification.

The Spirit of God: Union

However, you are not in the flesh but in the Spirit, if indeed the Spirit of God dwells in you. But if anyone does not have the Spirit of Christ, he does not belong to Him.
—*Romans 8:9*

WORD STUDY

In Romans 8:9, the Greek word used for "dwells" is *oikeō*. It means, "to occupy a house, i.e., reside," and figuratively means "to inhabit, remain" (Strong, #3611). This verse tells us that whether we are in the flesh or the Spirit depends on whether the Spirit of God dwells in us or not. Here, *oikeō* is written in the present tense, indicating a continual action (Rogers, 330), and the indicative mood, indicating the strongest level of certainty of the indwelling of the Spirit of God (Wallace, 748). In other words, we could think of the first half of this verse in this way: "If the Spirit of God truly and certainly dwells in you, you are not in the flesh but in the Spirit."

REVELATION AND APPLICATION

Our experience of sanctification is never apart from the

Spirit. Some Bible scholars have said that as Romans progresses, God is gradually revealed more and more. We could say that in chapter 1, He is the God of creation. In chapter 3, He is the God of redemption. In chapter 4, He is the God of justification. In chapter 5, He is the God of reconciliation. In chapter 6, He is the God of union. Now in chapter 8, He is God in our human spirit.

In chapter 5, Paul mentioned the grace of God (v. 21); here in chapter 8, he mentions the Spirit of God (v. 9). Both of these are related to the triune God. Grace is the triune God enjoyed in our spirit, and the Spirit of God is the triune God Himself living and dwelling in us. Paul describes the Spirit of God further, calling Him the Spirit of life (v. 2), the Spirit of Christ (v. 9), the Spirit of Him who raised Jesus from the dead (v. 11), and the Spirit who dwells in us (v. 11). This entire section of verses in chapter 8 testifies that our experience of sanctification is totally related to our experience of the Spirit of God.

The Spirit of Life

The first phrase Paul uses to describe the Spirit of God is the "Spirit of life" (8:2). This is because as we experience the process of sanctification, the goal is life (6:22). Life and the Spirit are inseparable. If we have the Spirit, we have life. If we do not have the Spirit, we do not have life (John 6:63). Through His incarnation, human living, crucifixion, resurrection, and ascension, God has gone through many experiences to become the applicable Spirit of life to us today.

The Spirit of life is the result of everything our triune God has passed through, and He is a living person dispensing the divine life into us today. We are saved in life (Rom. 5:10), will reign in life (v. 17), are unto the justification of life (v. 18), live and walk in newness of life (6:4), bear fruit of sanctification unto eternal life (v. 22), and receive the gift of God which is eternal life (v. 23). All of these experiences are for life, and all are related to the operation of the Spirit of life.

Three Aspects of the Spirit

Again, the reality of sanctification totally lies in the Spirit. In our experience, the Spirit has three aspects:

1. The Spirit of God dwelling in us (Rom. 8:9). This indicates our union with the triune God.
2. The Spirit of Christ possessing us (v. 9). This indicates our mingling with the triune God.
3. The Spirit of Him who raised Jesus from the dead supplying us with life (v. 11). This indicates our incorporation with the triune God.

The first aspect of the Spirit will be covered here, and the last two aspects will be considered in the next two chapters.

A Permanent Dwelling

The key word in Romans 8:9 is "dwells" (*oikeō*). The Greek word for "dwells" means to occupy a house. This indicates the thought of staying permanently. For example, a family renting an apartment can move out at any time, even though we would say that they live in that apartment. If they buy a house, they dwell there without the thought of moving, because the house belongs to them. Since we have been purchased by the precious blood of the Lord Jesus (1 Cor. 6:20; 1 Pet. 1:18-19), the Spirit of God dwells in us and makes His home in us.

At the moment of our regeneration, the Spirit of God entered us and was united with our spirit. Now the Spirit of God dwells in our spirit, the deepest part of our being.

According to Romans 8:9, since the Spirit of God dwells in us, we are not in the flesh.

In our experience, it seems we often live in the flesh and not in the Spirit. However, the Word of God is absolute. As long as the Spirit of God dwells in us, we are not in the flesh but in the Spirit. Since believers all have the Spirit of God dwelling in them, which is a matter of regeneration, they are in the Spirit. Praise the Lord for such an absolute and wonderful fact!

109

The Spirit of Christ: Mingling

However, you are not in the flesh but in the Spirit, if indeed the Spirit of God dwells in you. But if anyone does not have the Spirit of Christ, he does not belong to Him. ¹⁰If Christ is in you, though the body is dead because of sin, yet the spirit is alive because of righteousness.

—Romans 8:9–10

WORD STUDY

In Romans 8:9–10, Paul mentions the Spirit of God, the Spirit of Christ, and Christ. It is important to realize that he is not referring to different spirits, but that all these terms are used of the Holy Spirit dwelling in the Christian (Alford, 2:389; see also 2 Cor. 3:17). It is our interaction with the Holy Spirit that is set in opposition to the flesh (v. 9) and death (v. 10). This interaction is described by the "dwelling" (*oikeō*) of the Spirit of God and "having" (*echō*) the Spirit of Christ. *Oikeō* means, "To occupy a house, i.e., reside," and figuratively means "to inhabit, remain" (Strong, #3611). *Echō* means "to have," and indicates the thought of holding or possessing (Strong, #2192).

REVELATION AND APPLICATION

Possessing Us for Christ

Romans 8:9 mentions both the Spirit of God and the Spirit of Christ. These are not two Spirits but two aspects of the same Holy Spirit. The Spirit of God is related to a mutual indwelling, while the Spirit of Christ is related to a mutual possessing. When we have the Spirit of Christ, He possesses us for Christ. In this way, we are mingled with the triune God. Not only so, but the Spirit of Christ brings us into the subjective experience of such ownership. This causes us to live Christ out in our daily life.

What does it mean to belong to Christ? In Galatians, Paul said, "Now those who belong to Christ Jesus have crucified the flesh with its passions and desires" (5:24). Paul did not say in this verse that our flesh has been crucified with Christ in a passive way. Rather, he describes this crucifying of the flesh as an action by those who belong to Christ. Of course, this is not done independently of Him. Rather, it is an application of the fact that our flesh has been crucified with Christ. Those who belong to Christ not only have the status of belonging to Him but also experientially apply the fact of the crucifixion of the flesh.

Filling Us with Feelings for Divine Things

In Romans 8:10, Paul relates the experiences of death and life to whether Christ is in us or not. What is the difference between "the Spirit of Christ" and "Christ"? Paul indicates that we possess the Spirit of Christ, but that Christ Himself is in us. In other words, if we have the Spirit of Christ, we possess and enjoy the very person of Christ Himself. In principle, the title "Christ" emphasizes His person and "the Spirit of Christ" emphasizes His feelings and essence. It is Christ—a living person, Savior, and anointed One—who dwells within every regenerated Christian. It is His Spirit who fills us with His feelings toward the divine things.

These feelings draw Christians to spiritual things, and cause them to be willing and able to enjoy and apply the reality of these things. The Spirit of Christ causes the Bible to inspire and infuse Christians with His heavenly supply. The Spirit of Christ causes the church life to become inspiring and enjoyable. All regenerated Christians have Christ as a living person and the Spirit of Christ as the One who fills them with feelings toward the divine and spiritual things.

Applying the Fact

The flesh of every regenerated believer has been crucified on the cross, but this fact of crucifixion must be applied. We must belong to Christ in order to put to death the flesh with its passions and desires (Gal. 2:24). How do we know if we are in the flesh? We should ask ourselves, "What is my relationship with the Lord—do I belong to Christ right now?" If we objectively belong to Christ, we can subjectively apply the fact that we are not in the flesh but in the Spirit.

According to the Bible, it is a fact that all regenerated Christians belong to Christ and have been crucified with Him (Gal. 2:20). Experientially, however, we often walk as if we do not belong to Him. Whenever we act as if we are not of Christ, the fact accomplished on the cross is not subjectively applied to us. In such times, we should be so thankful for the objective facts and boldly declare, "I am of Christ! Though my flesh is still here, it has nothing more to do because I belong to Christ. My passions and desires are still here, but they have nowhere to go, because I belong to Christ! My flesh with its passions and desires has been crucified! I am of Christ and have the Spirit of Christ!"

Forgetting the Flesh

Those who belong to Christ, who have applied the effectiveness of the cross and the fact of the crucifixion of the flesh, will forget about the existence of their flesh in experience. This is the relationship between those of Christ and their flesh. When we belong to Christ, our flesh, passions, and desires all go to the cross. Our flesh still exists, but we are no longer debtors to it and can set it aside. In our sensation, it is as if the flesh ceases to exist!

When we apply our belonging to Christ, the flesh seems to fade away. Only Christ remains with His sweetness, supply, nourishment, enjoyment, and experience. We forget about everything and simply enjoy being mingled with Christ. This is actually the normal experience of those who belong to Christ.

Alive Because of Righteousness

Romans 8:10 says, "If Christ is in you, though the body is dead because of sin, yet the spirit is alive because of righteousness." The spirit here is not the Holy Spirit but the human spirit (Vincent, 3:90). Yet the verse begins with the condition that Christ is in us. Christ is in us, and thus, our spirit is life because of righteousness. We not only have the Spirit of God and the Spirit of Christ dwelling in us (v. 9), but also Christ (v. 10). Christ is not only the propitiation (3:25), and He is not only in resurrection (4:24-25, 6:5); He is even in us today!

The righteousness Romans 8:10 talks about is the person and accomplishment of Christ. Every Christian's spirit is alive because of Christ and everything He has accomplished. This righteousness is the ground and basis for the triune God to mingle with us by dispensing Himself into us. If we are not righteous, God cannot dispense Himself into us as life to make our spirit alive. Yet if there is no Christ, we have no righteousness. For God to dispense Himself into us as life, we need Christ, because righteousness can never be separated from Him.

Many people have heard the story of the prodigal son who returns home, is clothed with the best robe, and given the fatted calf to enjoy (Luke 15). We are like this prodigal son. The robe typifies Christ as our righteousness, and the fatted calf typifies Christ as our life. It is because of Christ in us that we can enjoy both life and righteousness. Thank the Lord that He dwells in us as both the Spirit of Christ and Christ Himself today!

110 | The Spirit of Him Who Raised Jesus from the Dead: Incorporation

But if the Spirit of Him who raised Jesus from the dead dwells in you, He who raised Christ Jesus from the dead will also give life to your mortal bodies through His Spirit who dwells in you.
—Romans 8:11

WORD STUDY

In Romans 8:11, another description is used of the Holy Spirit—"the Spirit of Him who raised Jesus from the dead." The usage of the personal name "Jesus" is a reminder of the historical fact of the resurrection of the one person, Jesus. This verse shows that the Spirit is powerful over death and that He renders us partakers of Christ's resurrection as He dwells in us (Alford, 2:389).

There are two different Greek words in this verse that are translated "dwells." The first ("from the dead dwells in you") is the Greek word *oikeō*, which is also used in verse 9. It means, "to occupy a house, i.e., reside," and figuratively means "to inhabit, remain" (Strong, #3611). The present tense indicates a continuous action (Rogers, 330). The second word ("through His Spirit who dwells in you") is *enoikeō*. Rather than emphasizing the action of dwelling, it emphasizes the influence of the dweller upon the one he dwells within (Thayer, 217).

REVELATION AND APPLICATION

In Romans 8, Paul describes four aspects of the rich divine life. First, the Spirit is of life (v. 2). Second, the mind of the Spirit is life (v. 6). Third, our human spirit is life because of righteousness (v. 10). Finally, our mortal body will be given life through the Spirit (v. 11).

The Life-dispensing Spirit

Within us dwells the Spirit of God, making us those who are "in the Spirit" (Rom. 8:9). We also possess the Spirit of Christ, causing us to be possessed by Him (v. 9). Verse 11 adds that "the Spirit of Him who raised Jesus from the dead" dwells in us. This Spirit will give life to our mortal bodies. There are two aspects to this: the future transforming of our corruptible bodies in the glory of resurrection and the present daily dispensing of life.

Our bodies are mortal, and death is very powerful in us, to the point that Paul wrote that our bodies are "dead because of sin" (v. 10). For this reason, it is not unusual to experience death even as we go through the process of sanctification.

I remember one time when a brother was going to speak in a church meeting, but he was very tired and did not know what to say. He felt very dead. At that moment, his only strength was what the Lord would supply. What was marvelous, however, was that as he began to open his mouth to speak, he experienced the dispensing of life into his mortal body by the Spirit of Him who raised Jesus from the dead. By this dispensed life, he was able to go on and speak what was on his heart.

Christians should not fear death. We should not fear the death produced by the fall, nor should we fear the death brought in by our own weaknesses, failures, and limitations. Rather, we should know that the Spirit of Him who raised

Jesus can rise above all of these things and dispense life into our mortal bodies.

The Economic Spirit

It is very precious that the Spirit is not only "of God" and "of Christ" but also "of Him who raised Jesus from the dead." Each description in Romans 8:9–11 relates to a different aspect of the same Spirit. The "Spirit of God" is related to God's essence. The "Spirit of Christ" is related to the person and accomplishment of Christ. The "Spirit of Him who raised Jesus" is related to the process the triune God has gone through for the sake of His eternal economy and for the work according to His eternal will.

In other words, the Spirit of Him who raised Jesus is the Spirit of God's divine economy. This economic Spirit is full of the operation needed to raise Jesus from the dead and accomplish the eternal purpose and will of God.

The Incorporating Spirit

In Romans 8:11, dwelling is mentioned twice, although two different Greek words are used. The first dwelling (*oikeō*) denotes the Spirit making His home in us. The second dwelling (*enoikeō*) means to indwell. This indwelling denotes a certain influence, indicating that the Spirit of Him who raised Christ Jesus makes His home in us according to His own desires.

If the Spirit can dwell in us in this way and influence us by His own preferences, we will become incorporated with Christ, able to bear fruit to God in resurrection (7:4). The Spirit of Him who raised Jesus not only makes His home in us (*oikeō*), but through His indwelling (*enoikeō*) also incorporates us with the living person of Christ. We could paraphrase the verse in this way: "If the economic Spirit makes His home in you, He who raised Christ Jesus from the dead will also give life to your mortal bodies through His Spirit who indwells you and incorporates you with Christ."

Bearing Fruit

This incorporation produces the fruit-bearing mentioned in Romans 7:4 and is related to our bodies. We may marvel here that in our experience of the process of sanctification, God still cares about our physical bodies, which are mortal and indwelt by sin. We may pray, "Lord, I have utterly failed, and I feel so dead within. Please save me!" God might reply, "The reason you fail and are dead is because of your body. This is why I am giving life to your mortal body."

Many brothers and sisters can testify that after many years of being saved, they still experience the dispensing of life to their mortal bodies through the Spirit of Him who raised Jesus from the dead. By such dispensing, we can continually bear unto God the fruit of life, even with the limitations of our mortal bodies.

111 | The High Peak of Sanctification: Our Living

So then, brethren, we are under obligation, not to the flesh, to live according to the flesh—[13]*for if you are living according to the flesh, you must die; but if by the Spirit you are putting to death the deeds of the body, you will live.*
—Romans 8:12-13

WORD STUDY

The Greek word most often used for "death" in the New Testament is *thanatos*. Its primary usage is for physical death. Its secondary usage is for the spiritual separation of man from God. In this way, death does not denote nonexistence but is simply the opposite of life. As spiritual life involves a conscious abiding in fellowship with God, death represents cutting off that fellowship (Vine, 149). Romans 8:13 says that if we live according to the flesh, we must die. Some Bible translations use the phrase, "you will die." However, in Greek this expression is stronger than the simple future tense of "will die." Rather, it indicates a necessary consequence and is better translated "must die" (Vincent, 3:91).

Verse 13 continues, "But if by the Spirit you are putting to death the deeds of the body, you will live." The Greek word used here for "deeds," *praxis*, can be translated "doings, acts, transactions" (Thayer, 534) and also indicates habitual practices (Vincent, 3:91). The "putting to death" of these deeds is written in the active voice, indicating the performance of the action by the subject (Wallace, 746). Thus, this forceful phrase could be translated, "slay, abolish, and annul the deeds of the body" (Alford, 2:391). Doing this by the Spirit causes us to live.

"To live," *zaō*, is written in the middle voice and indicative mood. The middle voice emphasizes the subject's participation, while the indicative mood denotes the highest level of certainty (Wallace, 746–748). Thus, Paul is giving a promise of living if the conditions of the verse are met.

REVELATION AND APPLICATION

Putting to Death the Deeds of the Body

In previous verses, Paul mentioned that the mind of the flesh cannot please God, and it neither is nor can be subject to God. It is also hostile toward God and resists Him (Rom. 8:7–8). Therefore, we should not live according to the flesh today. Is the flesh still here? Yes, it is. Is the mind of the flesh still here? Yes, it is. Is the mind of the flesh still active? Yes. Should we live according to it anymore? No. The Word of God is very clear that if we live according to the flesh, we must die.

The phrase "putting to death" is used in verse 13. This is a very strong phrase, because it indicates an action on our side. What does it mean to put to death the deeds of the body? It means to create an environment in which the deeds of the body cannot help but die. Practically, this means we should learn to ignore the flesh. We should not feed the flesh, communicate with the flesh, or contact the flesh. By such treatment, the flesh will have nothing to do and will be cast aside. By isolating the flesh in this way, the deeds of the body will lose any active ability and will be put to death.

Putting to Death by the Spirit

If we do not live according to the flesh, the deeds of the body will be put to death. What is the secret to this action? It is accomplished by the Spirit. When the Spirit comes in and operates by isolating the flesh, the flesh will say, "How wretched this is! Here I am in my office, with only my desk and chair, and I have nothing to do! I am so lonely I could die!"

However, we sometimes go to this office and talk with the flesh again. What should we do when we realize we are feeding the flesh in this way? We should just come out of the office immediately. We should not have self-pity, praying, "Lord Jesus, I sinned again. Please have mercy upon me. Please save me!" This kind of prayer is not bad, but it is not the merciless "putting to death" mentioned here. Whenever we find that we are communicating with the flesh, we should simply cut off this communication immediately by the Spirit, return to the Spirit, and allow the Spirit to be Lord of our mind. Only this can bring in the reality of "putting to death" the deeds of our body.

A Transcendent Living

It is interesting that Romans 8:13 does not say that we should put to death the deeds of the flesh, but the deeds of the body. "Deeds" means intentional and habitual behavior. The deeds of the body not only indicate the behavior of the body but also involve every aspect of our daily life. It is not only the evil deeds; even good behavior must be put to death if it is apart from Christ or causes us to leave the presence of Christ.

Our experience of sanctification involves not living according to the flesh as well as putting to death the deeds of the body. We should have an indescribable transcendence over every aspect of our daily lives. Nothing of this world should have any ground in us, whether these things are necessary or unnecessary. If we are so worried about necessary items that we run from store to store, calculating prices and considering deals, can we say we are living a transcendent life? If yesterday our life was consumed with buying furniture, today with carpet, and tomorrow with clothing, is that a transcendent life? It is not! We need to put to death all the deeds of the body by the Spirit in order to live the transcendent life of sanctification.

When the Lord was on the earth, though His living was simple and poor, it was transcendent. He eventually did not even have a place to lay His head (Matt. 8:20). Yet in the absence of such things, He did not set His mind on the things of man but cared for the things of the Father. Here was a holy pattern without blemish. By the Holy Spirit, He always lived a life under the termination of the cross.

The High Peak of Sanctification

The Word of God is very clear that if we put to death the deeds of the body, we will live. Romans 8:13 is essentially the end of the discussion of sanctification in Romans. Thus, the experience of sanctification ends with a living which testifies of our experience of sanctification. The one who lives is the one who has experienced sanctification. How do we know if we have been sanctified? We should ask, "What is the source of my living?" If we live according to the flesh, we must die. If we live and walk in our spirit by the Holy Spirit, the deeds of the body will be put to death, we will live, and the reality of sanctification will be manifested through us.

The high peak of sanctification is our living. Christians who experience sanctification and bear fruit to God have a transcendent living. They simply live in their spirit, united with the Lord by the Spirit of God, mingled with the Lord by the Spirit of Christ, and incorporated with the Lord by the Spirit of Him who raised Jesus. They have put to death the deeds of the body, allowing everything good, bad, necessary, and unnecessary to be put to death by the Holy Spirit. They live according to the divine life, allowing the Spirit to give life, reign, and lead in everything. Theirs is a living incorporated with God for the accomplishment of His will, just as Christ lived on the earth in His body (Heb. 10:5–7). What a transcendent living! What a glorious living! This is the high peak of sanctification.

Section Five

Glorification

112

An Overview of Glorification

And if children, heirs also, heirs of God and fellow heirs with Christ, if indeed we suffer with Him so that we may also be glorified with Him. ¹⁸For I consider that the sufferings of this present time are not worthy to be compared with the glory that is to be revealed to us.

—*Romans 8:17-18*

WORD STUDY

The Greek word for "glory" is *doxa*, which can also be translated "dignity, honor, praise, worship" (Strong, #1392). The verb form, *doxazō*, can be translated "to magnify, extol, praise, honor, make glorious." Describing glory, W. E. Vine says, "It is used of the nature and acts of God in self-manifestation, i.e., what He essentially is and does, as exhibited in whatever way He reveals Himself in these respects....The glory of God is the revelation and manifestation of all that He has and is" (Vine, 267).

In the latter half of Romans 8, glory is mentioned in several verses, including verse 17, in which Paul declares that our suffering with Christ will lead to our being glorified with Him. This glorification is our exaltation "to the same glory to which Christ has been raised" (Thayer, 602). The latter half of chapter 8 (vv. 14–39) makes up a section that deals with glorification as the final fact in the salvation provided by God, both in terms of its process and its certainty (Morgan, 125).

REVELATION AND APPLICATION

God's Full Salvation

Romans 8:13 was the end of the section dealing with our sanctification. Now, Romans 8:14–39 covers our glorification. It is good to remember what Paul first covered before coming to this topic: condemnation, justification, and sanctification. This order is very meaningful. We all begin in condemnation, need to be justified, and require the process of sanctification before we can reach glorification.

God Himself is righteous, holy, and glorious. His work is righteous, His nature is holy, and His manifestation is glorious. Justification makes us righteous before God and deals with the human spirit. A believer's spirit is alive because of righteousness (v. 10). Sanctification relates to God's holy nature. The process of sanctification mingles God's nature with ours and deals with our soul. The mind of the Spirit is life and peace (v. 6). Glorification relates to the manifestation of God Himself and deals with our bodies. We are eagerly awaiting the redemption of our bodies (v. 23), when our bodies will be conformed to the body of His glory (Phil. 3:21).

Thus, God's full salvation of man's spirit, soul, and body is accomplished through the full process of justification, sanctification, and glorification.

A Process of Glorification

What is glorification? On one hand, our ultimate glorification will occur in the future, on the day our bodies are redeemed. On the other hand, glorification is a continuous process today. In this process, the children of God are constituted with His divine life which, when manifested, is the glory of God.

Paul writes later of the "freedom of the glory of the children of God" (Rom. 8:21). In this phrase, "glory" is a noun. Our glorification is a process resulting in glory. Our daily growing and maturing as children of God will eventually result in the future manifestation of our glorious new constitution.

The Crucial Role of the Spirit

Directly before addressing glorification, Paul made some profound statements about the Spirit. We have the Spirit of God dwelling in us (Rom. 8:9), the Spirit of Christ possessing us for Christ (v. 9), and the Spirit of Him who raised Jesus dispensing life to our mortal bodies (v. 11). Furthermore, it is by the Holy Spirit that we put to death the deeds of the body (v. 13).

We should not get carried away and think these are all different Spirits. The Spirit of God, the Spirit of Christ, the Spirit of Him who raised Jesus, and the Holy Spirit are all one and the same Spirit (Eph. 4:4). These descriptions all refer to different aspects of the Spirit's operation.

Our glorification is totally based on the operation and work of the Spirit in us. This section on glorification contains such a sweet verse: "The Spirit Himself testifies with our spirit that we are children of God" (Rom. 8:16). This shows a subjective participation of the Holy Spirit with our spirit. He is not distant from us but is in us and with us.

Our lifelong experience of glorification can never progress apart from the Spirit. In fact, glorification is experienced only in the Spirit. As the Spirit operates in us, constituting us with glory, our whole life becomes one of glorification, continuing unto the day our bodies are redeemed.

113

Led by the Spirit of God

For all who are being led by the Spirit of God, these are sons of God.
—Romans 8:14

WORD STUDY

Romans 8:14 has two parts: the first describes an action, and the second describes the subjects of the action. The Greek word used here for "led" is written in the present tense, portraying the Spirit's leading as a progressive event, without regard for beginning or end (Wallace, 751).

This verse says that those who are being led by the Spirit are the "sons of God (*huios theos*)". Notice that the term, "children of God (*tēknon theos*)," is not used in this verse. H. Alford explains the difference between these two descriptions in the following way: "["Sons of God"] differs from ["children of God"] in implying the higher and more mature and conscious member of God's family. Hence our Lord is never called the 'child,' but always the 'Son' of God. Applied to a Christian, this signifies 'one born of God' in the deepest relation to Him, and hence a partaker of His nature" (Alford, 2:391).

REVELATION AND APPLICATION

After writing so much on justification and sanctification, the apostle Paul now moves on to glorification. Romans 8:14 is the beginning of this section on glorification, and this beginning verse opens with the matter of being led. Our experience of justification and sanctification, from Romans 3:21 to 8:14, results in our being led as sons of God by the Spirit of God. We should allow the Spirit of God to take the lead in us. Once the Spirit can lead us, we will experience the reality of being sons of God.

Proof of Sonship

As we follow the Lord, we usually experience being a child of God more than we experience being a son of God. There is a difference between these two terms. "Child" indicates our status. Once we are saved, we are the children of God (John 1:12). However, "son" goes beyond our status and indicates a deeper application, experience, and enjoyment of all the riches of God the Father.

A child of God has been born according to the divine life. A son of God has experienced the growth of the divine life (see Gal. 4:1-7). A person led by the Spirit of God is a son of God who applies, experiences, and enjoys all the riches promised by God the Father.

The Bible is so wonderful, even in the fact that it uses the matter of leading to prove who the sons of God are. Many questions can arise regarding our spiritual growth. Are we really sons of God? Do we live in a healthy and vital spiritual situation? Are the riches of God subjective, applicable, and experiential to us? The answer to these questions lies in whether we have the leading of the Spirit of God or not.

The Manifestation of God's Operation

From the moment the Spirit of God came to dwell in us, we automatically had the leading of God. "To lead," *agō*, is here written in the passive voice and present tense—*agontai*. The passive voice shows that we are not leading ourselves but are being led by someone else, and the present tense indicates that this leading is constantly operating and working in us.

The leading of the Spirit is a manifestation of the healthy operation of the triune God in our spirit. If we allow the triune God to actively live in us, He will lead us in a living way. If we allow Him ground in us, He will lead us in His sovereignty. If we have a fresh relationship with Him, He will lead us in a fresh way.

A Most Normal Life

Some may think the leading of the Spirit is an unusual thing or that it is only experienced by more mature Christians. In fact, the leading of the Spirit of God is a most normal thing. For a physically healthy person, it is very normal to eat and sleep because these things are matters of our natural life. In the same way, the leading of the Spirit is normal for a healthy Christian because it is a matter of the divine life. The Spirit of God desires to be our Master so that through His healthy operation He can guide us and lead us in all things. The operation of the Spirit of God in us is always according to who God is and what He desires. The more intimate our relationship with God is, the more the Spirit of God can live and operate in us, and the stronger and more manifest His leading will become.

An Indicator of Our Healthiness and Maturity

Believers should be led by the Spirit as sons of God. However, the degree of the Spirit's leading is not always the same in all sons of God. The degree to which this leading is rich and manifest shows how healthy we are before God and testifies of our maturity before Him.

The leadings of the Spirit in us reveal the health of our Christian life. We should be able to be led by the Spirit in everything we do, from what time we wake up, to what we eat, how we dress, how we work, and how we talk. When there is not much leading in us, it is an indicator of an expanding distance between us and the Lord.

Additionally, saints at different spiritual levels will be led in different ways. For example, a mature brother who has been saved for many years may be led by the Spirit to properly fulfill his ministry before the Lord. However, a newly saved brother may be led to be separated from the things of the world. In this way, the kind of leading we receive from the Spirit testifies of our maturity in life.

The Process of Leading: The Anointing

The leading of the Spirit of God follows the principle of the dispensing of life. It is not forceful or sudden. This process is called the anointing.

In the Old Testament, all the utensils for the tent of meeting were sanctified by being anointed with the holy anointing oil (Exo. 30:25-29). In the New Testament age, the children of God all have an anointing from the Holy One (1 John 2:20), which not only dwells in us but also teaches us about all things (v. 27). The more we obey the leading of the Spirit of God, the more we will experience this anointing. The stronger the anointing is, the richer the presence of God becomes, and the more we are constituted with Him so that we become more one with Him, appreciative of Him, and obedient to His leading.

When the Lord leads us a certain way, and we respond positively to His leading, we will feel the nourishment of the anointing within us. The more we say, "Lord, if You want this, I also want this," the more we will experience the anointing. The more we say, "Lord, I consecrate myself to You and am willing to follow You; I do not choose my own things but only want to be one with You," the more we will be anointed within.

There is a hymn by Watchman Nee with lines that read, "Tears cloud my eyes, yet sweetness fills my heart. May I decrease. May Thou increase in me!" (Martin, #319). Wherever we are, and however we feel, when we tell the Lord, "May Your will be done; I am willing to obey You," the anointing will come and bring sweet nourishment to us.

The source of the Spirit's leading is the operation and working of the divine life within us. The process of being led is according to the divine anointing. Our obedience does not leave us feeling like we are shedding our blood and forsaking our life. Rather, it is sweet, nourishing, and enjoyable.

Life and Peace

The leading of the Spirit of God is totally a matter of the divine life. This is one way to determine whether the Spirit is leading us in a certain matter: His leading is always accompanied by the dispensing of His life. If we obey the leading, the result will be life and peace (see Rom. 8:6).

Unfortunately, many Christians pay attention to everything but the leading of the Spirit of God. It seems very few can genuinely declare, "The Lord led me in this way!" Also, few can say, "Because the Lord is leading me in this way, I am full of life and peace within." Inward peace has nothing to do with whether something seems right or wrong. Many saints have testified that in outwardly confusing or chaotic situations, they have still felt very peaceful within. Other situations may seem outwardly proper or logical, yet the inward sense of peace can be lost. We should learn not to over-analyze what seems right or wrong in our outward environments. Rather, we should pay attention to the anointing and inward feelings of life and peace.

An example of this is a brother who, years ago, wanted to buy a house. He was scheduled to look at several houses one day, but as he left for these appointments, he did not feel peaceful within. Although he inwardly felt like there was no need to go, he still decided to keep his appointments. After looking at the houses, he thought he had found the one he wanted. It was a small house, well maintained, and not far from where the church met. However, as he considered this house more, there was no anointing within him, and there was no life or peace. A few days later, he looked at another house, yet did not like it much. However, he later felt that he needed to see it again. This time the anointing was very strong within him, and he felt like the Lord was telling him, "This is it!" He eventually bought this house and had a very peaceful feeling within. This peace was the result of his obedience to the Spirit leading him.

According to Holiness

The matter of the Spirit's leading is crucial to the beginning of this section of Romans which deals with glorification. If we have not gone through the test of being led by the Spirit, it will be very hard for us to experience glorification. We must learn to receive the leading from the Lord, to live according to the anointing by obeying His leading, and to live in life and peace. We will have the experience of glorification only if we have learned these lessons well.

The leading of the Spirit of God is according to the divine life and the operation of the law of the Spirit of life (8:2). This leading never has anything to do with things of sin and death. God never leads us to sin or to do things to offend Him. His leading in us is always holy and according to His holy nature (1 Pet. 1:16). This is another way to recognize the leading of the Spirit.

The Full Experience of the Gospel of God

The Spirit's leading is also related to the gospel. According to the Greek language, "leading" (*agō*) is a distant root of *euaggelion*, the Greek word for "gospel" (see Strong, #2097, #32, #71). If we are short of the Spirit's leading, we will be short of the experience of the gospel. The richer His leading is in us, the richer will be our enjoyment and application of the gospel. If the Lord has not spoken to us in a long time and we have not had any leading from Him, we can be sure that our experience of the gospel has been lacking during that time.

Consider how wonderful this connection is between the Spirit's leading and the gospel. Romans 1:1 began with the gospel of God, and here at Paul's highest peak in chapter 8, he talks about the leading of the Spirit of God in us. This leading is according to the realization of all the riches of the gospel in us. Justification, sanctification, the renewal of our mind, transformation, and our conformation to the image of the Son of God are all included in this gospel. When the gospel of God comes to its peak, its focus is no longer our sins or fallen nature but the leading of the Spirit of God in us.

Glorification is the highest peak in Romans, and the emphasis of glorification is to be led by the Spirit of God. A person who is led in such a way dwells in the gospel. Only as we continually accept and enjoy the leading of the Spirit of God will we be able to fully accept and enjoy the gospel.

The Purpose of the Spirit's Leading

The leading of the Spirit of God is not only for our sake but is chiefly for God's eternal economy, which includes not only His eternal purpose but the work to accomplish that purpose. The purpose of the Spirit's leading is to bring us into this economy. No leading should be for the leading itself.

Rather, it must be related to God's economy and must further the work of His eternal purpose.

For example, if we are clear that the Lord is calling us to serve Him, this is the Spirit's leading. However, if this leading does not go further and develop, it is not enough. Our existence is not to simply serve God in whatever way we feel is right. Our existence is for God, His gospel, and His economy. It is for the sake of the economy of God that the Spirit leads us to earnestly serve God. The result of our leading should always be related to this purpose.

Many seek the Spirit's leading and are eager to obey, but few concern themselves with the purpose of the Spirit's leading. Those who have given their lives to serve the Lord and those who are considering to do so should pay close attention to the following: Whether or not we serve the Lord in such a way is a matter of His leading, yet we cannot stop there. Rather, we ought to ask, "Why do I serve? What is my serving for?" If we stop at the initial leading itself, we will come short of the Spirit's purpose. A healthy leading always brings us into God's economy.

If we stop at an initial leading by the Spirit, it can actually be quite dangerous. For example, a brother sought the Lord in his prayer over the matter of his service. He asked the Lord whether he should continue to work for his company or if he should drop the job to serve the church full-time. Eventually, he felt led to drop his job and serve the church. After serving like this for some time, he ran into a problem. At his former job, he had always worked under a boss who handed out assignments and demanded production. Now he had no such boss. In fact, almost no one knew what he specifically did! No one knew whether he had led anyone to the Lord in the past year or if he had helped anyone love the Lord more over that time. He could have done nothing all day, and no one would have known it!

The problem was that this brother felt led to serve the Lord in a certain way, yet never asked what that service was for.

In a sense, he followed the leading of the Spirit but stopped with that leading. Without understanding how his service related to God's economy, it was easy to become lost in the abstract idea of a "full-time servant of the Lord." Many full-time Christian workers find themselves in similar situations, and if their living is sloppy, they will ruin their character and operation within a year.

The Spirit desires to lead all of us in every aspect of our lives. Christians should be led by the Spirit of God in all things, resulting in a normal, healthy, and vibrant spiritual life. The problem is that our lives are not always related to God's economy. Please allow me to share my testimony. I began to learn to accept the leading of God in everything from a young age. The first thing I did every morning was pray, "Lord, which route do You want me to walk on my way to school today?" If I knew my route was from the Lord's leading, my walk to school would be filled with prayer, praise, and the enjoyment of His presence. This practice eventually became my habit. No matter what I've faced in the years since my youth, I can always return to the presence of the Lord to pray, look unto Him, and seek His leading. Seeking His leading is normal, healthy, and beneficial, but our following can potentially be unrelated to God's economy. A healthy leading is always related to God's economy and will work to bring in the accomplishment of God's eternal will.

114

The Spirit of Sonship

For you have not received a spirit of slavery leading to fear again, but you have received a spirit of adoption as sons by which we cry out, "Abba! Father!"
—Romans 8:15

WORD STUDY

Paul states in Romans 8:15 that we did not receive a spirit of slavery, but a spirit of adoption as sons. W. E. Vine says, "Believers are said to have received 'the Spirit of adoption,' that is, the Holy Spirit who...produces in them the realization of sonship and the attitude belonging to sons" (Vine, 14). This spirit could also be a combination of the objective Spirit of God with our own subjective human spirit (Alford, 2:391).

The Greek word used here for "received," *lambanō*, means "to take" or "to receive" (Thayer, 370–371). In order to determine how to translate *lambanō* accurately, the context must be considered. Did we take the spirit of adoption as sons, or were we given the spirit of adoption as sons? Scholars and commentators generally agree with the latter statement. In this case, *lambanō* would express gaining or obtaining (Thayer, 371).

The Greek word translated here "adoption as sons" is *huiothesia*. It is comprised of two words: *huios*, meaning "son"

(Strong, #5207), and *theō*, meaning "to place, establish" (Strong, #5087). Therefore, *huiothesia* can be translated "sonship" (Strong, #5206) and can be thought of as "the placing of one in the position of a son" (Vincent, 3:91). It signifies giving the place and condition of a son to one to whom it does not naturally belong. Rendered "adoption" by many scholars, *huiothesia* does not stress being put into the family of God by spiritual birth (as the term "children" might), but being put into the position of sons (Vine, 14). *Huiothesia* emphasizes the matter of position rather than life. In this position, the believer not only has the life of God but is also a partaker of the rights, privileges, and responsibilities of His sons (Rogers, 330).

REVELATION AND APPLICATION

As Paul introduces glorification here in Romans, he emphatically mentions the matter of adoption as sons, or sonship. Romans 8:14 described the sons of God as those who are led by the Spirit of God. Romans 8:15 continues by saying we have received a spirit of adoption as sons, or a spirit of sonship. We can conclude that our experience of glorification strongly relates to this matter of sonship.

Paying a Price

Paul uses the Greek word *lambanō* in Romans 8:15, which is a very subjective Greek verb that implies gaining, experiencing, and applying. Paul uses an intensified version of this word (*katalambanō*) in Philippians 3:12 to express his "laying hold of" that for which Christ laid hold of him. This "laying hold of" in Philippians involves pressing on (3:12), counting all things to be loss (v. 8), and conformation to the death of Christ (v. 10). For sure, this "laying hold of" required Paul to pay a price.

The Bible is very clear that our salvation is not by our own effort but through faith and by grace (Eph. 2:8-9). The Spirit we received when we were born again is the same spirit of sonship we obtain, experience, and apply. However, we must pay a price to enjoy and apply the reality of sonship. God is so willing to give this sonship to everyone, yet some Christians experience the reality of this sonship while others do not. The difference is that some have not only received God's grace and Spirit but have also paid a price to lay hold of the sonship obtained in the Spirit.

The Growth unto Sonship

A healthy Christian eagerly awaits the consummation of sonship (Rom. 8:23). However, in Romans 8:15, Paul did not say that we receive "sonship" directly, but rather we receive the "spirit of sonship." The spirit of sonship is what we receive, obtain, experience, and apply. This phrase shows that the reality of sonship is not simply obtained by us at the moment of our regeneration, but is related to the subjective experience, enjoyment, and application of the Spirit in our spirit day by day.

The word "sonship" implies that a child has grown up and become a legal heir to all the riches of his father. We used to be prodigal sons living in sin and far away from God (Luke 15:11-32). However, one day God found us and took us back home to enjoy the reality of our sonship. In this position, we can enjoy all the riches of our Father's house, grow up to be His heirs, and inherit His full divine inheritance. This is the sonship we have received.

Our status changed the moment we were regenerated. We were no longer apart from God, but rather became the sons of God (Gal. 3:26) and objectively obtained the spirit of sonship (Rom. 8:15). The more we experience, enjoy, and apply the spirit of sonship, the more this sonship is manifested in us and the more mature its expression will become.

This sonship does not have a subjective reality within us at regeneration. It is not until we begin to love the Lord, consecrate ourselves to Him, and pay a price to follow Him that we begin to obtain the reality of sonship in the spirit. The more we pay a price, the more the divine life will grow in us. The more this life grows, the more we experience the spirit of sonship. The more we experience the spirit of sonship, the more our subjective reality of sonship grows.

In resurrection, Christ became the firstborn Son of God (Acts 13:33; Rom. 1:4). By His resurrection, we have become the many sons of God, those who have a life relationship with Him and share in His nature. Our sonship is not simply the result of a legal process but is the result of being constituted with the divine life. As the divine life constitutes us, we cry out, "Abba! Father!" Such a cry is so sweet to our God and Father.

115 The Testimony of the Spirit with Our Spirit

The Spirit Himself testifies with our spirit that we are children of God, ¹⁷and if children, heirs also, heirs of God and fellow heirs with Christ, if indeed we suffer with Him so that we may also be glorified with Him.

—*Romans 8:16-17*

WORD STUDY

Romans 8:16 describes an aspect of the relationship between the human spirit and the Spirit of God: His testimony with our spirit that we are children of God. The Greek word used here for "testifies," *summartureō*, means "to testify jointly, i.e. corroborate by (concurrent) evidence" (Strong, #4828). It is often used in a legal sense to indicate a testimony in a court of law in support of someone (Rogers, 330). A root of the word is *martureō*, meaning, "to be a witness" (Strong, #3140). This word grew in importance in the second century when, following the impulses found in the New Testament, it came to designate all who would seal the seriousness of their witness by death (Kittel, 4:504–505). This is the root of the English word "martyr."

REVELATION AND APPLICATION

When considering glorification, we should understand that we who have been saved are the glorious heirs of God (Rom. 8:17). Concerning our being heirs of God, there are three main points: our identity, status, and experience. Our identity is that we are children of God (v. 16), which we will consider in this chapter. Our status is that we are fellow heirs with Christ (v. 17a), which we will consider in chapter 116. Our experience is that we suffer and will be glorified with Christ (v. 17b), which we will consider in chapter 117.

The Spirit and Our Spirit

Let us first consider our identity described in Romans 8:16. The Spirit of God bears witness with our spirit that we are children of God. This verse can be hard to comprehend if we do not rightly understand the two spirits mentioned.

What is "the Spirit"? Paul wrote, "The last Adam became a life-giving Spirit" (1 Cor. 15:45, NKJV®). The last Adam, Christ, was born, lived a human life, died, was buried, and resurrected to become the life-giving Spirit. What is "our spirit"? This refers to the spirit of man, regenerated by the life-giving Spirit, and joined to the Lord to become one spirit (1 Cor. 6:17).

In Paul's consideration of God's organic salvation in Romans, the key is "the Spirit...with our spirit." The Spirit and our spirit testify together that we are the children of God. Additionally, in our spirit mingled with the Spirit of God, we can enjoy, apply, and obtain all of God's supply reserved for His children.

A Strong Testimony

In Romans 8:16, the word "testifies" is a verb. In Greek, the noun form of this word, *martus*, means "a witness," and is the root of the English word "martyr." A martyr is one who not only outwardly witnesses and testifies, but who also has a heart and a commitment to stand for the truth, whatever the consequences. The Spirit and our spirit together bear this strong testimony that we are children of God, and in so testifying, they are firm, unyielding, and strong. When we feel unsure about our status with God, we can remember that the Spirit and our spirit unflinchingly stand together to testify that we are children of God.

A Declaration and Commitment

Romans 8:16 shows that the Spirit and our spirit testify together. This testimony is a combination of a declaration of the Spirit and a commitment within our spirit. When the Spirit declares, we also receive a commitment. When this declaration and our commitment are in one accord, the testimony that God desires will be produced—a testimony that we are children of God.

The word *martureō* ("to witness, testify") was sometimes used in the ancient Greek world in connection with events at amphitheaters. After watching a performance or competition, some of the audience were so deeply affected that they would "witness" to everyone about what they had seen. In the spiritual realm, a true testimony involves seeing something, a vision, and then becoming constrained by this vision. What we see through the Spirit in our spirit makes a deep impression that controls our living and constrains our interactions with others. The testimony that comes from such an experience is more than a declaration of doctrine; it is a rich testimony with content and substance.

The testimony that the Spirit and our spirit bear together is a testimony with rich content, which comes from the vision imparted to our spirit. This content is the Spirit's declaration and becomes our spirit's commitment. The testimony that the

Spirit and our spirit bear together is borne with the attitude and persistence of a martyr. Paul expressed this spirit of a martyr when he said, "I am ready not only to be bound, but even to die at Jerusalem for the name of the Lord Jesus" (Acts 20:13). What a witness! This is the strong testimony and commitment that becomes reality in our mingled spirit.

116 | Heirs, God's Heirs, and Fellow Heirs with Christ

The Spirit Himself testifies with our spirit that we are children of God, ¹⁷and if children, heirs also, heirs of God and fellow heirs with Christ, if indeed we suffer with Him so that we may also be glorified with Him.

—Romans 8:16–17

WORD STUDY

Used three times in Romans 8:17, the word "heirs" is a translation of the Greek word *klēronomos*, which means "an inheritor, by implication a possessor" (Strong, #2818). In verse 17, this position of an heir of God is directly linked to being a child of God and is even confirmed by such a status (if children, heirs also). It is God's children who are heirs of their Father's wealth and home (Morgan, 121).

The Greek word for "fellow heirs," *sugklēronomos*, is created by adding the Greek prefix *sun* to *klēronomos*. When used as a prefix, *sun* denotes association, community, fellowship, and participation. In this sense, "together" is a good translation of the word, indicating "several persons or things united or all in one" (Thayer, 599). The stress of this word sets forth the New Testament view that the redeemed saints are equal to Christ as regards the inheritance, and His possessions are theirs (Alford, 2:392–393). This is truly a wonderful truth regarding the children of God.

REVELATION AND APPLICATION

There are three main points in Romans 8:16–17 concerning our being heirs of God: our identity, status, and experience. Our identity is that we are the children of God (v. 16), our status is that we are fellow heirs with Christ (v. 17a), and our experience is that we suffer and will be glorified with Christ (v. 17b).

In our experience of the process of glorification, we are brought to a wonderful position as heirs—we are heirs of God and fellow heirs with Christ! The word "heir" appears three times in verse 17. First, we are heirs if we are children. Second, we are God's heirs. Third, we are fellow heirs with Christ.

If Children, Heirs Also

An heir is a legal inheritor. This term becomes precious when we consider it within the context of our relationship with God. We are God's legal inheritors and will inherit all His riches. These riches include God Himself and everything He possesses. Our position as legal heirs is an unchangeable fact.

The phrase "if children, heirs also" (Rom. 8:17) shows that this inheritance occurs because we have the divine life in us. It is not only judicial and legal but also organic. Unlike the many legal heirs in the world today who inherit the possessions of a deceased person, as children of God, we become heirs of the living God in the divine life. In this life, we enjoy God, apply Him, and receive a never-ending spiritual supply from Him.

Heirs of God

As heirs of God, we are God's inheritors! But what will we inherit? Many Christians would say we will inherit heaven. A general Christian thought of heaven is a place where God's power and wisdom unite to form a perfect physical realm. Is there really such a place? This understanding of heaven is based on the description of the New Jerusalem (see Rev. 21). God's relationship with us, however, is not focused on physical things but on the divine life. As God's heirs, we will organically inherit everything that is His. When we fully gain this inheritance, the result will not be to live in a physical realm in the clouds, but it will be our enjoyment of "the freedom of the glory of the children of God" (Rom. 8:21). Just as God is glorious, we will be given the same glory and will testify of this glory for eternity. This is our glorious hope!

Fellow Heirs with Christ

The divine life has been given to us, making us children of God (John 1:12). Since we are children, we are heirs. Yet we are not common heirs but heirs of God! As God's heirs, we will be given the same glory and will testify of this glory for eternity. Even more, we are fellow heirs with Christ. We will be incorporated with Christ in His person, and we will be glorified together with Him as fellow heirs (Rom. 8:17).

Our incorporation with Christ makes us like Him. We will want, think, and seek what Christ wants, thinks, and seeks. Oh, praise the Lord for this! We not only have the divine life and a glorious hope, but we also have Christ as our person so that we would become fellow heirs with Him!

Paul's burden in verse 17 is totally focused on the word "heirs" and is expressed in three phrases related to life, glory, and incorporation. We are the children of God—this is related to life. We are heirs of God and will manifest and testify of God's glory—this is our hope of glory. We will be fellow heirs with Christ—this is related to our incorporation with Christ in His person.

117

Glorified with Christ

And if children, heirs also, heirs of God and fellow heirs with Christ, if indeed we suffer with Him so that we may also be glorified with Him.

—*Romans 8:17*

WORD STUDY

At the end of Romans 8:17 is the phrase, "glorified with Him," translated from the Greek word *sundoxazō*, which is a combination of the Greek words *sun* and *doxazō*. *Doxazō* means "to render glorious" and can be translated, "to glorify, honor, magnify" (Strong, #1392). In discussing "glory," W. E. Vine translates *doxazō*, "to magnify, extol, praise, honor, make glorious." He says, "[Glory] is used of the nature and acts of God in self-manifestation, i.e., what He essentially is and does, as exhibited in whatever way He reveals Himself in these respects....The glory of God is the revelation and manifestation of all that He has and is" (Vine, 267).

When used as a prefix, *sun* denotes association, community, fellowship, and participation. In this sense, "together" is a good translation of the word, indicating "several persons or things united or all in one" (Thayer, 599). *Sundoxazō* does not point to a personal experience, but to a corporate glorification, an exaltation to the same glory to which Christ has been raised (Thayer, 602).

REVELATION AND APPLICATION

Glory: The Manifestation of God

In Romans 8:17-27, Paul talks about our suffering and glorification with Christ as our experience of the process of glorification. It is interesting that Paul puts suffering and glory together. Such a combination runs contrary to the thought many people have of glory, but the Biblical picture is that the more suffering there is, the more glory there will be. The more we experience suffering with Christ, the more we may be glorified with Him.

To be glorified with Christ, we must suffer with Him. According to position, we are heirs, God's heirs, and fellow heirs with Christ. According to experience, however, we must pass through suffering to be glorified with Christ.

What is glory? When people think of glory, they may imagine a white light shining forth, so bright that people fall to the ground as it shines on them. However, this is not what glory really is. Glory is the manifestation of God Himself. Glory comes when the God of glory is revealed.

No person has ever seen God (John 1:18), but many believers can testify today that when they pray, read the Bible, meet with the saints, or listen to Bible messages, they touch the Lord with their spirit and meet Him in a substantial way, giving them a glorious feeling. Such a feeling comes from glory—God manifesting Himself to them.

The Process of Glorification

Glorification is a process. We accumulate glory every time we meet, experience, and gain God. Then, as we gain God and accumulate glory again and again, our experience of this process deepens.

Paul told the Corinthians, "We all, with unveiled face, beholding as in a mirror the glory of the Lord, are being transformed into the same image from glory to glory, just as from the Lord, the Spirit" (2 Cor. 3:18). The process of glorification is found in this verse: "with unveiled face, beholding as in a mirror the glory of the Lord." We are looking into a mirror which is reflecting the glory of the Lord. As we gaze into the mirror, we allow the Lord to shine upon us. Whenever we behold the Lord in the mirror, He is reflected to us, and we are transformed into the image of the Lord. This is "from glory"—the glory of the Lord—"to glory"—the glory manifested from us.

The Accumulation of Glory

Glory is God revealed and manifested. As believers meet God, experience Him, and gain more of Him time after time, they accumulate glory (see 2 Cor. 3:18). The manifestation of glory from us is not a miracle that instantly happens. It is impossible for a drunkard or a gambler to manifest God's glory in a moment. Manifested glory comes from daily accumulations. The little glory we accumulate today, tomorrow, and the next day eventually becomes the glory that is manifested in the day of the Lord's coming (2 Thess. 1:10).

There was a brother who left his job to spend a full year studying and learning the Bible with other believers. In the beginning, he had very little facial expression, but after a few months, he was different. He not only carried a joyful smile wherever he went, but also became quite capable of speaking for the Lord! This was evidence that he had accumulated some of the glory of God.

Do not look down on our pursuing of God today. Whenever we pray, come to the Lord, obey Him, or contact Him, we are accumulating more glory. As we allow God to add Himself more and more to us, we are actually allowing glory to accumulate in us. One day, when the Lord returns, the glory of God will radiate from us. This manifested glory will be the result of all the glory we have accumulated over the days, months, and years we have followed Christ.

Following the Lord is very romantic. Someone once asked an older brother if there was anything that brought him joy after so many years of following the Lord. His answer showed the romantic side of such a life. He said, "Outwardly speaking, there are not many things that cause me to be joyful. On the contrary, there are many things that bring a great deal of pressure to me. I dare not say that I have lost hope of living, but many times I do not know how to go on. However, there is one thing I have that brings joy to me, whether in the morning or evening: by the Lord's mercy, I have accumulated some glory of God every day, and I believe this accumulation will be the capital for the glory of God to be manifested from me in the day of His appearing. This brings me great joy."

Awaiting Glorification

The glorification spoken of by Paul in Romans 8:17 is a glorification with Christ. On the one hand, Christ has entered His glory in resurrection (Luke 24:26). On the other hand, He is waiting to be glorified with us.

Today He is the glorious and heavenly Christ, reigning over all things. He also continually dispenses Himself into us and sovereignly measures out to us all kinds of outward environments, including suffering, to the point that we can be glorified with Him. This glorification is echoed in Paul's second letter to the church in Thessalonica: "When He comes to be glorified in His saints on that day, and to be marveled at among all who have believed" (2 Thess. 1:10).

Christ is patiently waiting for His glorification in us on the day of His return. We have nothing to boast about regarding ourselves outwardly, and our outward man is indeed decaying. By the Lord's mercy, however, He lives in us, and our inner man is being renewed day by day (2 Cor. 4:16). Our outward man is decaying, yet the Lord would say, "I, the glorified Christ, will be glorified in and through you, and My glory will radiate from you."

It is when Christ is glorified in us that we can be glorified with Him. The one to be glorified is Christ, not us. We have nothing worthy of glory from ourselves. We do nothing but offend, disobey, and displease God. However, the wonderful thing is that He repeatedly gives us opportunities to come close to Him, contact Him, experience Him, enjoy Him, and gain Him. Through God's mercy and grace, He will one day be glorified in us—a people who have only failed, sinned, offended, and fallen. That moment of glorification, when we are glorified together with Christ, will be a most sweet and wonderful moment.

118

The Revealing of the Sons of God

For I consider that the sufferings of this present time are not worthy to be compared with the glory that is to be revealed to us. ¹⁹For the anxious longing of the creation waits eagerly for the revealing of the sons of God. ²⁰For the creation was subjected to futility, not willingly, but because of Him who subjected it, in hope ²¹that the creation itself also will be set free from its slavery to corruption into the freedom of the glory of the children of God. ²²For we know that the whole creation groans and suffers the pains of childbirth together until now.
—Romans 8:18-22

WORD STUDY

In Romans 8, the word "reveal" is used in both verses 18 and 19. First, the present sufferings are not worthy to be compared with the glory that is to be revealed (*apokaluptō*) to us. Second, all creation is waiting for the revealing (*apokalupsis*) of the sons of God. The first "reveal" is a verb, and the second is a noun. The Greek root is composed of two words: *apo*, meaning "off" (Strong, #575), and *kaluptō*, meaning "to cover, hide" (Strong, #2572). *Apokaluptō* literally means "to take off the cover" (Strong, #601) or "to uncover or unveil" (Vine, 532), and the noun form can be translated "revelation" (Strong, #602). Thus, there will be a revelation of glory to us and a revelation of the sons of God to the whole creation.

Scholars and commentators debate over the use of "creation" in this passage. Although various interpreters limit the word in different ways, there is no obvious reason to exclude any part of creation from Paul's meaning, animate or inanimate. It is safe to take the word in the sense of the whole creation, which includes all nature—the animals and plants. This is not surprising in light of other Bible passages, such as Isaiah 11:1–10, 2 Peter 3:13, and Revelation 21:1–7 (Alford, 2:393–394).

The Greek word used in Romans 8:19 for "anxious longing," *apekduomai*, indicates an eager watching with an outstretched head. This word, strengthened by the prefix *apo*, "denotes diversion from all other things and concentration on a single object and indicates a patient waiting" (Rogers, 330). This anxious longing of creation is for the revelation of the sons of God because even creation itself will enter into the freedom of the glory of the children of God (v. 21). In this way, freedom is described as a component of the glorified state of the children of God. Freedom belongs to glory (Alford, 2:395). This glorious state will arrive at the end of time, when the kingdom of God is manifested on the earth (Rev. 11:15–19, 21:21–26).

REVELATION AND APPLICATION

Suffering and Being Glorified

The first section regarding glorification in Romans 8 (vv. 14–17) provides necessary knowledge about our being glorified with Christ: our identity as children of God, our status as fellow heirs with Christ, and our experience of suffering leading to glorification with Christ.

This experience of suffering and being glorified with Christ is the major experience of this section (vv. 18–27) and has three aspects. The first aspect is that it is under God's sovereignty. A realization of this aspect allows for the reality of verse 18 to become ours: "For I consider that the sufferings of this present time are not worthy to be compared with the glory that is to be revealed to us." The second aspect involves the divine dispensing of the Spirit (vv. 23-25), and the third involves the divine operation (vv. 26-27). In this chapter, we will consider the first aspect of our experience of suffering and glorification—God's sovereignty.

The Proper Attitude Regarding Suffering

Romans 8:18 says, "For I consider that the sufferings of this present time are not worthy to be compared with the glory that is to be revealed to us." The word "consider" is the same Greek word used in Romans 6:11 for "reckon." It literally means "to take an inventory" and can be translated "to count, take account of, reason, reckon" (Strong, #3049). Like using a balance sheet, we should take account of our sufferings today and consider the glory to come. If we do such counting, we will find that our current sufferings cannot be compared to the glory to be revealed to us in the future. The grief and sorrow of today are nothing when compared with the glory in that day.

On one hand, there should be a consideration of the future—that the sufferings of the present time are not worthy to be compared with the glory that will be revealed to us. On the other hand, the suffering we have today under God's divine and sovereign hand is for us to receive more glory today. Glorification is a process of the growth of life which continues each day. Without sufferings, it is very hard for life to grow and develop. It has been said that it is in times of stress and hardship that trees develop deeper roots. We do not need to ask God to give us sufferings, but when hard environments come, we should learn to welcome them. James and Peter wrote such things in their epistles:

> Consider it all joy, my brethren, when you encounter various trials, knowing that the testing of your faith produces endurance. (James 1:2-3)

> In this you greatly rejoice, even though now for a little while, if necessary, you have been distressed by various trials, so that the proof of your faith, being more precious than gold which is perishable, even though tested by fire, may be found to result in praise and glory and honor at the revelation of Jesus Christ. (1 Peter 1:6-7)

God is sovereign; He knows our needs and will perfectly measure out to us many different environments to further gain and constitute glory in us. Such a measuring out is according to His good pleasure. As we are in the midst of our current sufferings, we should remember that they are not worthy to be compared with the glory that will be revealed to us.

Revelation, Glory, Attraction, and Following

Glory comes from revelation and is the manifestation of God Himself. Romans 8:18 says that glory will be revealed to us in the future. Yet as God manifests or reveals Himself to us today, we gain more glory.

The appearing of God is revelation. When Abraham lived in Mesopotamia, the God of glory appeared to him (Acts 7:2), revealing Himself to Abraham. Every appearance of God to us is a revelation. Each revelation brings glory to us, attracts us, and draws us to follow the Lord. These four things compose a cycle in our Christian life: revelation, glory, attraction, and following.

Every revelation of God reveals glory to us. This will attract us to God. As we are attracted to Him, we will follow Him. As we follow the Lord, we will be brought to higher revelations and further glory, attraction, and following. This cycle is very normal. When God reveals Himself to us, glory, attraction, and following are automatically produced. Eventually, this leads to even higher revelations.

Why do some Christians feel so tired as they follow the Lord? It is because their revelation is not sufficient, and the glory they have seen so far is not enough to sustain them. If Christians feel it is too hard to follow the Lord, it shows that their relationship with the Lord is not healthy or intimate enough. Without the revelation of the Lord, we cannot be attracted to Him or follow Him. When we lack intimacy with the Lord, this leads to insufficient revelation and glory.

Sometimes we feel that following the Lord is hard and stressful. However, as soon as our revelation is clear and we see that the Lord is so good and glorious, we are willing to drop everything to follow Him. We should pray, "Lord, please reveal Yourself to me more and more, that I may gain even more of Your glory. Please attract me unceasingly, absolutely, and so deeply that I have no choice but to follow You. As I follow You, Lord, grant higher revelations and more glory."

Revelation produces glory, glory produces attraction, attraction produces following, and following produces more and higher revelations. This is a healthy and normal process. Yet, it does require something—the price of obedience, just as in Abraham's time. If we receive a revelation that attracts us to the Lord, yet we do not actively follow Him, this revelation will soon disappear. Once this revelation is gone, our vision and commitment will not be as clear as before. Unless we are willing to pay a price to follow the Lord according to the revelation we have seen, it is very hard for the Lord to lead us to experience glorification in a deeper way. In the process of glorification, we should not fail to notice, obey, and pay a price for any revelation of the Lord.

The Revelation of Glory

Romans 8:19 says, "For the anxious longing of the creation waits eagerly for the revealing of the sons of God." Creation is eagerly waiting for the revelation of the sons of God. Glory is not only incomparable to our present sufferings, but it will also be revealed by the sons of God in the future.

Verses 18 and 19 provide us with two steps of revelation. The first step is the revelation of glory to us. God reveals Himself to us and becomes the glory revealed to us. The second step is the revelation of the sons of God to creation. We, the sons of God, will be a revelation of God's glory to all creation. God is revealed to us today, and we will be revealed to all things in the future. God is our revelation today for the sake of making us a revelation one day to the whole creation.

The revealing of God to us is continual and ever greater, higher, and richer. It will produce in us the reality of the glorious revelation all creation is waiting for. This process does not happen overnight. It is an accumulation in us through many months and years, and it is the result of our faithful daily following of God. This is the glory that the sufferings of this present time are not worthy to be compared with, and it is the glory for which all creation is eagerly waiting.

The Eager Waiting of Creation

Because the glory in us has not been revealed yet, the entire creation is "subjected to futility" (Rom. 8:20) and "groans and suffers the pains of childbirth together until now" (v. 22). Today, all plants, beasts, birds, fish, and insects groan and suffer together in the hope that the glory of God might one day be revealed through the sons of God.

Creation's subjection to futility is the result of the curse that came from man's fall (Gen. 3:17). Man's fall brought about a curse of bondage, and all creation is enslaved under the bondage of corruption. Consider even grapes and oranges. One grape may be very sweet and another very sour. One orange may be very sweet, but another may be very sour. Why are some grapes sour, and why are oranges not all sweet? It is because they are under a curse. If there were no curse, every grape and orange would be sweet and delicious.

The creation did not willingly subject itself to futility, and it desires to come out from under its slavery to corruption. How can this happen? It is through us, the sons of God, becoming a glorious revelation to the entire creation. We become this glorious revelation by constantly seeing God's glory and allowing this glory to be added to us. By this process, all creation will one day be released from the curse.

Right now, all creation is eagerly waiting with anxious longing for the revelation of the sons of God so that it may be delivered. We should not criticize the creation for its subjection to corruption. If we could talk with grapes, we might accuse them for being so sour. But the grapes would say back to us, "I am not a sour grape because I want to be, but because you are not living up to expectations! I am a sour grape today because you are a sour Christian!" If we live in revelation and allow revelation to restrict us, attract us, and lead us, one day grapes will no longer be sour. All creation will be released from its slavery to corruption when the glory of God is revealed through us!

The Freedom of the Glory

The entire creation is waiting for us today. The flowers, trees, beasts, birds, fish, and insects are all eagerly awaiting the revelation of the sons of God. In that day, all the roses and lions will thank us for loving the Lord with our whole heart, pursuing Him earnestly, continually receiving revelation, and eventually becoming a glorious revelation.

When the sons of God are revealed to all creation, the age of God's kingdom will have arrived. At that time, the wolf will dwell with the lamb, the leopard will lie down with the young goat, the calf and the young lion and the fatling will be together, and a little child shall lead them. The cow and the bear will graze, their young ones will lie down together, and the lion will eat straw like the ox (Isa. 11:6–7). What a sweet picture this is! Today the grapevines are waiting with an expectation: "My fruit will be ever sweet one day!" The tigers are also waiting with the expectation: "I will not hurt men or hunt for animals one day. I will be released from the bondage of corruption when the age of the kingdom has come!"

One day, the sons of God will be revealed and glorified, and they will usher in a realm of glory in which there is freedom. At that time, all creation will be released from the curse and enjoy "the freedom of the glory of the children of God" (Rom. 8:21). The creation itself does not have glory, because only the manifestation of God is glorious. However, the children of God will enter into glory one day and bring in a glorious kingdom. Even if the creation itself does not have glory, it can still enter into the realm of the glory of the sons of God where it will be revived and released.

In that day, all the flowers, grasses, trees, beasts, birds in the air, and fish in the sea will be revived in the realm of the glory of the sons of God. At that time, a pear will say, "I am free. I can be as sweet as you want!" A flower will say, "I am free! I can be as beautiful as you want." A deer will say, "I am free! I can leap as much as you want!" The entire creation will shout, "We are free! We have been set free from the bondage of corruption!"

The Glorious Kingdom of Freedom

Glory is the realm and domain of the kingdom of God. Freedom is what we experience in this realm. In such a glorious kingdom, the children of God testify of the glory of God and enjoy and experience the freedom found in the person of Christ. What a result of Romans 8:17! If we suffer with Christ, we will be glorified together with Him. At the moment of our being glorified with Him, we will enjoy Him and all that He has. We will never be separated from Christ, because we will be fully incorporated with Him in person.

In such a glorious kingdom filled with freedom, there is no futility, groaning, slavery to corruption, or pains of childbirth. Today we have all of these things. In that day, there will be only the glory testified of by the children of God and the freedom enjoyed by us through our incorporation with Christ. When the creation sees us, it will see glory and freedom. This glory is not our own but is the glory of God, and it will shine from us because of our incorporation with the person of Christ. This is what creation will see!

Oh, what a picture this is! No one can tell how wonderful it will be when the myriads of saved saints are constituted to be the glorious kingdom of freedom! Every child of God will manifest the radiant glory of God and enjoy the freedom of this glory. No matter how much suffering we experience today, it is not worthy to be compared to the glory in that day. Oh, how good, beautiful, transcendent, and heavenly such a revelation of glory will be!

119

The First Fruits

And not only this, but also we ourselves, having the first fruits of the Spirit, even we ourselves groan within ourselves, waiting eagerly for our adoption as sons, the redemption of our body.
—*Romans 8:23*

WORD STUDY

The Greek word used in Romans 8:23 for "first fruits," *aparchē*, primarily denotes the first portion of the harvest, which was offered to God (Thayer, 54; see Lev. 23:9). This portion was regarded both as a first installment and as a pledge of the final delivery of the entire harvest (Rogers, 331). *Aparchē* is also used in the Bible to describe Christ (1 Cor. 15:23) and His believers (Rom. 16:5, Rev. 14:4) (Vine, 241). The genitive phrase in this verse, "of the Spirit," indicates that the Holy Spirit is a pledge to those who have Him that they will be saved in the end. Thus, the Spirit is seen as an anticipation, or foretaste, of our final salvation (Rogers, 331).

REVELATION AND APPLICATION

The experience of suffering and being glorified with Christ

has three aspects. First, it is under God's sovereignty; this was considered in the previous chapter. Second, in our experience of glorification with Christ, we experience God's compete salvation in the dispensing of His Spirit (Rom. 8:23-25). The third aspect involves the divine operation and will be covered in chapter 121. We will consider the second aspect in this chapter.

Our Organic Model

We have the first fruits of the Spirit (Rom. 8:23). This phrase does not indicate that the Spirit has the first fruits, but that He is the first fruits. This verse assures us that even as we are inwardly groaning, we have the Spirit. We have a hope—our "adoption as sons," or sonship.

"First fruits" is a very important term in the Bible, used by God to indicate a particular principle of growth. The first fruits were the first stalks of mature grain harvested and offered to God. This grain was the beginning of the harvest, a model the rest of the harvest would match as it matured. Thus, the principle of the first fruits is that there is an organic pattern for the rest of the harvest to be modeled after as it matures. Spiritually, Christ is the first fruits of the new creation (1 Cor. 15:23), and in Him is the new creation (2 Cor. 5:17).

Christ is the first mature One in the new creation. All the believers in the new creation will eventually become like Him. The apostle John wrote, "Beloved, now we are children of God, and it has not appeared as yet what we will be. We know that when He appears, we will be like Him, because we will see Him just as He is" (1 John 3:2). One day we will be like the Lord. He is the first fruits, the organic model for us to match in that day of His coming.

The Spirit as Our Foretaste

Christ is not only the first fruits of the new creation, but He also became the life-giving Spirit (1 Cor. 15:45). Now in our spirit, He is our foretaste of God's full salvation and of our full enjoyment of God.

If someone asks us if we have gained, experienced, and enjoyed Christ, we should say, "Yes." If someone asks if we have completely gained, experienced, and enjoyed Christ, we should say, "Not yet, but I have the foretaste of the Spirit!" Today we have the Spirit as the first fruits, but because we only have a foretaste, we can joyfully look forward to much more gaining, experiencing, and enjoying of Christ.

The Progression of First Fruits

The book of Revelation describes a special group of 144,000 people who are first fruits unto God and the Lamb.

> *And they sang a new song before the throne and before the four living creatures and the elders; and no one could learn the song except the one hundred and forty-four thousand who had been purchased from the earth. These are the ones who have not been defiled with women, for they have kept themselves chaste. These are the ones who follow the Lamb wherever He goes. These have been purchased from among men as first fruits to God and to the Lamb. And no lie was found in their mouth; they are blameless. (Revelation 14:3–5)*

Yet even all the saints are considered "a kind of first fruits," as James writes in his epistle:

> *In the exercise of His will He brought us forth by the word of truth, so that we would be a kind of first fruits among His creatures. (James 1:18)*

Putting all of these verses together, we can say that there is a sequence of first fruits. First, Christ became the first fruits of the new creation. Second, the resurrected Christ became the life-giving Spirit, who in our spirit is the first fruits of full salvation, a foretaste for us. Third, the 144,000 are first fruits to God from among the saints. Finally, all the saints are a kind of first fruits among God's creatures. By God's dispensing of life through His Spirit, we are brought into this progression of first fruits. Now all creation is waiting for us, the first fruits, to be manifested and revealed.

120

The Redemption of Our Body

And not only this, but also we ourselves, having the first fruits of the Spirit, even we ourselves groan within ourselves, waiting eagerly for our adoption as sons, the redemption of our body. ²⁴For in hope we have been saved, but hope that is seen is not hope; for who hopes for what he already sees? ²⁵But if we hope for what we do not see, with perseverance we wait eagerly for it.
—Romans 8:23-25

WORD STUDY

The Greek word used for "adoption" in Romans 8:23, *huiothesia*, is the same word found in 8:15: "you have received a spirit of adoption." This word can literally be translated, "the placing of one in the position of a son" (Vincent, 3:91). Verse 15 shows that we have already received the spirit of adoption, or, sonship. However, here in verse 23, adoption is something we are waiting for and is linked to the redemption of our body. H. Alford writes, "Our adoption is come already (v. 15), so that we do not wait for it, but for the full manifestation of it, in our bodies being rescued from the bondage of corruption and sin" (Alford, 2:395).

The "redemption" of our body in verse 23 can be thought of as a release, a deliverance from all the negative things inherited in our flesh. This redemption is the final and complete deliverance of our earthly bodies (Rogers, 331).

REVELATION AND APPLICATION

The first aspect of our suffering and being glorified with Christ is the aspect of God's sovereignty. The second aspect involves the dispensing of the life-giving Spirit to us, who is our foretaste of the full enjoyment of God. Although we have this foretaste, joy, and satisfaction in our spirit, we also have an outward body that is mortal, corrupted, and limited. This causes us to groan inwardly and wait eagerly for our sonship, the redemption of our body. A person experiencing the process of glorification is a groaning person. However, our groaning is actually full of the hope that our body will soon be redeemed.

The Process unto Full Sonship

According to Romans 8:23, the redemption of our body and our adoption as sons, or sonship, are the same thing. Waiting eagerly for sonship is the same as waiting eagerly for the redemption of our body. This redemption of our body is the fullness of sonship. Sonship will not instantly happen to us. Instead, we must pass through a process of becoming full sons of God. This process begins with the regeneration of our spirit, continues with the transformation of our soul, and ends with the redemption of our body, which is our glorification.

In Romans, Paul gives three steps of this process of salvation. The first step is our justification in Christ by faith in Him, thus becoming children and sons of God (3:24-26; see also Gal. 3:26). The second step is God's sanctifying and leading us in the Spirit of life, in order that we would grow unto the reality of sonship (Rom. 8:2, 14). The final step is

God's glorifying us in the Spirit which brings us unto the fullness of sonship, the redemption of our body (vv. 17, 23).

A Redeemed Body

It may surprise us to think that our body is related to God's complete salvation, but this is absolutely the case! In following the Lord, our greatest frustrations, limitations, and hindrances come from our body. Within our body dwells sin and the sinful nature (Rom. 7:17-24). Our body has all kinds of limitations and is continually decaying (2 Cor. 4:16). Our fallen body prevents us from completely manifesting the glory of God while we follow the Lord.

Our body is sinful, perishable, and mortal (1 Cor. 15:53). However, one day when this sinful, limited, and destructible body is redeemed, we will obtain full sonship. In that day, all the limitations of the body will be no more. There will be no more pain, no more tears, and no more exhaustion, since our whole person—spirit, soul, and body—will enter the unending, eternal glory of God.

Even more, the Lord will transform our lowly body and conform it to His glorious body, according to "the power that He has even to subject all things to Himself" (Phil. 3:21). It is wonderful that God is so concerned with our body! His salvation is truly a full salvation! It is a glorious salvation that He has both accomplished and will reveal in a day to come. This salvation will be full and complete when our body has been redeemed and our sonship fully gained.

121

The Help of the Spirit

In the same way the Spirit also helps our weakness; for we do not know how to pray as we should, but the Spirit Himself intercedes for us with groanings too deep for words.
—Romans 8:26

WORD STUDY

In Romans 8:26, the Greek word translated "helps," *sunantilambanomai*, is composed of three Greek words:

1. *sun*, meaning "with or together" (Strong, #4862),
2. *anti*, denoting contrast, substitution, or correspondence (Strong, #473), and
3. *lambanō*, meaning "to take, accept, obtain" (Strong, #2983).

Together they mean "to lend a hand together with, to help, to come to the aid of someone" (Rogers, 331). This means that in this verse, the Spirit is not presented as the One to bear our weakness *for* us, or even the One who lifts our burdens *from* us. Rather, this verse indicates that the Spirit is the One who is *with* us who are weak in order to help us bear the burden of verse 23—the inward groaning (Alford, 2:397).

REVELATION AND APPLICATION

As we experience the process of being glorified with Christ, we will suffer in order that we may be glorified. This experience has three aspects. The first aspect is that these sufferings are under the sovereignty of our triune God. Seeing this allows us to welcome our present sufferings in the hope of the coming revelation of glory (Rom. 8:17-18). The second aspect is our experience of complete salvation by the dispensing of the triune God into us through the Spirit. This will one day result in the redemption of our body, at which time we will possess full sonship (v. 23). In the third aspect, covered in this chapter, we have the Spirit of God. Through the Spirit, God operates to help us bear our weakness, interceding for us with groanings too deep for words (v. 26).

Working Together with the Spirit

The word "help" in Greek conveys the thought of mutual gaining, holding, or possessing. From the side of our experience, to say that the Spirit helps us means that we hold, possess, gain, and win the sonship together with the Spirit.

The Spirit does not need to obtain sonship for Himself. Rather, He intercedes for us in order that we would gain full sonship. The Spirit is striving together with us to gain our sonship. On one hand, we obtain and grasp our sonship; on the other hand, the Spirit obtains and holds it with us. There is a mutuality produced. As the Spirit obtains more of the sonship for us, we obtain it. As we obtain more, the Spirit helps us further. Each side works together to effectively gain and possess the full sonship for us, the children of God.

The Spirit Matching Our Desire

In chapter 114, we saw that *lambanō* can indicate obtaining or possessing through the process of paying a price (see Phil. 3:8–12). In our experience, to whatever degree we are willing to pay a price, the Spirit is also willing to pay that price for us to obtain the full sonship of God.

The Spirit is willing to be limited by our desire. He never desires less than we do, but He helps us exactly where we are in our weakness. As our desire grows, the Spirit matches that desire and is eager to help us grow more, all the way unto the day of the redemption of our body. When our desire is to gain the best, to experience God's complete salvation, and to speed the day of the redemption of our body, the Spirit also has such a desire for us and will help us unto that end. Hallelujah that we have the Spirit of God to help us in such a way!

122

Groanings Too Deep for Words

In the same way the Spirit also helps our weakness; for we do not know how to pray as we should, but the Spirit Himself intercedes for us with groanings too deep for words; ²⁷and He who searches the hearts knows what the mind of the Spirit is, because He intercedes for the saints according to the will of God.

—Romans 8:26-27

WORD STUDY

Romans 8:26 says that the Spirit intercedes for us with "groanings too deep for words." The Greek word used here for "groanings" is *stenagmos*, which means "a sigh" (Strong, #4726). The verb form, *stenazō*, means "to make or be in straits, i.e. (by implication) to sigh, murmur, or pray inaudibly" (Strong, #4727). *Stenazō* is used to indicate an inward, unexpressed feeling of sorrow (Vine, 282). These groanings by the Spirit are too deep for human words, meaning they are unable to be spoken out (Rogers, 331). However, God understands them because He knows the mind of the Spirit, whose intercession is not according to the will of man but according to the will of God (Alford, 2:397).

REVELATION AND APPLICATION

A Universal Groaning

In Romans 8, the apostle Paul mentions "groaning" three times. All of creation is groaning (v. 22), we are groaning (v. 23), and even the Spirit is groaning (v. 26). In our experience, all of these groanings are "too deep for words."

According to these few verses, it seems that the whole universe is groaning! Such a universal groaning is because our body has not yet been redeemed, and we have not yet fully received our sonship. The whole creation seems to cry out, "Oh! If only you Christians could mature faster!" We who have the Spirit as the first fruits also groan inwardly, "Lord, it is so sweet to taste You, yet when will I have the full enjoyment of You?" The Spirit also groans for us, "Oh that they would grow more and become more mature!"

The whole creation groans because of its "slavery to corruption" (vv. 21–22). We who have tasted the Spirit as the first fruits also groan inwardly, but our groaning is because of our hope for the full enjoyment of sonship (v. 23). The Spirit helps us, bears us who are weak, and intercedes for us with groanings according to God's will (vv. 26–27). The whole universe is filled with groanings and will be until our body is redeemed.

The Reason for Groaning

Groaning is our response when we feel there is no alternative to or way around a dire situation. Do we groan when we are joyful? Do we groan when we have other options? When our future looks good, do we groan? What person groans after being admitted to Harvard University? Or what person groans after getting married, finding a job, or buying a house? Groaning comes when a husband and wife argue, when a person is fired, or when a house has a leaky roof. When we feel that the situation is so hard and that there is no other way, then we begin to groan.

The whole creation is groaning today because it feels there is no other way than slavery to corruption. The fruit trees groan, "I want all of my fruit to be sweet, but I cannot do it because I am under slavery to corruption. There is no other way for me." The lions groan, "Why should I eat meat? Yet I have no other way." Wolves also groan, "Why should I eat sheep? Yet I have no other way." All of creation is groaning today because it feels that it has no other way than slavery to corruption.

Just like all of creation, we who have the Spirit can sense our limitations, and this causes us to groan inwardly. On one hand, we have tasted both the Lord's grace and the Spirit as the first fruits, and we know how good and how rich our Lord is. On the other hand, our experience and foretaste of sonship are so limited. We yearn for a full enjoyment of Christ today, but because of our limitations, we have no way to enjoy such fullness. We can only groan as we have this sense that there is no other way.

To a certain degree, we can understand why we are groaning and why creation is groaning, but it is harder to understand why the Spirit is groaning. What is He even groaning for? His groaning is surely for people. He may see so many people talking about Christ, discussing Christ, and even preaching Christ, yet He also sees how short we come in truly handling Christ. The manifestation of Christ among us, our enjoyment of Christ, and our experience and application of Christ are all so small and limited. The Spirit may look at us and wonder, "When will they grow well? When will they reach full and mature sonship?" As One who knows God's heart's desire, all the Spirit can do is groan as He considers our situations and sees that there is no other way.

Groaning according to God's Will

All three parties mentioned in Romans 8:26-27 are groaning because God's children have not yet obtained full sonship. The groaning of the creation can be described as selfish groaning. Creation only hopes to be released one day from its slavery to corruption. Our groaning is somewhat different; it is not only for our own situation but also for the Lord. Our groaning is not for our sonship only but also for the full satisfaction of God.

The groaning of the Spirit, however, is different. The groaning of the Spirit is beyond our understanding. It is holy and heavenly, and it becomes His intercession for us. Paul did not simply say that the Spirit intercedes for us; rather, he said that the Spirit intercedes for us "with groanings too deep for words." Paul uses these words because groaning describes the feeling of the Spirit. It seems that even the Spirit is affected by the seemingly impossible situation we are in. It may seem that there is no way to deal with us, no way to help us, no way for us to grow, and no way for us to be more useful. All He can do is groan for us to be led according to the will of God.

Verse 26 relates the Spirit's groanings to our weakness. Though His intercession and groanings are related to our weakness, they are not according to our weakness. They are "according to the will of God" (v. 27), God's eternal purpose and economy.

The Spirit groans within us because we are so far from God's heart, need, will, and hope. These groanings are His intercession for us. As the Spirit intercedes, God, who searches the hearts, knows the mind of the Spirit. This is because the Spirit's groaning and interceding are according to the will of God. The Spirit does not groan simply because we are good or bad, but because He wants God to reach the goal He wants to reach, gain what He wants to gain, and testify what He wants to testify.

We need to learn to feel the support of the Spirit's groaning. No matter how many years we have loved, followed, and served the Lord, we still need the Spirit to intercede for us with groanings too deep for words. The groaning of the Spirit for a brother may be, "Oh God, discipline him! Strike him!" Or, it may be, "Support him! Strengthen him! Comfort him!" This kind of groaning for us becomes prayer and intercession on our behalf to bring us to the heart and economy of God.

A Secret for Spiritual Survival

Learning to groan is the most important thing to learn in a Christian's whole life and is the first secret for spiritual survival. The plants and animals groan; we must also learn to groan. We begin to groan when we consider who we are and how little we have matured spiritually. We may tell the Lord, "I have tasted Your sweetness, seen Your beauty, known Your value, and realized how glorious and free the future will be. Still, Lord, I have not grown well or learned much. I am still so soulish, so self-centered, so independent from You, and so unable to follow the Spirit. Lord, have mercy on me!" The more we groan in this way, the better and healthier our life will be before the Lord.

We should learn to groan in all situations. When we look at the work of the Holy Spirit among the churches and their situation today, we should groan. When we look at the sanctification experiences of the believers, we should groan. All our prayers may be groanings: "Lord, what can we do? How will Your churches go on? How will the saints go on? What will our situation become?"

Additionally, groaning is a way to admit our lack and need before the Lord. It is unwise to use words such as, "I know what to do," "I have decided what to do next," or "I know what the result will be in the future." Rather, we should groan,

"Lord! Have mercy on me!" Groaning to the Lord, whether regarding the church or simple matters of life, brings us to the presence of the Lord.

We must learn to groan. A Christian who is short of groaning is not healthy. Watchman Nee wrote a hymn in which he expressed the sensation that even on sunny days, thick clouds are always near. In other words, even in the best times there are thick clouds that restrict the Lord's shining upon us. One line of the hymn speaks of an inability to sing sweet songs or recite poetry. Yet the hymn concludes with the realization that such experiences and sensations force us to learn patience and to seek God's heart and pleasure. This process is full of groanings that bring us into the presence of the Lord and before His face.

A Lifelong Experience

Christians who do not love or pursue the Lord have very little to groan about. They may groan about their stock values decreasing or about a missed promotion, but these are only superficial groanings. Their real groaning will come at the Lord's second coming, when they exclaim, "Lord, why is my glory so small?" The Lord will answer them, "You did not love Me, pursue Me, or pay a price to buy from Me gold refined by fire. Therefore, you only have a little glory" (see 1 Cor. 15:41-42; Rev. 3:18).

A person who loves the Lord and pursues Him always groans in this life, "Lord! I have believed You, loved You, pursued You, and served You for so many years. I have participated in so many church meetings and have consecrated myself to You many times. Yet I am still the same as I ever was! Lord, I have not allowed You much room to work in me. I have so often limited Your manifestation through me, and I have given You so little satisfaction. Oh Lord, have mercy on me!"

A life of following the Lord is a life full of groaning. However, one day this groaning will cease—the day our body is redeemed and we fully receive our sonship. On that day all groanings will cease, whether they were uttered by us, by creation, or by the Spirit. In fact, the Spirit will no longer have any reason to groan in us! What peace that day will bring!

A Crucial Spiritual Practice

It is hard to believe how emphatically Paul talks about groaning in the midst of a section on glorification. This shows how crucial groaning is to our real experience of God's life. If we are not groaning, our spirituality is fake. We may know so much doctrine, but it is all theoretical if there is no response of groaning in us. We must pay attention to life and the matters of life. Spiritual things are not merely doctrinal but involve the experience of groaning before the Lord.

There is a very serious problem among Christians today. We talk about Christ, but are we actually filled with His life after talking so much about Him? We must be watchful and careful that we do not gain so much knowledge and doctrine yet lose the flow of His life within us.

If we desire to continually experience the life of God, we should learn to groan. By groaning, we can experience the Lord, enjoy Him, touch Him, abide in His presence, hear His speaking, and live before His face. By these experiences, we become full of life and spiritual health, and we can experience the deep intercession of the Spirit. Though seemingly basic, groaning to the Lord leads us into ever deeper experiences of glorification.

123

All Things Work Together for Good

And we know that God causes all things to work together for good to those who love God, to those who are called according to His purpose.
—*Romans 8:28*

WORD STUDY

In Romans 8:28, the Greek word translated "all things," *panta*, means "all, any, every, the whole" (Strong, #3956). The phrase "all things" is an accurate translation indicating every aspect of life, especially adverse events and circumstances (Alford, 2:397).

The Greek word translated "work together" is *sunergeō*, meaning "to be a fellow worker, i.e. co-operate; to work together" (Strong, #4903). The Greek prefix *sun* denotes association, community, fellowship, and participation, and indicates several things united or all at once (Thayer, 599). Thus, "all things" are seen as co-workers, working together as one unit for good to those who love God. This close cooperation is also seen in the fact that although *panta* ("all things") is a plural word, *sunergeō* ("work together") is singular.

As to the importance of this verse, Martin Luther wrote, "This passage is the foundation on which rests everything that the Apostle says to the end of the chapter; for he means to show that to the elect who are loved of God and who love God, the Holy Spirit makes all things work for good even though [these things may be] evil (in themselves)" (Luther, 128).

REVELATION AND APPLICATION

In our experience of the process of glorification, the Spirit intercedes for us "with groanings too deep for words" that are "according to the will of God" (Rom. 8:26–27). Verse 28 adds that all things are also working together for good to those who love God. The groanings and intercession of the Spirit, plus the working together of all things, bring us to a deeper and more subjective experience of glorification.

All Things

What are "all things" in Romans 8:28, and how many are "all"? When people read this verse, most will only think of all the things that happen to themselves. However, such a personal focus limits the phrase in our understanding, and it no longer means all things. We must realize that the Bible does not say here, "only the things that happen to you." The Bible clearly states that it is all things.

"All things" includes everything that exists, all events that take place, and every experience. To those who love God, all objects, all events, and all experiences are working together. This includes things like a church's meeting place, the community around it, and even the flowers, grass, and trees! Even a car works together with all other things. A car is a thing that exists, a car accident is an event, and there is an experience of this event. All of these things work together for good to those who love God.

All Things Work Together

In Greek, the noun translated "all things" in Romans 8:28 is plural, but the verb translated "work together" is singular. It could literally be translated as, "all things works together." This shows that from God's point of view, "all things" are working together as one entity, even though this entity is made up of many elements. There is nothing that exists, no event, and no experience that is alone or isolated.

If two people are talking to each other, one may say, "I was not very lucky yesterday." The other might reply, "Oh, I was very fortunate yesterday!" In God's view, there is nothing called "luck" or "fortune." All the people, things, and events we will face are a single entity working together for one purpose—"for good to those who love God." The things we pass through are not by chance or random.

We often feel discouraged over our failures, such as when we lose our temper. We may wonder why our anger bursts out so easily. It is because God allows us to be angry in order to give us an opportunity to repent, turn to Him, and rely on Him more. Through our anger, God is able to conform us more to the image of His Son. To be clear, God does not desire that we would sin. He hates sin, so He does not like when we are angry apart from Him. However, we should realize that even our failures, weaknesses, and insufficiencies are included in "all things."

The same is true in the church. Why are there so many disheartening situations in the church? Why are there so many bothersome saints? It is because we need them as part of the "all things" that work together for our good.

We must learn to trust God who is faithful and steadfast and who operates according to His own will. In order to carry out His heart's desire, He gives us all things. When we see things happening around us, whether positive or negative, we should feel totally assured before the Lord because all things are continually working together for good to us.

Working Together for Good

Romans 8:28 tells us that "all things work together for good to those who love God," but what is good? In the gospel of Mark, Jesus explained to a man what is good. The man came to the Lord Jesus and asked, "Good Teacher, what shall I do to inherit eternal life?" (10:17). The Lord answered him, "Why do you call Me good? No one is good except God alone" (v. 18). The Lord seemed to be saying, "If you want to call Me good, you must confess that I am God because God Himself is the only One who is good."

So what does "for good" mean? It means "for God and Christ." There is only one purpose for all things working together—to help us gain Christ Himself. There are no lucky or unlucky things for us. The purpose behind all things that happen to us is our gaining of Christ. When we consider the environments around us, we should realize they are for good to us—for us to gain more of Christ. With such an understanding, we can appreciate every environment and situation, and say with simplicity in each of them, "All things are working together for good to me because I love God."

The Experience of Those Who Love God

Nothing is more important than loving God. If we love Him, all things work for good to us. As long as we do not love Him, we will not obtain the good Romans 8:28 speaks of. Loving God allows all things to help us gain more of Christ for our growth, maturity, and stature in Him.

Those who do not love God will not experience the preciousness of this verse. Through all events and in all environments, we should learn to say, "Lord, I love You!" Even in the midst of our sufferings, we should still say, "Lord, I love You!" If we can learn to tell the Lord of our love for Him, we will realize that all things work together to cause us to gain more of Christ.

Those who love God always have the assurance that He is above every environment and is arranging all things for those who love Him. All Christians experience things measured by the Lord's hand and have experiences of strength, weakness, victory, and defeat. Yet, many Christians often receive nothing good from these experiences. They do not grow. Why is this? A major reason is that they have left their first love (Rev. 2:4).

Some Christians grow very well, even after following the Lord for three or four years. Others do not. Some Christians experience much growth and maturity by going through a hard environment. Others remain the same. Not everyone experiences the same things in life as others, but who has never suffered? Who has never felt troubled? Every believer has experiences of the "all things" in this verse. Why, then, do some Christians gain so little and change so little, while others grow? We can only say that some fall into the realm of judging their environments as "right and fair" or "wrong and unfair," while others maintain love for God in every kind of environment.

What It Means to Love God

Practically speaking, loving God means to focus on Him. It does not just mean having a certain feeling about Him; it means that our focus is on Him. Many people miss the good—the Christ—they could have gained through an environment or experience because their focus was not on God. Those who love God focus on Him because He is everything to them. Their desire, enjoyment, pursuit, and purpose are all directed toward and found in God.

If we focus on God, all things become our blessing. Why would we reason or complain? All things do nothing but cause us to love God more, live before Him more, see His blessing more, and become more related to His eternal will.

124

Those Whom He Predestined

*For those whom He foreknew, He also predestined to become conformed to the image of His Son, so that He would be the firstborn among many brethren; *³⁰*and these whom He predestined, He also called; and these whom He called, He also justified; and these whom He justified, He also glorified.*
—Romans 8:29–30

WORD STUDY

Within Romans 8:29–30 is a chain of actions that encompasses the entire process of God's full salvation. This chain starts with God's foreknowledge, indicating His awareness before time began of each person He would designate for salvation (Rogers, 331; Vincent, 3:95). Following God's foreknowledge is His predestination, followed by His calling, justification, and glorification. All of the Greek words for these actions are written in the aorist tense, which is a snapshot of the action taken (Wallace, 753). We can say that although it is carried out in time, God's plan of salvation was eternally decreed and has already been accomplished in His eyes. H. Alford wrote, "These persons, thus foreknown and predetermined, He, in the course of His providence…called, bringing them through justification to glory; and all of this is spoken of as past, because to Him who sees the end from the beginning—past, present, and future are not, but all is accomplished when determined" (Alford, 2:399).

The Greek word for "predestined," *proorizō*, is composed of two Greek words—*pro*, meaning "before, in front of" (Strong, #4253), and *horizō*, meaning, "to appoint, decree, specify" (Strong, #3724). *Proorizō* is a "pre-designation," which for God is based upon His foreknowledge (Vine, 482). This pre-designation leaves little room for "doubt that the sons of God will at last be conformed to the image of the Son," Jesus Christ, and is thus a great assurance of the "finality of glory" (Morgan, 132–133).

REVELATION AND APPLICATION

The Purpose of God's Great Plan

Romans 8:29 states with certainty that we will eventually be conformed to the image of the Son of God. This is the glorious end to the process of God's full salvation! Verses 29 and 30 give a wonderful summary of this section on glorification. God's foreknowledge, predestination, calling, and justification are for one purpose—that we might be glorified!

All of the verbs describing God's actions in these two verses are written in the aorist tense, showing us that God's plan—His foreknowledge, predestination, calling, justification, and glorification—has already been accomplished in His eyes. However, our experience of His plan is in the realm of time. It was before time that God knew us and predestined us according to His will, and in time that He called and justified us. God has also arranged all things to work together for good to those who love Him. This is so that we could be continually conformed to the image of the Son of God, that Christ might be the firstborn among many brothers, and that we might be glorified with His glory.

These two verses are so wonderful! Here is a chain that shows the unalterable will of God concerning us: that we would be glorified with Him!

Our Designation by God

God's actions in Romans 8:29 are both simple and profound. His foreknowing shows that God knew each individual person in His eternal will. The word for "predestined" in Greek means "to appoint or designate beforehand." In other words, God's pre-destination was a pre-designation. He not only foreknew us, but before we were born, He also designated us to be conformed to the image of His Son. Now, in time, we are experiencing and realizing that designation.

Designation (*horizō*) was also used in Romans 1, where it says that Christ "was declared," or designated, "the Son of God with power by the resurrection from the dead" (v. 4). Now this word appears again in chapter 8, this time in reference to us. Before we experienced anything, we were first foreknown and designated by God (v. 29). This designation was for us to be conformed to the image of His Son, Jesus Christ our Lord. We were not designated by God solely for a status or position but to be conformed to the image of a person. The outworking of this designation is organic and of life.

Christ is the organic seed of life with both divine nature and human virtue. This seed of life is now planted and hidden within our humanity. This seed puts to death all the negative elements of human life through the effective operation of the cross. By the power of resurrection, this seed revives and uplifts all the positive elements of human life.

Our experience of the power of resurrection matches the experience of the Lord Jesus in resurrection. Just as Jesus was designated in resurrection, our designation is realized through our experience of His resurrection life. Yet, this does not happen overnight. Rather, we experience this process over the course of our whole life.

The Lord Jesus went through resurrection to be designated. So also we who have been predestined by God will realize our designation by our experience of resurrection. The Lord Jesus was designated as the Son of God, and we have been predestined by God to be conformed to the image of the Son of God. This designation is the will of God.

Our High Value to God

Dear brothers and sisters, do you marvel that we were designated by God to be fully conformed to the image of His Son? We would probably say, "I am an unworthy person and unworthy of such designation." We may even feel, "Father, who am I before You? I am nothing but a worm without value. Like a worm, I live my entire life in a pile of earth. All I eat is of the earth, and all that comes out of me is earthly. My entire life is wasted in this world. Who am I, that You would designate me to bear the image of Your Son?"

We may be nothing but worms, but this is simply our own valuation of ourselves. God's plan and will are focused on man. We will be fully designated just as the Lord Jesus was. This is beyond what we would dare to dream. We can only say, "Lord, I am not worthy, able, or sufficient. But since You have predestined me, what can I say? I can only thank You and worship You. Your will and economy are truly magnificent."

God predestined us because of His desire that we would one day bear the image of His Son. This designation will be a testimony that will declare and represent God to the entire universe. One day, God will point to us and say to Satan, "Look! These are My glorious sons! They have been gained and formed by Me, and I declare today that they are fully My sons!"

When we look at ourselves today, we still feel, "Who am I? What do I have? What can I do? What can I boast of?" In one sense, this is true; we are nothing, have nothing, and cannot boast in anything of ourselves. Yet, God has predestined us, and He is able to bring us one day into the full realization of that designation!

In that glorious day, God will point us out to the angels and say, "Angels, look at these people! I am not ashamed of them at all. Even though they failed many times, had many weaknesses, and offended Me in so many ways, today they are manifesting the glorious image of My Son!" To Satan, God will also say, "Satan, look at these people! You did your best to torture and destroy them, but you do not realize how often your attempts to destroy only caused them to further realize their designation." At that time, Satan will be put to shame, God will be glorified, and we will become an overcoming and glorious testimony of God Himself.

125

Conformed to the Image of His Son

For those whom He foreknew, He also predestined to become conformed to the image of His Son, so that He would be the firstborn among many brethren; ³⁰and these whom He predestined, He also called; and these whom He called, He also justified; and these whom He justified, He also glorified.
—*Romans 8:29-30*

WORD STUDY

Romans 8:29 tells us that God predestined us for something—to become conformed to the image of the Son of God. The Greek word used here for "conformed," *summorphous*, is composed of two Greek words: *sun*, meaning "with, together," and denoting "union" (Strong, #4862), and *morphē*, meaning "shape, nature, form" (Strong, #3444). Together, the words can be translated "having the same form." However, the "union" aspect of sun denotes not only superficial conformity but also an inward conforming (Rogers, 331). M. R. Vincent calls this "inner and essential conformity" (Vincent, 3:96).

The Greek word used here for "image," *eikōn*, means "a statue, profile, or figuratively a representation" (Strong, #1504). It is the same word used of Christ in Colossians 1:15, "He is the image of the invisible God." In the context of these verses in Romans, our conformation to the image of Christ is not simply to His moral purity or sufferings but to His glorified body. Thus, Christ is seen as the perfect pattern or model for the accomplishment of His people's sanctification and transformation. At the end of verse 29, it is revealed that Christ is not only our glorified Head and model but that He is also our eldest Brother (Alford, 2:399).

REVELATION AND APPLICATION

The Experience of Conformation

The word "conformation" indicates our union with the Son of God according to His image. The apostle John wrote, "Beloved, now we are children of God, and it has not appeared as yet what we will be. We know that when He appears, we will be like Him, because we will see Him just as He is" (1 John 3:2). Christ is indeed the firstborn, and in the end, we will be just as He is. Jesus Christ is our model, and we will eventually become totally and perfectly like Him.

However, the process of being conformed to the image of the Son of God is very messy. We are somewhat like pieces of art. A studio where artwork is produced is always very messy, but the final product has great value. Our experience of the process of conformation is likewise quite rough and messy. Therefore, we should take our focus off our "mess" and focus on God! We should tell God all the time, "Father, thank You. All things are working together for me to be conformed to the image of Your dear Son. In the process of this work, many things discourage me, many environments perplex me, and many experiences pressure me. However, I worship You! You are my Maker and the Potter. You clearly know what You want. Thank You for the ability to rest in the fact that even in this messy process, You are, by Your mercy, working to conform me unto the glorious image of Your Son."

Christ, the Image of God

The Greek word for "image" in Romans 8:29 is the same Greek word used in Colossians 1:15: "[Christ] is the image of the invisible God." In Colossians, this image is the Lord Jesus, who, in His person, manifests God's life, divine attributes, and very being.

God's creation of man was according to His image and likeness, so that man could rule over all things (Gen. 1:26). For this, God created a spirit inside of man, in order that every part of a person, from the inside to the outside, would be like God and manifest Him. Unfortunately, sin came into man and began to live and manifest itself in a fallen image. Some people manifest "good" images of morality, righteousness, or honor. Others portray a very different image. Some bear the image of a drunkard or a gambler. Some people's images even project the reigning of sin through their faces. However, whether a fallen image is "good" or "bad," it is still only of a fallen person and does not manifest God at all.

In this fallen situation, God performed the greatest miracle in the universe—His incarnation. God became a man, the Lord Jesus Christ. This Jesus lived as a most perfect image. When there was a need for a touch of compassion, He was that compassion. When there was a need for the outflow of love, He was the love. When there was a need to testify of meekness or manifest righteousness, He was that meekness and righteousness. He is the same to us today. Jesus Christ is truly the most holy and beautiful image—the very image of God.

Conformed to Christ

The image of God is a wonderful person! Today, Jesus, who is both God and man, is our Savior through His death and resurrection. At the moment we believed, He gave us

His being (including all the divine attributes) and His living (including all the human virtues) and united them with our deepest part, our spirit. In Romans 8:29, we are conformed to the image of the Lord Jesus in order that we would manifest all of His attributes and virtues.

Our initial confession of the Lord may have been selfish. We may have believed into Him so that we would not perish eternally, so that our life would have meaning, or to gain God as our protector and trustworthy One. These are all fine, but God is not satisfied with our stopping at these reasons.

When we say that believing into the Lord is so good and beautiful, and that we are so peaceful and joyful now, God might say, "There is so much more! I saved you so that I could live and work in you. I forgave your sins, justified you, and released you from all bondage so that My work could begin in you. I will give you both smooth and rough environments, and I will cause you to be encouraged, discouraged, abundantly joyful, and hopelessly lost. All of these are My work in you, and all of My work is according to Christ, who is resurrected, ascended, and full of abundant life. My work in you is to fully conform you to His image so that you might be completely like Him!"

Our Lord is so good, and the work of God within us is so good! God not only saved us, justified us, and sanctified us, but He will also conform us to the image of His Son, Jesus Christ. He is our wise Maker, and He is making us according to the organic model of our Lord and Savior. Every touch of His hand, every cut of His knife, and every period of time in the furnace is totally according to this model This is all so that we would be completely like Him from our inside out.

126

The One Who Is For Us

What then shall we say to these things? If God is for us, who is against us? ³²He who did not spare His own Son, but delivered Him over for us all, how will He not also with Him freely give us all things?

—Romans 8:31-32

WORD STUDY

Verse 31 begins the closing section of Romans 8. Paul offers the question, "If God is for us, who is against us?" The Greek word translated here "for," *huper*, is a widely used Greek preposition that most literally means "over" (Strong, #5228). Used here with the genitive case, it is conceived of as God's standing or bending "over" the one He would shield or defend. It indicates that God is on our side and favors and furthers our cause (Thayer, 638). Martin Luther wrote, "If God be for us, who is the Judge of all and whose omnipotence calls into being all things, no one can be against us" (Luther, 133). G. Campbell Morgan also wrote, "Already [Paul] had demonstrated the fact that the very forces of sorrow and of suffering which seemed to be opposed [to us], are working together for good. In the light of that assurance he looked out through all space and all ages, and demanded 'Who is against us?' The answer is really an exposition of the assumption of the question—that God is for us" (Morgan, 134–135).

The realization that God is for us is closely linked by Paul to an appreciation of God's unsparing treatment of His Son. The word "spare," *pheidomai*, is elsewhere used only in Acts 20:29 and 1 Peter 2:4–5, describing wolves as not sparing the flock and God's unsparing judgment upon fallen angels and the ancient world. The thought here in Romans is clear—if God would give His Son in such a way for us all, it is inconceivable that He would withhold anything from us (Morgan, 135).

REVELATION AND APPLICATION

Romans 8:31–32 is a wonderful pronouncement of God's heart toward us. God has called us according to His will in order that we would be conformed to the glorious image of His Son. God designated us for this before time existed! Since this is the case, can any adversary stand against us? Did God not justify us? In fact, He did not spare His own Son, but delivered Him up for us all. Now, "how will He not also with Him freely give us all things?" Oh, what a marvelous declaration!

God Stands with Us

"For us" and "against us" are opposing phrases that bear the idea of standing on someone's side. We could think of this verse as, "If God is standing with us, who can stand against us?" Consider such a thought: our God, who is for us, is standing at our side!

God is always for us and standing with us. He stands with us and shields us in all environments. He stands with us whether we are weak or strong. He stands with us whether we overcome or fail. In peace and security, He stands with us. In turmoil and despair, He still stands with us. Our God is always standing beside us, ready to defend us and to freely give us all things.

God Not Sparing His Son

The God of love, who is for us and stands with us, did not spare His own Son but delivered Him over for us all. This is reflected elsewhere in the Bible when Abraham offered up his son Isaac to God. At that time, the Lord said to Abraham, "You...have not withheld your son, your only son" (Gen. 22:16). To "not withhold" is to "not spare." When God did not spare His Son, He was not withholding His Son for Himself.

The beginning phrase of Romans 8:32, "He who did not spare His own Son," has an almost cruel feeling to it. Certainly, the Son of God was never pampered by His Father in the flesh on earth. Jesus was not born in a palace where He could enjoy a royal life. He was not enthroned to reign as an earthly King. Such a life would have been the opposite of the cruelty Jesus Christ suffered on our behalf.

God was cruel to His Son. Yet, He was cruel to His Son for our sake. God gave His Son to us and caused Him to die on the cross. It was for us that He forsook His beloved Son. As the Lord Jesus hung on the cross, He prayed to the Father, "My God, My God, why have You forsaken Me?" (Matt. 27:46). This prayer revealed that God did not withhold His Son. He did not spare Him such a cruel life and death.

The idea of "not sparing" is also found in Acts, describing wolves who would not spare the flock (Acts 20:29). On the one hand, God's treatment of His Son was like Abraham, who did not withhold Isaac his son. On the other hand, God's treatment of His Son was like a wolf among the flock. This does not mean God stopped loving His only begotten Son (Matt. 3:17). In fact, God never withdrew His love from Him.

For the sake of our sins, however, God had to treat His Son with unsparing cruelty by laying Him aside and judging Him on the cross. Oh, who can tell how deeply this hurt the Father? Yet, He delivered over His own Son for us all. In the cross of Christ, we see that God did not spare His Son and that our sins have all been attributed to Him (2 Cor. 5:21; John 1:29).

What God Gives to Us

It is easy to misunderstand the phrase, "God is for us." When we think about this phrase, we may imagine that God is like a department store where we can get whatever we want. If we want strength, wisdom, or money, we expect God to give us as much of these as we want.

However, this is not how God wishes to give! To understand what it means that God is for us, we must read Romans 8:32 and consider what His gift is. It tells us that the Son of God was delivered over for us all. What does it mean that God is for us? It does not mean God is a department store. His greatest gift to us is His Son, Jesus Christ our Lord, and it is for the giving of this gift that "all things" work together (Rom. 8:28). Everything God gives to people is for giving them His Son.

Just because we have a need or are short in something does not mean God will come to meet that need and supply our shortage. God is on our side, standing with us, and is willing to give His Son to us. His hope for us involves nothing more than our continual gaining of His Son.

In our experience, this giving by the Father is not only something in the future but is also relevant today. On the one hand, we will inherit all things and obtain full sonship at a point in the future; on the other hand, the working together of all things continually allows us to gain the Son of God today (v. 28)! God freely gives all things to us for only one purpose—to give His Son to us. The reason God did not spare, withhold, or treat His Son with mercy is that He wants to give us His Son. This is the love God has for us and has demonstrated to us (5:8).

127

The One Who Justifies

Who will bring a charge against God's elect? God is the one who justifies.

—Romans 8:33

WORD STUDY

The Greek word used in Romans 8:33 for the phrase "bring a charge" is *enkaleō*. It is composed of two Greek words—*en*, most simply meaning "in" (Strong, #1722), and *kaleō*, meaning, "to call" (Strong, #2564). *Enkaleō* could literally be translated "to call in" or "to call something in or against someone" (Vine, 10). This word was often used in a legal sense to indicate a charge brought against someone in court (Rogers, 332). A good sense of this word is "to accuse," as it is used in Acts 19:38: "So then, if Demetrius and the craftsmen who are with him have a complaint against any man, the courts are in session and proconsuls are available; let them bring charges (*enkaleō*) against one another."

The legal sense of the word may lend more context to the answer—that God is the One who justifies—to the question posed in the verse. In other words, God is the One who makes us judicially righteous before Himself.

REVELATION AND APPLICATION

A Charge against Us

What is the "charge" mentioned in Romans 8:33? On the one hand, it implies an accusation brought against God's elect. Surely, it is Satan who would accuse us before God. On the other hand, the Greek word for "charge" could imply that Satan wants to call us in to stand before the court of God. This is like how a court would use a subpoena today. When a person is accused regarding a legal matter, the court may issue a subpoena—a written command ordering the defendant to come and testify before the court.

Satan entices us with many things. He entices us with riches, fame, promotions, the world, and the vainglory of nations. Yet all of this is for the purpose of calling us to the divine court and accusing us before God.

God Justifies Us

Romans 8:33 begins with a question and ends with an answer to that question. The answer is that God is the One who justifies. Do not forget Paul's question two verses earlier—"If God is for us, who is against us?" (v. 31). The God who is for us and stands with us is the same God who justifies us.

Although God is for us, there is one who is against us. This one is Satan, who loves to accuse us day and night (Rev. 12:10). Because God justifies us, however, no accusation can ever hold up against us. Satan may say to us, "Look at yourself, you pathetic worm! You offended God again, this time beyond anything you've ever done before. You are weak, low, and helpless. You are finished; you cannot go on. God will never accept you anymore! You are not capable of following the Lord, and you will never please Him." However, our God justifies us. Satan's accusations are full of words, but what can he do to us? Because God is for us, stands with us, and justifies us, Satan's accusations are worthless.

When we face Satan's accusations, we should learn to say, "Satan, get behind me!" We were chosen by God, He is for us, and He stands with us. He will never leave our side, whether we are strong, weak, victorious, or defeated. Neither our worthiness nor our unworthiness matters; God always stands with us. We have been chosen and justified by God! We can boldly declare, "Satan, neither you nor anyone else can ever successfully accuse me again!"

Two Callings

Both God and Satan call people. However, God's calling is to glorify people while Satan's calling is to accuse them. God calls people for one purpose: those whom He predestined, these He also called, justified, and glorified (Rom. 8:29–30). Satan only calls people for the purpose of accusing them (Rev. 12:10). He calls people to sin so he can accuse them of their sins. He calls people to love the world and the lusts of it, yet he also accuses people of loving the world! Day and night, Satan is accusing.

God is for us, Satan is against us, and they oppose each other. God's calling is the opposite of Satan's accusation. Satan calls people into his world to accuse them with it. God calls people into His glory to share it with them. The way we can live a victorious, spiritual life is to abide in the glorious calling of God. When we see God's calling, hold fast to it, and abide in it, every accusation against us will fall short. Since God has called us, who can accuse us? The answer is no one, because God is the One who justifies us.

128

Intercession for Us

Who is the one who condemns? Christ Jesus is He who died, yes, rather who was raised, who is at the right hand of God, who also intercedes for us.
—*Romans 8:34*

WORD STUDY

Paul not only emphasizes Christ's death in Romans 8:34 but also that He has been raised. Regarding the word "rather," M. R. Vincent quotes J. Bengel: "Our faith should rest on Christ's death, but it should *rather* also so far progress as to lean on His resurrection, dominion, and second coming" (Vincent, 3:97, italics original). It is in connection with His resurrection that Christ's intercession on our behalf has meaning.

The Greek word used here for "intercedes" is *entunchanō*. Since it is written in the present tense, it indicates a current action by the living Christ. It is composed of two Greek words—*en* and *tuchanō*. *En* is a Greek preposition most often translated "in," and used to denote spatial position. Yet, it can also denote a relation of rest, as it is the intermediate between *eis*, "into," and *ek*, "out from." In this case, *en* would denote "continuing or remaining" (Strong, #1722;

Wallace, 742). *Tuchanō* properly means "to affect" or "to attain or secure an object or end" (Strong, #5177). It implies a specific end or goal to obtain (Vine, 44).

By understanding the parts of *entunchanō*, we can think of intercession as continually affecting or entreating someone to obtain a specific goal.

REVELATION AND APPLICATION

The Goal of Christ's Intercession

The intercession of Christ is His prayer for us. No one can accuse us whom God has chosen, because God has justified us. No one can condemn us, either, because Christ Jesus has died, been raised from the dead, and is now at the right hand of God interceding for us.

Intercession is not without purpose. In fact, it is continually working toward a target or goal. This target is mentioned very clearly in previous verses: God has predestined us to be conformed to the image of the Son of God. This is the goal of the resurrected Christ's intercession for us.

The Effectiveness of Christ's Intercession

The intercession of Christ is continuous and has a specific target. It is because of this intercession by Christ at the right hand of God that Paul could so confidently say, "God causes all things to work together for good to those who love God" (Rom. 8:28).

Christ intercedes in a way completely different from the way we intercede. Since we often do not know the purpose of our intercession, we do not know what to intercede for. However, when Christ intercedes for us, His purpose is very clear. He clearly knows why He intercedes for us, and He is very clear about what our real need is. This is why His intercession is so effective.

If His intercession was without a goal, like our intercession often is, nothing would work together at all, and things would not be unto the good of those who love God. In His intercession, Christ only desires to accomplish the eternal purpose of God, which is to conform us to the image of the Son. This intercession effectively results in the working together of all things.

Intercession and the Triune God

Paul declared in Romans 8:27 that the Spirit intercedes for us according to the will of God, yet here in verse 34 he says that Christ intercedes for us at the right hand of God. Christ and the Spirit are not interceding separately but bring the same intercession from two sides. On one side, the Spirit is in us and initiates the intercession for us (v. 27). On the other side, Christ completes this intercession for us at the right hand of God (v. 34). The Spirit initiates, Christ completes, and eventually God the Father fulfills this intercession. All this intercession, which constantly operates and works in a strong way, is toward one goal.

Brothers and sisters, do you see the wonderful cooperation of the triune God? The Spirit initiates the intercession that is according to the will of God in His groanings too deep for words. Christ—who is at the right hand of God, understands our situation, and knows how to help us—completes this intercession in His resurrection. The Father fulfills this intercession in His powerful operation and working, causing all things to work together for the good of those who love God. Oh, the cooperation of the triune God is so wonderful!

In this entire process, the divine intercession has only one goal—to accomplish the eternal purpose of God, which is to have many sons conformed to the image of God's firstborn

Son. The intercession initiated by the Spirit, completed by Christ, and fulfilled by the Father is focused on us. Its purpose is that we, the sons of God, might be conformed to the glorious image of the Son of God. Praise Him!

129

The Love of Christ

Who will separate us from the love of Christ? Will tribulation, or distress, or persecution, or famine, or nakedness, or peril, or sword?
—*Romans 8:35*

WORD STUDY

Having asserted in Romans 8:31–34 that in God's great love none can accuse nor harm us, Paul now writes that this love from God is permanent, even under all adverse circumstances (Alford, 2:401). He begins with a rhetorical question dealing with separation from the love of Christ. The Greek word used here for "separation," *chōrizō*, means "to place room between two things" (Strong, #5563). The root of this word is *chōra*, meaning "a space of territory" and carries "the idea of empty expanse" (Strong, #5561). Paul's rhetorical question conveys the idea of distance—"can anyone or anything cause any distance or space to come between us and the love of Christ?"

REVELATION AND APPLICATION

In Romans 8:34, Paul talked about the intercession of Christ, and now in verse 35, he talks about the love of Christ.

The intercession of Christ ushers us into the experience His love and the appreciation of the work and value of His love. All of the items in this verse—the tribulation, distress, persecution, famine, nakedness, peril, and sword—are parts of the "all things" that "work together for good to those who love God" (v. 28). Rather than separating us from the love of Christ, they bring us to appreciate His love more and more.

A Love That Cannot Be Separated

The Greek word Paul uses in Romans 8:35 for "separate" means to put distance between. To be separated by any of these things—tribulation, distress, persecution, famine, nakedness, peril, or sword—is for them to have put distance between Christ's love and us. Though we can never be completely cut off from the love of Christ, we may sometimes feel that there is a distance. We sometimes feel like the love of the Lord is far away from us and no longer as vivid, fresh, clear, intimate, real, or tangible as it once was. This can be our feeling regarding the love of Christ.

We must learn to abide in the truth given to us in the Bible. No matter how we feel, the word of the Bible is that nothing can separate us from the love of Christ. Tribulation cannot, distress cannot, and neither can persecution, famine, nakedness, peril, or sword. Though we may sometimes feel that we are distanced from the love of Christ, the Bible is clear that this is not possible, for nothing can separate us from the love of Christ.

Satan's Tool to Wear Us Down

It is interesting that the first item Paul mentions in this list in Romans 8:35 is tribulation. According to the definition of the Greek word used here, "tribulation" means "pressure"

(Strong, #2347). In our experience, tribulation is anything that pressures us and wears us down. Watchman Nee once explained that Satan's campaign against us is to wear us down (Nee, 79-87). At a certain point, we may be very sensitive toward God and filled with the divine life, but Satan's strategy is to wear us down to the point we become insensitive, discouraged, and dark. This wearing down is both inward and outward. From within ourselves and from the things around us, we can be made to feel harassed and opposed and so become calloused. Whenever Satan works, he uses tribulation to wear us down.

Tribulation is Satan's war of attrition with us. Christians should not fear a direct attack from Satan but should be guarded against his unrelenting stream of tribulation. For example, there was a brother who began working for a certain company. On one hand, his going there to work was very good and proper. On the other hand, his working there caused him to be worn down. After only a few years, this young man who had been full of strength and vitality had lost all of his energy and freshness. We must see that Satan's goal is to wear us out, whether through our jobs, our families, or even our church life. His desire is to afflict and destroy us, and his method is tribulation.

However, for those who love God, tribulation is an opportunity to strengthen their resolve to follow and serve the Lord, even as they face many limitations and difficulties. According to our logic, every round of tribulation should leave us worn out and wasted away. However, those who love God emerge from tribulations like polished precious stones. Some saints have weathered many storms and high waves; they have experienced much tribulation and affliction. By any measure, the outward situation would be discouraging. Yet amazingly, these saints emerged from their tribulations still able to serve the Lord. They were not worn out or wasted away but only shone brighter than ever before. Their burden was clearer, their subjective assurance of the Lord was greater, their confidence in following the Lord was deeper, and their trust in the Lord was more unshakable than ever.

Dear brothers and sisters, tribulation is Satan's tool for wearing us down. Yet because we love the Lord, even this can become our benefit and boasting.

130

Overwhelmingly Conquering

Just as it is written, "For Your sake we are being put to death all day long; we were considered as sheep to be slaughtered." ³⁷But in all these things we overwhelmingly conquer through Him who loved us.

—Romans 8:36-37

WORD STUDY

In Romans 8:37, the phrase "overwhelmingly conquer" is derived from one Greek word, *hupernikaō*. This word is composed of two other Greek words: *huper*, meaning "over, above, beyond" (Strong, #5228), and *nikaō*, meaning, "to conquer, overcome, prevail" (Strong, #3528). Together they mean, "To vanquish beyond, that is, gain a decisive victory" (Strong, #5245). Some Bible translations, like the New King James Version, translate this phrase, "more than conquerors."

According to G. Kittel, *nikaō* belongs to a powerful word group in the New Testament. However, here in Romans 8:37, the rare word *hupernikaō* is used in place of *nikaō*, which although powerful is still "almost too weak a term." *Hupernikaō* evokes the image of a warrior unbothered by earthly affliction or defeat, and it seems Paul's point is to say, "We win the supreme victory through Him who loves us" (Kittel, 4:942–945).

REVELATION AND APPLICATION

In Romans 8:35, we saw that nothing could separate us from the love of Christ, whether tribulation, distress, persecution, famine, nakedness, peril, or sword. Paul's use of the Old Testament in verse 36 shows that when these things come to us, we will feel that we are being put to death all day long. However, verse 37 reveals that through the Lord, the One who loves us, we overwhelmingly conquer in all these things.

The Fruit of Victory

The Greek word *nikaō* means both to overcome and to conquer, but *hupernikaō*, the word used in Romans 8:37, indicates that we are those who more than overcome and conquer! What does this mean? In Old Testament warfare, the Israelites were more than conquerors when they not only won the battle but also gained much spoil. Today, for us to more than conquer in our experience means not only to overcome our environments and situations but to also gain the fruit of victory within us. As this fruit of victory abides in us, the overcoming life becomes constituted in us.

We should be inspired regarding conquering. We may not have many overcoming experiences to boast of as we follow the Lord, but every year we should have a few. These experiences are for us to be constituted with our overcoming God. We should not take each matter in our lives as a separate situation to be overcome. Rather, we should let God's overcoming life be dispensed into us in every situation and environment. The constitution of this life within us is the fruit of our victories and conquering.

A Christian's life is an overcoming and conquering life. Yet, it is not a conquering of the world in an outward way by becoming successful. Do not admire others who have conquered business, wealth, or fame. Rather, we should say, "What is my career, business, or fame? I do not regard them at all." Under God's sovereignty, we are led through many different environments to overcome and conquer in all things. This is not to gain wealth or fame but that the fruit of these victories through Christ would abide in us and fully constitute us. This is the true overcoming of the world, and this is a life worthy of admiration and pursuit.

Overwhelmingly Conquering in Any Environment

Romans 8:37 says that we overwhelmingly conquer "in all these things." What "things" is Paul talking about? According to the context, these things are the situations brought up in verse 35—tribulation, distress, persecution, famine, nakedness, peril, and sword. These situations fall into three categories: suffering (tribulation, distress, and persecution), poverty (famine and nakedness), and martyrdom (peril and sword).

Even in times of suffering—when we face tribulation, distress, and persecution—we can still overwhelmingly conquer. There is no doubt that tribulation, distress, and persecution will come to those who love the Lord and follow Him. Tribulation attempts to wear us down, distress causes us to feel there is no hope, and persecution pressures us to the uttermost. These sufferings can come from any environment, from those around us, and even from within us. Yet, in this suffering, through the Lord who loves us, we are more than conquerors.

In situations of poverty, like famine and nakedness, we still can overwhelmingly conquer. In today's world, especially the western world, even the poor are relatively wealthy. There are very few in the western world who must endure famine and nakedness. Yet even so, Christians can still experience lack or shortage. In environments of poverty, we are still more than conquerors through the Lord who loves us.

Finally, when facing martyrdom through peril or the sword, we still overwhelmingly conquer. The heart of one who loves and follows the Lord ought to be willing to face even peril and sword. We should be willing to be a martyr for the Lord. From our youth, it is good to pray, "Lord, for the sake of the gospel of God, I am willing to go to the ends of the earth, to the poorest region where no one has preached the gospel, and I am even willing to be a martyr for You there!" Watchman Nee had such a will. He declared that his future was either to be raptured or to be martyred.

In His love, the environments the Lord measures to us may be of suffering, poverty, or martyrdom. It is just as the Scripture says: "For Your sake we are being put to death all day long; we were considered as sheep to be slaughtered" (v. 36). However, our victory is in Christ. In all of these environments, we should always believe, declare, and boast that through the Lord who loves us, we overwhelmingly conquer.

131

The Love of God in Christ Jesus

For I am convinced that neither death, nor life, nor angels, nor principalities, nor things present, nor things to come, nor powers, [39]nor height, nor depth, nor any other created thing, will be able to separate us from the love of God, which is in Christ Jesus our Lord.
—Romans 8:38-39

WORD STUDY

With verses 38-39, Romans 8 is brought to a close, and Paul's point is further illustrated that nothing can "separate us from the love of God, which is in Christ Jesus our Lord." The Greek word he uses for "convinced," *peithō*, is written in the passive tense and can mean "to assent (to evidence or authority)" (Strong, #3982). H. Thayer defines the use of *peithō* in this verse as, "to be persuaded of a thing concerning a person" (Thayer, 497). In other words, Paul's experience of God Himself had given him enough evidence to persuade him that none of the things he lists can separate us from the love of God.

In conclusion to Romans 8 and in response to the great work of redemption described up to this point, G. Campbell Morgan wrote, "On account of sin, God was against man, and man was silent. Through His salvation God is for him, and the opposing forces are silent. By reason of sin God was the supreme Accuser. By the way of His salvation He has become the Justifier....The inevitable issue of sin was that God had excluded man from fellowship with Himself. The equally inevitable result of salvation is the restoration of man to such fellowship with Him in love that no force in the universe can separate between them" (Morgan, 138).

REVELATION AND APPLICATION

In previous verses, we saw that many kinds of harsh environments may come to us, and we may even feel that we are considered as sheep to be slaughtered. Yet, none of these things can separate us from the love of Christ (Rom. 8:35—37). Paul now further says that no created thing can separate us from the love of God because this love is in Christ Jesus our Lord. In fact, it is because of the intercession of the resurrected Christ at the right hand of God (v. 34) that we are able to overwhelmingly conquer in all of these things, which are under God's sovereignty.

Nothing Is Able to Separate Us from God's Love

In Romans 8:38, Paul first mentions two opposite things—death and life. Our experience is of death, but we gain life. We continually experience death, but we also continually obtain the divine life. Yet, whether we experience death or gain life, we are not separated from the love of God.

Paul next mentions angels and principalities (v. 38). Angels are ministering spirits who are sent to serve those who will inherit salvation (Heb. 1:14). Principalities are the fallen angels who are under Satan and rule over the dark world from the air (see Eph. 2:2, 6:12). Angels and principalities are also opposites of each other. The principalities try to rule over us continually while the angels continually serve us. The principalities are occupied with dark, evil, and rebellious activity, whereas the angels provide better, more beautiful, and higher service to us. Yet, whether we are attacked by principalities or served by angels, we are not separated from the love of God.

Paul also mentions things present and things to come (Rom. 8:38). The things present include everything of this life, whether buying a house, studying for a degree, or finding a job. Even our church life today is a present thing. The things to come are our coming glory (v. 18). Yet, whether we are in the wonderful day of glory or taking care of present things, we are not separated from the love of God.

Life Issuing in Love

What Paul says in Romans 8:38-39 is so rich! From our point of view, we have tribulation, distress, persecution, famine, nakedness, peril, and sword. From God's point of view, we have death, life, angels, principalities, things present, things to come, powers, height, depth, and every created thing. All these items, whether positive or negative, have only one purpose—to bring us to the experience of the inseparable love of God in the Lord Jesus Christ (v. 39). What a picture of our God who is love bringing us to know and experience His love for us through all our environments and all created things.

Our God is full of love. Love is one of His attributes and issues from the operation of His divine life. As believers, we enjoy God's divine life, and in this enjoyment, we experience His love. When His life is infused into us, we gain love.

No matter how many years we have been saved, we can still ask the Lord today, "Lord, why do You still love me so much?" For as long as we have been saved, we have enjoyed His life and felt His love. His life entered us, and as it operates within us, we obtain, experience, and enjoy His love. The love of God has become something we can hold fast to, and nothing can separate us from it. Oh, thank the Lord!

The Sweet and Rich Love of God

Our experience of glorification is not only to "overwhelmingly conquer" but also to enjoy the love the God in the Lord Jesus Christ. Following the Lord is not a matter of gritting our teeth and trying to overwhelmingly conquer. Rather, it involves an inexpressible sweetness in all our experiences, which causes us to tell the Lord, "I love You! Your love is so good, so rich, so deep, and so sweet! I want to enjoy Your love in every environment You measure to me!" We are inseparable from God's love. This love causes us to willingly experience every environment arranged for us by our sovereign God, whether it seems positive or negative.

We ought to marvel that at the end of Paul's description of the experience of glorification is the love of God. This love is the source of God's judicial justification of us and His work of sanctification and glorification in us. Where is such love found? This love is found only in Christ Jesus our Lord. Oh, praise the Lord for His great love for us!

Works Cited

Alford, Henry. *Alford's Greek Testament: An Exegetical and Critical Commentary.* Grand Rapids, MI: Guardian Press, 1976.
Brown, Colin, ed. *The New International Dictionary of New Testament Theology.* Grand Rapids, MI: Zondervan Publishing House, 1986.
Griffith, Thomas. *St. Paul's Epistle to the Romans.* Grand Rapids, MI: Wm. B. Eerdmans Publishing Company, 1974.
Jamieson, Robert, A.R. Fausset, David Brown. *A Commentary on the Old and New Testaments.* Peabody, MA: Hendrickson Publishers, Inc., 1997.
Kittel, Gerhard, ed., Gerhard Friedrich, ed., Geoffrey W. Bromiley, trans. and ed. *Theological Dictionary of the New Testament.* Grand Rapids, MI: Wm. B. Eerdmans Publishing Company, 1964.
Luther, Martin, J. Theodore Mueller, trans. *Commentary on the Epistle to the Romans.* Grand Rapids, MI: Kregal Publications, 1976.
Martin, Del, ed., Richard Yeh, ed. *Songs and Hymns of Life.* Ann Arbor, MI: Good Land Publishers, 2009.
McDowell, Josh. *The New Evidence that Demands a Verdict.* Nashville, TN: Thomas Nelson, Inc., 1999.
Morgan, George Campbell. *The Analysed Bible: The Epistle of Paul the Apostle to the Romans.* Eugene, OR: Wipf & Stock Publishers, 2001.
Nee, Watchman. *Let Us Pray.* New York, NY: Christian Fellowship Publishers, Inc., 1977.
Rippon, John, ed. *The Psalms and Hymns of Dr. Watts.* New York, NY: Moore & Payne, 1835.
Rogers, Cleon L., Jr., Cleon L. Rogers III. *The New Linguistic and Exegetical Key to the Greek New Testament.* Grand Rapids, MI: Zondervan Publishing House, 1998.

Strong, James. *Strong's Exhaustive Concordance of the Bible.* Peabody, MA: Hendrickson Publishers, Inc., 2009.

Thayer, Joseph H. *Thayer's Greek-English Lexicon of the New Testament.* Peabody, MA: Hendrickson Publishers, Inc., 2009.

United Methodist Church (U.S). *Book of United Methodist Worship.* Nashville, TN: United Methodist Publishing House, 1989.

Vincent, Marvin R. *Word Studies in the New Testament.* Peabody, MA: Hendrickson Publishers, Inc., 2009.

Vine, W. E. *Vine's Complete Expository Dictionary of Old and New Testament Words.* Nashville, TN: Thomas Nelson, Inc., 1996.

Wallace, Daniel B. *Greek Grammar Beyond the Basics.* Grand Rapids, MI: Zondervan Publishing House, 1996.

Wuest, Kenneth S. *Wuest's Word Studies from the Greek New Testament.* Grand Rapids, MI: Wm. B. Eerdmans Publishing Company, 1973.

Online Ministry by Titus Chu

MinistryMessages.org is the online archive for the ministry of Titus Chu. This includes audio messages, articles, and books in PDF format, all of which are available as free downloads.

"Daily Words for the Christian Life" is an e-letter sent out every Thursday. It features selections from the writings of Titus Chu. To subscribe, visit http://ministrymessages.org/mailing-list/.

Books by Titus Chu

The books listed below are available in print, Kindle, or iBook format. To purchase them, go to MinistryMessages.org/order. They are also available via Amazon.com and iTunes.

Born Again

David: After God's Heart

Elijah & Elisha: Living for God's Testimony

Ruth: Growth unto Maturity

Philippians: That I May Gain Christ

A Sketch of Genesis

Two Manners of Life

www.ingramcontent.com/pod-product-compliance
Lightning Source LLC
Chambersburg PA
CBHW022057090426
42743CB00008B/634